Driven

Driven

The Secret Lives of

Drivers

MARCELLO DI CINTIO

Biblioasis
Windsor, Ontario

FIRST EDITION

10 9 8 7 6 5 4 3 2 1

Library and Archives Canada Cataloguing in Publication
Title: Driven : the secret lives of taxi drivers / by Marcello Di Cintio.
Other titles: Driven (2021) | Secret lives of taxi drivers
Names: Di Cintio, Marcello, 1973- interviewer.
Series: Untold lives.
Description: First edition. | Series statement: Untold lives
Identifiers: Canadiana (print) 20210129050 | Canadiana (ebook) 20210129247 | ISBN 9781771963848 (softcover) | ISBN 9781771963855 (ebook)
Subjects: LCSH: Taxicab drivers—Canada—Interviews. | LCGFT: Interviews.
Classification: LCC HD8039.T162 C3 2021 | DDC 388.4/13214092271—dc23

Edited by Daniel Wells
Copyedited by Emily Donaldson
Cover and text designed by Michel Vrana

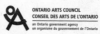

Published with the generous assistance of the Canada Council for the Arts, which last year invested $153 million to bring the arts to Canadians throughout the country, and the financial support of the Government of Canada. Biblioasis also acknowledges the support of the Ontario Arts Council (OAC), an agency of the Government of Ontario, which last year funded 1,709 individual artists and 1,078 organizations in 204 communities across Ontario, for a total of $52.1 million, and the contribution of the Government of Ontario through the Ontario Book Publishing Tax Credit and Ontario Creates. This is one of the 200 exceptional projects funded through the Canada Council for the Arts' New Chapter program. With this $35M investment, the Council supports the creation and sharing of the arts in communities across Canada.

PRINTED AND BOUND IN CANADA

Contents

In loving memory of

Amedeo Sorrentino,
Gabrielle Cran,
and
Wayson Choy

Author's Note:

On a few occasions, I have changed the names of cabbies' family members due to privacy concerns. The identities of all drivers, however, remain unobscured.

Introduction

BETWEEN STORY AND SILENCE

I HATE TAKING TAXIS.

My near quarter century as a travel writer has landed me in the backseats of countless taxicabs around the world, and their drivers have been my most common nemeses. Nearly every ride I have taken in the Middle East, Africa, and South Asia, where taxi meters are either nonexistent or conveniently "broken," has sparked a squabble over the fare. For me, taxis represent a necessary evil at best, and a cause for angry conflict at worst. Once, at the end of a ride in Ouagadougou, Burkina Faso, I recklessly called the driver a thief and he lunged out of the car at me, ready for a fight. An Iranian driver almost punched me, too, when I petulantly slammed his door after I thought he overcharged me. Luckily, both men calmed down before throwing their fists. My stature hardly matches my temper, and I would've lost those fights.

My most potentially dangerous taxi ride, though, occurred in eastern Turkey during my honeymoon. I sat up front and my new bride sat in the back, next to a strange man who appeared to be a friend of the driver. As soon as we left the border, our cabbie pulled a tall can of Efes Lager from beneath the driver's seat and drained it in one long pull. Then he drank a second. The driver also kept a knife with a five-inch blade on the armrest between his seat and mine. I was convinced that he and his backseat buddy planned to rob us at knifepoint, or worse, if he didn't first drunk-drive us off the road into the Black Sea. I picked up his knife and held it my hand for the duration of the ride, pretending to admire it, just to ensure he remained unarmed. Thanks to these kinds of experiences, I now possess a lingering dread of taxis in general—a Post-Taxi Stress Disorder.

Cabbies engender more sympathy from me than suspicion in places where the meters work and I don't fear being cheated or stabbed. As an enthusiastic traveller, I can hardly imagine anything worse than being in constant motion but never really going anywhere. Still, at home, I'd rather use public transit and car-share services than hail a cab, and I always accept offers of rides from family and friends. I adore cities like New York and Montreal as much for their extensive subway systems as their restaurants and cafés. And I walk a lot. I miraculously dropped ten pounds during a month-long trip to Belfast, where I mainly subsisted on draft beer and things made from potatoes, as a side effect of walking everywhere.

When I do end up taking a taxi, I tend to slip into the backseat and blurt out a destination. If I'm feeling beery and chatty, I might try to geolocate my cabbie's name or accent in case he comes from somewhere I've been. This is less an attempt at camaraderie than a clumsy excuse to boast about my travels. "Is your accent Persian? I've been to Iran twice," I might say. Or "You're from Nigeria? I spent a year in West Africa. Never made it to Nigeria, though." I am not proud of these inane exchanges. They're a more pompous version of "where are you from?"—the question I've learned taxi drivers hate the most.

More often, though, I don't speak at all, opting instead to mutely stare at my phone. I know I am not alone in this; a cabbie once told me his silent fares sometimes make him feel like he's simply another part of the car. As passengers, we rarely wonder at the lives of those we know only by the reflection of their eyes in a rear-view mirror. We don't inquire about the lives of our baristas or butchers or bank clerks, either, but the physical closeness between cabbie and passenger makes such silent disinterest feel unnatural. Antisocial, even.

I suspect this has always been the case. I doubt Thornton Blackburn, who became Upper Canada's first taxi driver in 1837, engaged much with his clients either. The configuration of Blackburn's cab did not lend itself to conversation. Passengers sat inside the red-and-yellow horse-drawn carriage while Thornton worked the reins up top. Had they spoken to Thornton at all, his clients might have glanced at his Black face, heard his unfamiliar accent, and asked him where he came from. "Kentucky," he'd have said. Thorton's clients, their brief pleasantries exhausted, might have returned to the pages of the week's *Upper Canada Gazette* in the same way today's passengers dissolve into the quiet glow of their Twitter feeds.

But Thornton's life history hints at what we might be missing. One's birthplace alone does not tell a story. Thornton and his wife, Lucie, didn't just come from Kentucky. They came from slavery. The Blackburns escaped their slave masters in high summer of 1831. They used forged documents to book passage across the Ohio River on a steamboat named the *Versailles*. Thornton and Lucie continued on to Detroit, where they lived for two years before getting arrested as runaway slaves. Then they escaped again. Lucie walked out of her prison cell after swapping clothes with a friend who agreed to take her place. Thornton was freed by a throng of Detroit's Black citizens, who armed themselves with pistols, knives, and clubs and overwhelmed the prison guards. The Blackburns reunited in Canada, but were jailed again while their American owners sued for their extradition. Since Thornton and Lucie had committed no crime in Canada, however, the court would not send them back. The Blackburns' exoneration established Canada as a safe haven for fugitive slaves from America.

Surely, none of Thornton's taxi clients could have imagined that their driver and his fearless wife had laid tracks for the Underground Railroad. They could not have known that many of the 35,000 escaped American slaves who found safe haven in Canada owed their freedom to the man sitting on their taxi's roof. They had no idea about the story they weren't hearing.

After reading about the Thorntons, I started to wonder what stories *I* was missing. I'd spent years crossing borders around the world to document suffering and injustice. Resilience and love. Yet I hardly needed to leave Canada for these stories. I could've found almost as many on my cab rides to and from the airport, because the taxi itself is a border. Beneath the roof light of every cab, a map of frontiers and dividing lines unfolds. The taxi occupies the margin between public and private space: accessible to all but simultaneously personal and intimate. The taxi is the border between autonomy and servitude. The cabbie has no superior to answer to; instead, each fare brings a new master to whom he briefly yields. Even a poor man is a boss in a taxi. The taxi can be the border between the wealthy and working class, and between white people and people of colour. Nowhere else do people so different share such close quarters and engage so little. If the US–Mexico border is, as writer Gloria Anzaldúa once described, the place "where the Third World grates against the first and bleeds," a taxi is the place where the First World rubs against the Third and stares at its phone.

4

For me, the most compelling taxicab borderline is drawn here, between silence and the stories that silence conceals. And so, in 2018, I decided to cross that border. I put away my passport and spent a year travelling around Canada to seek out the life stories of the nation's taxi drivers. I would speak with cabbies outside their cars, for fear the enclosed space and running meter would transform our discourse into a costly interrogation rather than a real conversation. I wanted to meet drivers somewhere they would feel comfortable, too. This meant spending a disproportionate amount of time amid the familiar brown tiles of Tim Hortons.

Not every driver wanted to meet me. In fact, most didn't. Some didn't want to divulge their personal lives. Others were simply too busy. The manager of Toronto's Beck Taxi, the largest taxi brokerage firm in North America, told me that drivers don't see any value in talking to a writer. One retired cabbie in Montreal was more blunt: "Most of the drivers I know are not willing to waste their time ranting about their interesting stories to a stranger." Fair enough.

I wasn't sure what kind of stories I hoped to find anyway, but I was sure of the kinds of stories that *didn't* interest me. I'd heard enough gritty tales of driving taxi after hours. We all know those stories. The intersection of taxi driving with sex, drugs, and violence is a long-standing cultural cliché. Robert DeNiro's Travis Bickle, pop culture's most iconic cabbie, describes his nocturnal world early in 1976's *Taxi Driver*:

> All the animals come out at night—whores, skunk pussies, buggers, queens, fairies, dopers, junkies. Sick, venal. Someday a real rain'll come and wash all this scum off the streets... Each night when I return the cab to the garage, I have to clean the cum off the back seat. Some nights, I clean off the blood.

Victoria-based comedian Sean Proudlove turned his experiences as a night cabbie into a stage show, *The Taxi Driver Is Always Listening*, billed as "tales of sketchy passengers buying crack, drunken fools getting sick and all the silly things people do in the back seat of his cab." Peter McSherry's 2002 memoir, *Mean Streets: Confessions of a Nighttime Taxi Driver*, includes chapter headings like "Me and the Prostitutes," "Druggies and Street Drug Dealers," "My Best Pimp Story," and "Sex in My Taxi." Less literary takes on the same theme can be found on a porn website called *Fake Taxi*, which, at last glance, offered around 250 videos of cabbies having sex with their passengers.

The clichés of taxi noir don't appeal to me. This surprised many of the drivers I met, who couldn't understand why I asked about their childhoods, say, rather than their late-night exploits behind the wheel. But I wanted to hear about their back stories, not their backseats. To be honest, I wasn't much interested in stories about taxi driving at all, titillating or otherwise. I wanted to know who these drivers were before they drove taxi.

There was another trite story I wanted to avoid: the sad tale of the overeducated immigrant taxi driver who was a doctor or a dentist or an engineer in his home country, but whose credentials weren't recognized here. These men never wanted to drive cab at all, and their stories are hardly new. Writing for *The Globe Magazine* in 1970, taxi-driving journalist Peter Churchill described such cabbies as "immigrants who have struggled to Canada bearing their glittering recommendations and qualifications from places with unpronounceable names: doctors of law, medicine or philosophy who suddenly find they must keep body and soul together while the New World figures out what to do with them—or to let them do for themselves." Many of these drivers resented their downward mobility. They knew they should be installing pacemakers or filling prescriptions rather than driving drunks home from Yonge

Street bars or shuttling Disneyland-bound vacationers to Trudeau Airport, their educations wasting away beneath their roof lights.

This trend didn't end in the 1970s, of course. The trope of the taxi-driving brain surgeon remains a cliché in Canada and elsewhere in the Western world. According to a study of the 2006 Canadian Census, the last time such an analysis was conducted, more than a fifth of immigrant taxi drivers held a post-secondary degree, compared to fewer than 5 percent of Canadian-born cabbies. Two hundred foreign-born taxi drivers had been doctors in their homelands. Ontario is said to have more foreign-trained doctors driving cabs than anywhere else in the world. There's an old joke still told in Montreal: Where are you least likely to die of a heart attack? In a taxi, because odds are your driver is a cardiologist.

When I first started my year among the cabbies, these are the drivers I feared I'd meet most often. No doubt I'd find uplifting tales of personal sacrifice and compromise. I'd find cabbies whose lingering bitterness over their wasted talent was sweetened, or at least tempered, by a daughter who started medical school, or a son who'd just passed his bar exam. I could describe these brown and Black men as "heroic," knowing I've never had to work as hard as they do. Nor would I ever want to.

These narratives didn't interest me any more than those ribald taxi-after-dark stories did. We've heard them all before, too; they're part of our national lore. In 2009, York University professor Lorne Foster wrote: "It is almost a rite-of-passage in contemporary urban Canada to know somebody, or at least to know somebody who knows somebody, with a prestigious academic degree and a huge talent from a foreign-Third-World country who is 'pushing cab.'" Such stories would hardly vary, differing only by country left and career lost. This driver was an engineer in Pakistan; that driver a dentist in Ethiopia.

I didn't want to typecast the cabbies as characters in stories everyone already knew. I wanted to see the range of their experiences. I wanted to learn what makes them unique. I wanted to know what drives them. Besides, pressing cabbies to reveal their unfulfilled potential and broken dreams felt cruel.

As it turned out, I didn't meet any of these overeducated "road scholars" anyway. Neither idle degrees nor nocturnal mischief defined the taxi drivers I would get to know. Their personal narratives were far more complex than these thin clichés. Some drivers had fled or fought wars I knew little about. Many suffered horrific violence. Some perpetrated it. They weren't all heroes. I met bullies and blowhards. Pranksters, weirdos, and misanthropes. My drivers weren't all family men, and they weren't all men. Perhaps the only thing they shared was that their cramped driver's seats couldn't contain their life stories. Each had crossed many borders, both real and metaphorical, before the first day they switched on their roof light. As one cabbie would tell me "No mother ever gave birth to a taxi driver."

One

THE OLD SCHOOL

I DECIDED TO START MY YEAR AMONG THE CABBIES WITH A veteran. I reached out to Peter Pellier, who drove taxi in Mississauga for thirty-four years. Now in his late seventies, and nearly two decades retired, Peter would be my oral historian of the taxi business. And he seemed excited to chat. Peter met me at Mississauga's commuter GO Train station. He was tall and thin and walked fast. I could barely keep up with him as he led me to the nearest Tim Hortons—my first of too many.

Emil Pellier, Peter's father, was born in Czechoslovakia. He served the British army as a liaison officer in a German POW camp in Italy during the Second World War, and moved to Toronto after the war. Emil worked in a tannery for a year before sending for his wife and Peter, who was three years old at the time. Peter's early resumé reads like a catalogue of old-timey child labour. He started delivering the *Toronto Star* in Mississauga when he was six. Later, he stocked shelves at a drugstore. He shined shoes, and worked as a "pin boy" at the five-pin bowling alley in his neighbourhood. "Back then, there were jobs for kids," Peter said. "These days? You gotta be kidding me. Kids get a hundred dollars a week from their dads."

In 1969, Peter studied sociology and psychology at York University. His college buddy Bob drove cab part-time out of a garage in Erindale. Bob loved the job and encouraged Peter to sign on, which he did, during his Christmas break. "I made a fortune," he said. "I loved the freedom and mobility. Nobody was forcing you." Peter enrolled in teacher's college after graduation, but his career in education lasted only a year. His school's principal passed away and was replaced by a vice principal who didn't appreciate Peter's "unorthodox" teaching style. He decided to quit teaching altogether and drive cab full time.

Peter partnered with Bob. They shared a taxi license and a car, a Dodge Monaco. Bob drove during the night, Peter during the day. The two men shared the cost of maintenance, insurance, and other expenses. "We came together perfectly," Peter said. After they racked up a half-million kilometres on the Monaco, Peter and Bob started buying used police cruisers. "Great big lumbering Plymouth Furies," Peter said. "Then the OPP switched to Chevys. Impalas and Caprices. This was long before small and beautiful was all the rage." He and Bob remained taxi partners for thirty years.

Many of Peter's cabbie brethren in the 1970s had spent years in the business. Some started driving after returning from the Second World War, when the taxi industry was a refuge for tradeless and uneducated men. In 1955, researcher and cabbie Edward Vaz wrote that while some professionals like doctors, lawyers, bank managers, and sea captains ended up driving cab temporarily, the business mainly attracted "the flotsam and jetsam of urban life." In particular "the youthful unemployed, the transients, the feckless, the disillusioned and the undesirable."

Desirable or otherwise, Peter adored these men. "Most were real characters," he told me. "I loved being around them." There were female drivers too, like Millie McClusky—who was "sharp as a tack" and just as good a driver as her husband, Kenny—and a woman Peter knew only as "The Duchess." "They were street smart. They were savvy. They had stories to tell," Peter said. A driver nicknamed Pappy, who Peter said "looked about 110," loved to talk about being at Toronto Harbour in 1949, the night the S S Noronic burned. The fire began in the ship's linen closet, and most of the Noronic's 525 passengers were sleeping when flames engulfed her. The city didn't have enough ambulances to transport the injured to the hospital, so taxi drivers were called to help. Pappy and the other drivers threw sheets down in their backseats and shuttled smoke and burn victims from the harbour to Toronto General and St. Michael's hospitals. At least 119 people perished. Many more would've died were it not for Pappy and his fellow cabbies.

Drivers earned good money during Peter's first decade or so in the business. On his predawn shifts, he cruised Mississauga's western neighbourhoods for airport runs. "Pearson International is on the opposite end of town," Peter said. "Those are terrific fares. And at 5 am there is no traffic. I am zip, zip, back and forth." At the time, taxi companies also secured lucrative corporate accounts. Peter had a contract with St. Lawrence Cement, for example, driving employees from the docks on Lake Ontario all the way to St. Catharines.

Cabbies drove schoolchildren, too. Then as now, big yellow buses brought most kids to school, but the schoolboards hired taxi brokers to transport their special needs students. Cab companies had contracts with both the public and Catholic school boards. If a driver was bringing a child to a public school and another to a nearby Catholic school, he would bill both boards and earn double the fare. "Talk about lucrative," Peter said. "Some drivers didn't want anything to do with those trips because they don't like kids. I like kids when it comes to driving them in my taxi, so I signed up for as many school runs as I could get."

And the taxi drivers weren't just delivering people. "We were delivering things," Peter said. These were the days before fax machines and package delivery companies. Peter drove for steel and trucking firms, bringing parts from supply warehouses to company garages. He also shuttled legal documents back and forth between law firms and registry offices.

Business started to decline in the 1980s, according to Peter. Courier companies surfaced to take over the parcel trade, and fax machines cut into the document delivery business. School boards stopped using taxis and hired smaller buses to ferry their special needs students. "The smorgasbord of business we were accessing gradually started to fall away once these specialists got onto the field," Peter said. New non-smoking policies chased some long-time drivers into early retirement, nicotine-addicted cabbies deciding they'd rather not work than not smoke.

At the same time, the feeling of camaraderie among cabbies started to fade. Peter partly blames technology for this. When he first started driving cab, companies used two-way radios. "They operated on tubes," Peter said. "In the winter time, once you turned the radio off, you'd have to sit there for ten to fifteen minutes while it warmed up to communicate with the dispatch office." The radios used an open channel so every driver could hear the dispatcher's communication with everyone else. In addition to fare assignments and traffic reports, taxi radios crackled with bad jokes and smart-assed chatter. Dispatchers would back off between transmissions to let drivers crack wise at each other, as long as they didn't take up too much airtime.

As Mississauga grew in size and dispatchers got busier, this village-style dispatch system became inefficient. Taxi companies in Mississauga finally shifted to closed channels, so the dispatcher communicated with only one driver at a time. The system was more streamlined, but far less fun. "I didn't like that," Peter said. "A lot of us didn't like that." He and his cabbie colleagues lost the sense of fellowship fuelled by endless crosstalk and sass.

But Peter believes the biggest change in the industry during his career was demographic rather than technological. "Until the 1980s," he said, "the industry was fairly monolithic and fairly stable." By this, he means drivers were white. As old-school drivers like Pappy and The Duchess started to retire, new immigrants from South Asia, Africa, and the Middle East took their place.

In other parts of the country, the change in cabbie demographics had started at least a decade earlier. In 1967, Canada introduced a new points-based immigration framework that eliminated restrictions based on race and national origin and that favoured newcomers with language fluency, education, and job skills. Ironically, the same point-scoring credentials that make someone a desirable immigrant were often not recognized by Canadian professional associations once the immigrant arrived. Hence all the cab-driving cardiologists. Regardless, immigration from South Asia, Africa, and the Middle East bloomed as a result of the new regulations.

Global conflict also helped propel immigrants in Canada's direction. Middle Eastern wars and revolutions—such as those in Lebanon, Iran, and Iraq—resulted in a spike in Arab and Persian migrants. After Canada accepted seven thousand South Asian refugees expelled by Ugandan strongman Idi Amin in 1972, high numbers of South Asians started arriving from other parts of eastern Africa. Between 1971 and 1980, the number of newcomers coming to Canada from South Asian countries more than tripled, and many ended up driving cab. According to Census data from 1971, the percentage of foreign-born cabbies matched Canada's immigrant population at about 15 percent. By 1981, Canada's immigrant population percentage hardly budged, while nearly a quarter of taxi drivers were born elsewhere.

As a result, the taxicab became a borderland between "old stock" Canadians and foreign-born newcomers—the frontier dividing white space and Black-and-brown space. Border relations were often strained. The warm welcome of federal immigration policies did not always translate into hospitality on the street. The abuse of taxi drivers by racist RCMP officers at Toronto International Airport, for example, made national news. In 1975, a Lebanese-born cabbie named Farouk Debaissi told the *Globe and Mail* that an RCMP officer at the airport had called him a "camel driver" and an "Arab animal." Cabbies from Spain and Palestine complained about RCMP officers suggesting they return to their own countries, and a Black driver broke down crying when an officer called him a "dirty ni**er." Inspector B L Campbell, who oversaw airport RCMP at the time, denied the force had a racism problem and showed little sympathy for offended drivers. "There are some people who would complain if it rained," he quipped.

Perhaps nowhere was the racism against cabbies of colour more blatant than in Montreal. In his book *A Place in the Sun: Haiti, Haitians, and the Remaking of Quebec*, author Sean Mills writes about the plight of Montreal's Haitian taxi drivers during the 1970s and '80s. So many white Montrealers refused to ride with Black drivers, the vast majority of them Haitians, that some taxi companies informally advertised as white-only. In the early 1980s, Mills wrote, two-thirds of Montreal's fifteen taxi companies refused to hire Haitians. On a single day in July 1982, a company called SOS Taxi fired twenty Black drivers because it could not compete with the all-white companies. Sixty white drivers also quit en masse from Taxi Moderne, which also employed a large number of Black drivers. Taxi stands known to be "white-only" sprung up around the city, and Haitian cabbies faced racist taunts and physical violence from their white colleagues.

The federal government abetted this de facto racial segregation. In what the Haitian community regarded as an attempt to "sanitize" Montreal's airport taxi stands of Black drivers, Transport Canada demanded a $1,200 fee for drivers to work at the airports, knowing most Haitian drivers couldn't afford to pay it. Airport cabbies, who'd been 90 percent Haitian, dropped to 3 percent. Haitian drivers organized protests and formed organizations to defend their interests, prompting the provincial government to launch a public inquiry into racism in the taxi industry in 1982. The inquiry acknowledged the rampant discrimination Haitian drivers faced. These findings, combined with the Haitian cabbies' own street-level activism, eventually led to changes that improved working conditions for Quebec's Black drivers.

In Mississauga, the number of immigrant drivers didn't rise until Toronto housing costs rocketed in the '80s, forcing new Canadians to seek more affordable homes elsewhere in the GTA. Peter remembers that the new drivers only socialized within their own cultural groups. "They knew each other. They came from the same place. They spoke the same language. Why wouldn't they?" Mississauga drivers still congregated in the regular cabbie hangouts, like the Orchard Restaurant parking lot in the middle of town, but even there ethnic groups huddled in their own corner of asphalt. This self-segregation sparked animosity in some of the senior drivers, Peter said. "Things were starting to become unglued."

Issues of language arose, too. Mississauga city councillor David Culham complained that he found it difficult, in at least one instance, to "understand" a taxi driver. As a result, the transportation and traffic committee recommended the city's taxi commission scrap a long-standing bylaw requiring cabbies to have at least a grade ten education. Instead, they directed the commission to place more emphasis on cabbies' English fluency and "their manners." The city started to test potential drivers' language skills before issuing taxi licenses, but many long-time cabbies accused the examiners of being too forgiving. According to Peter, city officials would overlook poor test scores and issue licenses to people who had families to support. "Better to give someone a license and keep him employed than have him go on welfare," Peter said.

These stories didn't sit well with me. Challenging newcomers' language and politeness, and accusing city officials of conspiring with English-challenged immigrants, smelled of old school bigotry. Peter must have noticed my discomfort. "I have to be careful with my terminology," he added. "Comments were made about drivers that were not complimentary. Racist comments. Derogatory comments. I always felt uncomfortable with that."

Cabbies of colour have long endured such invective. Racial abuse from passengers, and even from other drivers, has always been commonplace. Many cabbies blame racism for why they are driving taxi in the first place. When a 2007 study examined why foreign-trained professionals in Toronto were driving cab instead of practicing their professions, most cited racism as the biggest barrier to the latter. They considered their purported lack of "Canadian credentials" to be a smokescreen for discrimination. Another study suggested that everyday racism in the taxi-cab usually manifests indirectly, with derogatory stereotypes rather than outright slurs. According to one driver, "rarely people are stating their racism clearly, calling you 'Hey you Paki,' for example, or 'You are a ni**er.' This stuff rarely happens.... But usually they do it differently. Like 'Oh, you're from Afghanistan. Great country. Can you bring me back some hash from there? Some opium?'"

Slurs and insults towards taxi drivers surged in the wake of September 11. Indeed, some Middle Eastern and South Asian cabbies in New York, especially those who wore turbans, so feared violent reprisals from their passengers that they stopped working altogether. Drivers could hardly afford this voluntary unemployment for long, though, and eventually returned to their cabs to face intimidation, racist slurs, vandalism, and violence. They reported being spat on, cheated, kicked, and punched. Tires were slashed. Windshields and side-view mirrors broken. Passengers interrogated drivers with Muslim names displayed on their hack licenses. "Are you in al-Qaeda?" "Who bombed the World Trade Center?" "Why are you here, and when will you go back to your country?" "All you Muslims are the same" "You're all terrorists." New York cabbies covered up the Arabic names on their licenses, even though they risked heavy fines for doing so. The taxicab's front seat became the front line in a new culture war.

The cloud of those fallen towers hung over taxi drivers for years, and not just in New York. In 2007, a Toronto driver told Dr Sarah Sharma, a researcher from the University of Toronto:

> Since 9/11 people treat me differently. When people are drunk they just say it outright "do you know Osama, how come you look like Osama, go back home terrorist." In the daytime I've noticed that people give orders now. Like, they don't talk to me like I'm a human, they don't treat me like a human but like an animal. Go here. Go there. Turn.

Provocative statements from people like Montana senator Conrad Burns hardly helped. During a campaign stop in 2006, Burns said his administration sought to ensure "we have a safe world and a secure world where our kids can go to bed at night and not worry about a guy that drives a taxicab in the daytime and kills at night."

Many Muslim cabbies found themselves educating their passengers about faith and geopolitics. Drivers felt obliged to debunk their passengers' misconceptions about Islam and to counter media propaganda about the "war on terror." They answered questions about conflict in their respective homelands—Pakistan, Palestine, Afghanistan, Bangladesh—and often pulled over at the end of a ride to finish a discussion with the meter turned off. Even drivers who would normally deflect questions about politics or their countries of origin were drawn into such conversations. An Afghan driver told University of Hawai'i researcher Monisha Das Gupta: "We lost our jobs; we lost our country. Now that I am in the US, I lost my dignity. I told someone I am not in the US just to do a job. I am here for some time because my country has been destroyed. I'm here to survive for a little while."

Two

THE MAN WITH
THE PLAN

I SPOKE TO MANY DRIVERS WHO HAD WATCHED THEIR countries destroyed and just wanted to survive. These cabbies didn't just feel the social and political reverberations of war from afar in their taxis, they'd felt the literal rumble of bombs in their bodies. I doubt there's an armed conflict anywhere in the world unrepresented by a Canadian taxi driver. In one way or another, men with guns had invaded the personal lives of most cabbies I spoke to. Some drivers bore arms themselves. All of them bore scars. And none had more obvious scars than Michael Sillah Kamara.

Michael met me at my Halifax B&B on an exceptionally frigid February evening after one of his cab-driving shifts. The B&B owner had made it clear that all guests must leave their shoes in the entryway before heading up to the rooms, but when I asked Michael to take off his boots he just smiled. "It is diffi-cult for me," he said. "Because of my leg."

In December 1998, boys with guns attacked Komrabia N'jla, Michael's home village. Weeks earlier, the rebel forces had crossed over the border into Sierra Leone from Liberia and started their westward march to the capital, Freetown. The rebels looted and destroyed every village they passed through. They set homes on fire. They abducted children, and raped women and girls. They drugged young men and forced them into their ranks. Located about thirty kilometres southeast of Freetown, Komrabia N'jla was in their path.

One night, the rebels took up positions around the village. Then they started to shoot. The villagers understood what the rebels' assault would bring, and they panicked. "You see bullets going like fire," Michael said. "Like how rain is coming."

Michael was in his mid-teens at the time. If he were captured, the rebels would either kill him or conscript him. He scrambled out a window and ran towards the surrounding forest. He had nearly reached the treeline when he heard a rebel shout at him to stop. He didn't, and a bullet blasted through his left leg just below the knee. Somehow Michael continued to run. Fear and adrenaline kept him on his feet for two miles, he said, before he collapsed on the forest floor. He lay there for two days, bleeding and praying, until Sierra Leonean soldiers found him. They brought him to a government hospital in Freetown. Doctors could not treat Michael's wound. He'd lain in the bush too long and an infection had set in. They amputated his leg.

Considering the horrors that would descend on the capital in the days that followed, Michael's surgical amputation seems, in retrospect, a strange mercy. He was lucky to be safely recovering in a hospital bed on January 6, when the war came to Freetown. Villagers who'd escaped the advancing rebels had fled to the capital, where they believed government soldiers and Nigerian-led peacekeepers would keep them safe. "But the rebels entered anyway," Michael said. "That was the dark day of our city."

The rebels launched a murderous assault on Freetown, which they named "Operation No Living Thing." Commanders with monikers like Mosquito and Superman ordered their charges to empty the city's prisons, set police stations ablaze, and lay siege to government military positions. Rebel units were named for their particular expertise: "The Burn House Unit," "The Blood Shed Squad," "The Cut Hands Commando," and "The Kill Man No Blood Unit." The latter specialized in murdering without leaving a mess. The death squads didn't distinguish between civilian and military targets. They killed entire families at a time, often burning them alive in their homes or cars. They massacred men, women, and children in churches and mosques. They gouged out eyes and flung people off rooftops. Rebels kidnapped girls as young as eight years old and, in the words of a rebel who later testified at trial, "used them as women."

From his hospital bed, Michael couldn't see the bloody streets of Freetown—another mercy—but he could hear the boom of bombs dropped on rebel positions by Nigerian Alpha warplanes and helicopter gunships. The rebels started to withdraw from the city after two weeks of street battles. They'd lost many men during the fighting and craved revenge. "Those that remained were like wounded lions," Michael said. "They won't spare anyone they see now." The rebels hacked and slashed their way out of the capital and set entire city blocks on fire.

Of all the horrors the rebels perpetrated on the people of Freetown, none characterized the war more than the mutilations. In *Vanity Fair*, journalist Sebastian Junger wrote about "amputation squads" assembled by the rebels:

> The squads were made up of teenagers and even children, many of whom wore bandages where incisions had been made to pack cocaine under their skin. They did their work with rusty machetes and axes and seemed to choose their victims completely

at random. "You, you, and you," they would say, picking people out of a line. There were stories of hands' being taken away in blood-soaked grain bags. There were stories of hands' being hung in trees. There were stories of hands' being eaten.

The rebels amputated limbs from twenty thousand civilians. For each that survived their wounds, three died from blood loss, infection, or shock.

The chaos in Freetown makes an accurate accounting of civilian deaths impossible. A Physicians for Human Rights report claimed at least five thousand civilians were killed during the occupation of the city, while the government's senior pathologist registered more than 7,300 burials. The most visceral reminder of that January in Freetown isn't a cold ledger of fatalities, but the mutilated survivors that remain. "You will not go two or three steps in Freetown without seeing a man who lost his hand or foot from the war in the country," Michael told me. Past violence exists in the present on Freetown's streets. "All those people who suffered from the war must finish dying before it becomes history," Michael said. "They are everywhere."

Michael stayed in the hospital for two months. He laughed when I asked him if his family came to visit him. "War separates people. War makes you forget about other people. You just try to get yourself to a safe place. If you have kids, you go with your kids. But everyone else runs for themselves," Michael said. "War is no good. War is definitely no good."

After the war, the Sierra Leonean government set up camps for citizens displaced by the fighting. Michael was sent to the Aberdeen Road Amputee Camp on the Freetown peninsula, which was built to house amputees and their families. Nearly five hundred residents lived in tents built of branches and blue plastic tarps. The place reeked of garbage and smoke from cooking fires. Dogs prowled the grounds after dark. According to rumours, so did rebel fighters.

Many amputees blamed Aberdeen's scant food and medical supplies on thieving rebels who infiltrated the camp at night.

The amputees of Aberdeen Camp became the war's photographic icons. Images of Aberdeen's legless and handless children flashed on televisions around the world. Sierra Leone hosted the largest humanitarian aid operation on earth. Journalist Linda Polman reported on the endless parade of journalists, government ministers, and aid workers who streamed through the camp "trying to capitalize on the publicity value of the amputees." Amputees became mascots of fundraising efforts. Each camp tour would conclude with a visit to the same little girl whose arm was hacked off by a rebel when she was only three months old. "For each foreign visitor the mother rolled up her daughter's sleeve," Polman wrote. "Like a professional child star, the toddler would pose with her naked stump thrust forward, her little face a picture of misery."

Michael thrived at Aberdeen. The camp offered refugees various training courses, and Michael enrolled in a tailoring program. The job suited him. Michael had apprenticed in a tailor shop back in Komrabia N'jla, where he'd learned basic stitches and earned the occasional dollar from his "boss man." "In the camp, tailoring is one of the things God blessed me with," Michael said. After he opened his own shop in Aberdeen, tailors who'd lost hands during the war started to visit. They longed to work with cloth and thread again, but felt their amputations had killed their careers. "They were discouraged," Michael said. "When they lose their one hand they say 'This is the hand I was using the scissors to cut. I am not able to cut again.'"

Michael decided to gather the tailors together and retrain them. His efforts drew the attention of Cause Canada, a humanitarian organization working at the camp, which provided sewing machines and paid Michael to give tailoring workshops to amputees. The Cause Canada project ended after six months, but Michael kept his tailor shop running. He worked alongside the tailors he helped train, and they earned a little money sewing clothes for customers in the camps. "I have a lot of friends that came back to life," Michael said. "You are able to do the job that you know before. And you are able to get small, small money out of it. And you can feed your family." During his time at Aberdeen, Michael trained and retrained more than twenty fellow amputees and their children to be tailors.

The Cause Canada program aimed to give the camp's amputees the skills and training to function outside Aberdeen's boundaries. But Canadian occupational therapist Quentin Ranson, who met Michael in the fall of 2000, found that many amputees became completely dependent on the camp's material offerings. They believed that the best opportunities lay not in the skills they could learn, but the stuff they could get. And stuff came constantly. Sacks of rice, piles of second-hand clothes, and crates of used toys from distant donors arrived at the camp gates every day. One morning, camp officials arrived at Aberdeen's gate to find a group of lab-coated foreigners handing out antibiotics like Halloween candy. And Quentin remembers a truck pulling up in front of the camp, dumping a load of cast-off artificial arms and legs, then driving away. Even though the amputees already had two custom-made prostheses each, such deliveries were common. "Artificial limbs were lying around all over the camp," Polman wrote, "gifts from generous souls the world over, flung into tangled heaps in corners."

Enterprising amputees sold whatever they didn't want. They earned money peddling UNHCR tarpaulins outside the camp gates and sold food and clothing donations in the Freetown markets. Quentin found bags of donated dates from Saudi Arabia for sale in market stalls alongside packages of the high-protein Bennimix porridge that amputee mothers were given to feed their children. Everyone agreed that Bennimix tasted terrible. Saudi dates didn't appeal to Sierra Leonean palates either. But the community that lived outside the camp would buy them anyway. They envied Aberdeen's amputees for what they received from international organizations and foreign donors. Each time a United Nations vehicle drove up Aberdeen Road towards the camp, all of Freetown wondered "What are the amputees getting now?"

Michael was just as keen as his fellow amputees to take advantage of whatever short-term opportunities came to him at Aberdeen, but he didn't believe he could build a life out of the camp's donation economy. "Michael stood out," Quentin said. "He had entrepreneurial spirit. Self-driven. He really didn't like having things handed to him." In the ten months Quentin worked at the camp, Michael was one of the only amputees who never asked him for a handout. "I don't say this with any contempt," Quentin said. "I don't blame the others. I can imagine it is hard not to see me as an opportunity. To see what I could do for them to improve their lives." Michael, though, never wanted anything for free. "He was savvy without that hustler mentality. He never exploited anyone." Quentin believes that Michael would've become the CEO of a successful business had he been born just about anywhere else.

When Michael learned that Quentin planned to return to Edmonton for Christmas, he had a proposition. Michael asked if Quentin knew anyone in Canada who might be interested in buying the sorts of clothing he made. If so, Quentin could ask them to email their measurements to him in Sierra Leone. Michael would make the clothes in Aberdeen and send them to Canada with Quentin , who would sell them to his friends. Quentin could use the profits to buy Michael a camera, then bring the camera to Freetown after his Christmas break. Quentin agreed. He travelled to Canada with twelve custom-made skirts and returned to Sierra Leone at the beginning of 2001 with a camera for Michael.

Later that year, an American single-leg amputee named Dee Malchow visited Aberdeen. She met with a local pastor and a gathering of camp residents, including Michael, to teach them about amputee soccer. Michael and his Aberdeen campmates had never heard of the sport and sat fascinated as Malchow explained the rules. In amputee soccer, outfield players must have a single leg, and goalkeepers a single hand. The game is played on crutches and without prostheses, but players cannot make contact with the ball using their crutches or stumps. The pitch and goals are smaller than in regular soccer, the games shorter. Malchow also showed the men fabulous action photos of players from around the world kicking and heading balls while suspended in mid-air on crutches.

Michael, already a soccer fan, was intrigued. "He just ran with it," Quentin said. "He was so excited. Just the notion of doing something physical again." Michael assembled a team from among the camp's soccer-obsessed young men and explained the rules. Quentin and Michael combined their respective skills—occupational therapy and tailoring—and developed leather stump protectors for players whose amputations were still healing. Cause Canada pitched in funds to add reinforced tips to crutches. The camp quickly proved too small for a proper soccer practice, so Quentin negotiated with a local chief to allow the team to train on a patch of land near the ocean. He also hired a United Nations bus to bring the team to and from their Sunday practice sessions.

Quentin remembers accompanying the team to their inaugural seaside practice. "For the first time, people were not staring at the amputees out of pity or disgust; they were staring with wonder and awe," Quentin said. Street vendors left their stalls to watch the amputees play. Taxi drivers and UN peacekeepers stopped their cars at the side of the pitch. "It is impossible to see these guys move with such agility and confidence and pity them," Quentin said. "They had astonishing skill that nobody could deny. And I think it was the first time many of them didn't pity themselves." The players formed the Sierra Leone National Amputee Soccer Team in 2002 and went on to compete internationally, including in Liverpool in 2003.

Between soccer and tailoring, Michael found time to locate the surviving members of his family in other displacement camps. During tearful reunions with his parents and siblings, he learned that his home in Komrabia N'jla had been looted and destroyed by rebels. They killed several family members, including two of his twelve siblings. But a new family had grown around Michael in Aberdeen. He met and married Hannah, whose mother had lost her arm to a rebel machete. He also gained a five-year-old nephew, Mark, whom Michael's sister had entrusted into his care. "In Africa it is common," Michael said. "They born too many kids. They give them away so other people can help with the responsibility." By the time he was nineteen, Michael had a wife and a young child to care for.

And he wanted to bring them to Canada. All Michael knew about the country was that he wanted to go there. "Just because of Quentin," Michael said. "He is so nice, I thought that everything is nice in Canada." Michael and his soccer teammate Joseph Largawo approached Quentin for assistance. They weren't the first or last of the amputees to ask Quentin for immigration help, but Michael was one of the only people at Aberdeen who Quentin believed could thrive outside the camp. Still, Quentin felt conflicted abetting their immigration. Michael and Joseph's departure from Aberdeen would deprive the camp, and the soccer team, of their strongest advocates and leaders. "I quickly realized it wasn't my place to decide that on their behalf," Quentin said. "It wasn't something I had a right to influence."

Quentin brought Canadian refugee application forms for Michael and Joseph. He told them they would have to fill out the forms themselves, and send them to the Canadian Embassy in

Ghana, the closest embassy to Freetown, rather than to Ottawa directly. Michael remembers Quentin being clear and firm with them. "Quentin said, 'Mail this. Don't joke. Mail it. I am not sure if they will approve you guys. But mail it.'"

Michael and Joseph didn't mail it. "We did not take it serious," Michael said. Two months passed before Michael and Joseph showed the documents to a pastor who was visiting the camp. The pastor was appalled that the men had been sitting on the completed documents for so long. He scolded them for their hesitation and helped them gather enough money to cover the postage. Then he asked Michael if he could add his own name to the application. Michael told him, simply, that there was no room left on the form.

The pastor's interest finally convinced Michael of the importance of the Canadian documents. From then on, he refused to let the papers out of his sight. "We are not going to give these forms to anyone," Michael said to Joseph. "If someone wants to post it for us, we will hold on to it and say 'You bring us to the place.'" The two men walked to the post office together. "We walk foot to foot. Foot to foot," Michael said. "They charge us. We post it. They send it." Then Michael abruptly forgot about the forms.

Eight months later, in April 2002, while in Freetown to purchase tailoring materials for his shop, Michael saw a UNHCR truck driving up the road towards Aberdeen. Michael knew the truck would cause excitement at the camp. "When they see white people, everybody goes to see. They know gifts are coming." The UNHCR vehicle had left by the time Michael returned from town, but one of his tailoring students told him two officials came looking for him. The men returned in the evening. They introduced themselves to Michael and told him to bring his family, and Joseph's family, to their office the next day for an interview. Their refugee applications were being considered, and the officials needed Michael and Joseph to confirm everything they had written on their original forms.

Because Michael and his family still lived in Sierra Leone, the UNHCR did not consider them refugees. The commission transferred their case to the International Organization for Migration, a UN partner organization. The wheels of such organizations grind forward slowly. By the time IOM summoned Michael to its Freetown office to tell him his family's visas were ready, nearly three years had passed. Michael was at that point splitting time between Aberdeen and a house in Masiaka, a town east of Freetown, provided by a Norwegian refugee agency. He lived at Aberdeen during the week so he could continue his tailoring work and his training with the soccer team, and spent his weekends with his family in Masiaka. Many resettled amputees like Michael lived in Aberdeen part time for fear they might miss out on the opportunities the camp offered.

The IOM official asked when Michael wanted to leave. "Right now," Michael said. "Put us inside a plane and we'll go." The man told Michael his family needed a final medical check before flying to Canada. When Michael brought Hannah and Mark to the office the next morning, the official was shocked to see Hannah's pregnant belly. "Why didn't you tell us your wife was pregnant?" the man said.

""I didn't know I was supposed to. I've been waiting, waiting, waiting."

"How far along is her pregnancy?"

"Seven months," Michael lied. Hannah was only a week from her due date.

The man shook his head and told Michael they would have to cancel the flight. Had the organization known about Hannah's pregnancy sooner, they would've arranged for a nurse to accompany them on the flight to Canada. Now it was far too late. As it turned out, Michael and Hannah's baby, a daughter they named Surria after Quentin's wife, was born on the day of their original scheduled flight to Canada. Had their trip not been cancelled, she might have been born on the plane.

Michael and Hannah were heartbroken. The family had to start the refugee process all over again and would wait another two years before finally flying to Canada. They landed in Toronto on a bitter day in January 2007, nearly six years since first filling out their refugee-claim forms. The family stayed in a Toronto hotel for a couple of weeks before flying to Halifax. I asked Michael why the family chose Halifax. They didn't. "There is an organization that welcomes refugees," he said. "They do everything. They find a place for you. That's the location they sent us. We have no option." The weather was horrible on the East Coast when Michael and his family arrived. Almost every taxi driver I met who had come from somewhere else, especially from tropical climes, told a similar story of landing during the cold dead of winter. No one ever seems to arrive in Canada in the summer, as if there were an official government policy to cruelly haze new Canadians with weather.

"That was a bad winter," Michael said. "The thing is, when you come here newly, there are certain things that make you discouraged. One, you come and you have no family here. You miss your family. And two is the weather, especially if you come here during wintertime. It discourages you. And three, the food. You miss the food you used to eat." Eventually, Michael and Hannah learned where to buy familiar yams, cassava, and other ingredients that reminded them of home. The Kamara family has lived in Halifax for a dozen years now, but Michael still misses the feeling of community he left behind. "Back home you don't have to call and make an appointment to come over. You just go and knock on the door and say 'I am here. Open the door for me.'"

Michael received his taxi license in 2012 and has been driving cab ever since. "When you come newly, you like driving. But as time goes you start to hate it." More transportation options make it harder to earn a good living driving cab. Maintenance and insurance costs continue to rise, and customers often treat him poorly. "Some days you get people who are frustrating you all the time. You understand? Some people are rude. They don't appreciate whatever you do for them." As a Black driver, he endures a fair amount of racism, and not just from passengers. "I get treated bad from the police. A lot," Michael said. "They pull you out because of your colour. They will give you a ticket just for that. Offences other people do and go free, you will never go free on that."

The discrimination didn't bother Michael much, though. Many of the taxi drivers I spoke to shared his stoic response to racism. In fact, none mentioned their experiences with slurs or bigotry unless I asked first. In her research on racism in Toronto's taxi industry, scholar Jessica Walters found that drivers tend to downplay incidences of everyday discrimination. Some cabbies are more apt to blame a passenger's drunkenness, or bad mood, or some miscommunication about the fare or route—as if getting stuck in traffic warrants insulting a driver's name or skin colour. Cabbies become so desensitized to bigotry that they shrug off racist treatment as one of the hazards of the job. More a nuisance than a crime. "In Nova Scotia people are good, but you can't say everybody should be good. People are nice here. Not everybody will be nice. Some will be stinky," Michael said. "Some people say racist things. In any community, there is problem. I just focus on the good side."

Despite the frustrations and challenges of pushing cab, the flexibility of the job allows Michael to make trips home to Sierra Leone every two or three years to visit family and friends for up to two months at a time. On one of Michael's trips, he met with a friend whose son suffered from a serious bone infection in his foot. The father, himself an amputee, could not afford the surgery that would save his son's foot from being amputated. He asked Michael for help. When he returned to Halifax, Michael sent $500 of his taxi earnings to Sierra Leone for the surgery and doctors saved the boy's foot. Michael continues to assist the family. "In September, when school opens, I will send money. They buy all the necessary things. They pay all the school fees for the school year. They buy books, pens, pencils, schoolbag, shoes," Michael said. He feels compelled to help people because of the generosity he and his family received. "We are here because people helped us," he said. "Today my kids are getting opportunity. They go to good schools. My family, we breathe well. We lie down in good conditions." Michael believes a person should never pass up a chance to do good, especially if that means saving a life.

In 2014, Michael saw another opportunity to do good. Growing up, before his amputation, he'd played soccer outfitted in ragged jerseys and shorts that rarely matched. In Canada, though, all the kids playing community soccer wore matching uniforms that always seemed clean and new. Realizing they must replace their entire kit every couple of years, Michael called all the soccer teams in Halifax. He told team managers the story about how he survived the war in Sierra Leone, about his life as an amputee and soccer player, and about the soccer-obsessed Sierra Leoneans who play without matching jerseys. He offered to pick up any used kit the teams might be willing to donate. Michael collected enough kit—along with cleats, soccer balls, and school bags—to outfit four amputee teams as well as three primary schools.

Michael also wanted to help out his own former amputee soccer team. He knew they could use a team vehicle, so he spent $500 on a grey Honda Odyssey that one of his retiring cabbie colleagues had driven as a taxi. Michael stuffed the donated kit he'd collected into the back of the van, drove the Odyssey into a 20-foot shipping container he'd rented, and sent the container to Sierra Leone on a cargo ship. Michael met the ship when it arrived in Freetown and drove the van from the port to the soccer club headquarters.

Quentin knows Michael's motivations aren't purely altruistic. "I would never deny that he would be treated like a hero going back to the village with all that stuff," Quentin said. "That is part of the incentive, for sure. He enjoys that." But neither would Sierra Leoneans fault Michael for expecting acknowledgment for his generosity. It's part of the culture. And the recognition goes both ways. In the winter of 2018, Michael travelled from Halifax to Edmonton to visit Quentin and his family. As they sat in Quentin's living room, Michael invited Quentin's nine-year-old son, Sahen, to sit next to him. "I want to talk to you," he said. "I want to tell you what your father did for me."

While Quentin listened in, Michael told Sahen the story of meeting his father in Aberdeen and how he helped him start his tailor shop. Then he told Sahen how his father helped his family come to Canada and how his family now lives a better life. Quentin thought Michael had just come over for a casual visit. Just a friend in from out of town. But as Michael shared his story with Sahen, Quentin realized Michael had planned this visit to formally honour him in front of his son. Michael wanted Sahen to recognize the kind of man his father was. Sahen was impressed, or as impressed, at least, as a nine-year-old boy can be by his father's munificence.

Quentin, though, recognized an uncomfortable irony in Michael's story and that of many of the amputees he worked with in Aberdeen. Their injuries, though horrific, granted them opportunities they would not otherwise have had. "Being an amputee actually elevated their status," Quentin said. In Aberdeen, amputees were given job training and funding. The camp introduced them to immigration and refugee systems they would never have imagined. Michael would've never met Quentin and would likely never have left Sierra Leone. "It is terrible to say, but Michael's life is better because he is an amputee than it would be if he was not a war-wounded person." Michael's forced investment in pain, blood, and bone eventually paid out.

Michael's success also makes Quentin wonder about the amputees he *didn't* help to come to Canada. Well-meaning foreigners fitted Sierra Leone's amputees with prosthetics and taught them new skills in an effort to make their lives better and inspire others. But they were supposed to remain in Sierra Leone: the NGOs believed the refugees could build capacity at home and lead a new wave of disabled citizens. "We had a naive perspective that we could help these people to be successful in that context," Quentin said. There was a notion, too, that these damaged men and women didn't have the skills, experience, or connections to succeed in Canada anyway. Without the kind of rare savvy Quentin observed in Michael, the amputees would be better off in Africa.

Looking back, Quentin questions this idea. He recalls a double-arm amputee in Aberdeen who travelled to Europe several times with an NGO to talk about the good work being done for amputees in Sierra Leone. The NGO insisted the man not embarrass the organization by applying for refugee status while abroad. "He toed the line everyone was feeding him," Quentin said. "You need to stay here in Sierra Leone. Integrate. Learn to use your limbs. Be a leader." When Quentin returned to Sierra Leone six years later, he found the man struggling to make a living for himself and his family. And he was justifiably bitter. He told Quentin he should have taken the opportunity to immigrate to Europe when he had the chance.

"He was right," Quentin said. "He should have. All the advice people gave him not to claim refugee status or asylum was wrong.

We were wrong." Quentin now feels he should've encouraged more of the amputees he worked with to apply to come to Canada. For his part, Michael owes his personal success as much to leaving Aberdeen's culture of good intentions as to the charity and training he received as a resident.

"God blessed us to be in this part of the world," Michael told me at the end of our talk. "But not for me. I am getting old. And I'm deformed. I don't worry about my life." Michael lives for his family now. Mark moved to Saskatchewan, but Michael still has two children at home: sixteen year-old Surria and eleven-year-old David. Michael will drive cab until Surria and David finish university, perhaps for another ten years. "I prayed my kids would be born in a place where we don't struggle for them to get good education," Michael said. "And I like this place. We've been here for twelve years. I don't want to move from here. I want to raise my kids to grow here. It is a peaceful place."

I'd never met anyone like Michael before. Not in Canada or anywhere else. No one I knew had ever been through so much. Getting to know Michael, even for the few hours we spent together, exhilarated me. I felt as if I'd been told some tremendous secret. But after our conversation, once Michael clomped his boots down the B&B stairs and back into the snow, I had an uncomfortable thought. Quentin told me a man of Michael's savvy and demeanor could've been a CEO had he been born somewhere else. I wondered how I would have fared as a Sierra Leonean. Would I have had the mettle to survive a gunshot on the forest floor? Could I have made a life in the face of such challenges? I don't know if I have Michael's resilience—I've never been tested this way, after all—but I doubt I have his drive.

Three

THE UPSTANDER

"I WAS BORN DURING THE HORRORS," ANDY RETI TOLD ME.
When Mississauga driver Peter Pellier recommended I meet
Andy, he said only that Andy was a senior member of the taxi
industry with a million stories. Still, when I sat down with Andy
in the common room of his condo building, I had no idea one
of those stories would be about surviving the Holocaust. For his
part, Andy was surprised I wanted to hear this story at all. In fact,
he interrupted his own telling a couple of times to laugh and say,
"I think you wanted to talk about taxis" as if I'd rather hear about
the vagaries of Toronto's taxi industry. He'd get to those eventually, but we needed to get through the horrors first.

Ibolya, Andy's mother, gave birth to him on a cold hospital
floor in Budapest in 1942. Because they were Jews, the doctors
would not allow Ibolya into a delivery room. "To them, I was
just another Jewish bastard," Andy said. The systematic killing
of European Jews by the Nazis had started the previous spring

following the German invasion of the Soviet Union. But while Hungarian Jews suffered economic and political repression, no atrocities had been committed against them. Ibolya would later write, in a memoir called *Stronger Together*, co-written with Andy: "Somehow, we hadn't paid attention to what had been happening for years to Jews everywhere in Europe. We were young and optimistic, hoping the terrible things would not affect us. Then they did."

Hitler's army met no resistance when it invaded Hungary in March 1944. After Hungary's regent, Miklós Horthy, invited the Nazis to cross the border, they quickly deported all Jewish men between the ages of eighteen and sixty, including Andy's father, Zolti, to forced labour camps. Ibolya and Andy moved in with Zolti's parents, Henrik and Janka, Ibolya's own parents having already been shipped by cattle car to Auschwitz, never to return. Neither did Zolti. Under Nazi occupation, all Jews over age six were forced to wear a yellow fabric star on their chest. The Nazis also affixed yellow stars on the buildings where Jews were permitted to live. Hungarian Jews could not leave their homes except for two hours in the evening and were banned from most public places. Along with dogs, they were also banned from many stores.

When Horthy signed an armistice with the Soviet Union and withdrew Hungary from the war on October 15, Ibolya and the rest of Budapest's Jews tore the yellow stars from their chests and trampled them underfoot. Their joy, though, would be brief. The Hungarian army ignored the armistice and the fascist Arrow Cross Party launched a coup the very same day. Their leader, Ferenc Szálasi, became president. "Szálasi was bloodthirsty," Ibolya wrote. "He swore he would help the Germans to annihilate the Jews."

Police and swastika-adorned soldiers stormed Ibolya's apartment building the day after the coup. "Every Jew down to the yard or I shoot!" a soldier yelled. Ibolya lifted Andy from his bed. She grabbed his coat, a blanket, some apples and crackers, then joined a crowd of hundreds of Budapest's Jews. Most were women and children; the men had already been shipped to the camps. Soldiers marched them to an open field, where they instructed everyone to toss their valuables onto a blanket spread on the ground and to hold their hands up to show they were bare of rings and wristwatches. Ibolya managed to hide her wedding ring in Andy's coat pocket. Then, with their hands still held over their heads, the captives continued their forced march. Onlookers lined the route and spat on the captives as they passed. Someone in the crowd punched Andy's grandfather in the face and crushed his eyeglasses. Someone else snatched Andy's blanket from Ibolya's arms.

Their procession ended at the Tattersall racetrack and arena. Jews continued to arrive throughout the day, and the crowd inside the arena swelled until there was nowhere left to sit. Ibolya and her family spent two days at the racetrack without food, water, or shelter. At three o'clock in the morning on the second night, soldiers switched on the arena lights and announced that the assembled crowd was allowed to leave. But as the crowd moved towards the gates, German soldiers started firing bullets randomly into their backs. Everyone panicked. "Many were wounded and killed," Ibolya wrote, "but somehow we got home."

The soldiers took Henrik away to a labour camp a few days later. Fearing she'd be taken soon as well, Ibolya hid with Andy at a Red Cross facility set up to house children whose parents had been murdered or taken to the camps. Ibolya hoped to find a bed for Andy, but the shelter was already filled beyond capacity. More than three thousand people—mostly sick and orphaned children—were crammed into a shelter designed to house six hundred. Ibolya managed to find an empty corner in the shelter's cold cellar. She spread her coat on the floor and laid Andy down on top of it. They stayed there for two weeks.

Ibolya brought Andy home when he fell ill, but they returned to the shelter with Janka after Ibolya heard rumors the police were rounding up the rest of Budapest's Jews. Indeed, the police soon discovered Jews hiding in the shelter. "I was sure our fellow Hungarians had denounced us," Ibolya wrote. On December 3, soldiers circled the building and commanded everyone to come out into the yard, where they robbed the terrified Jews of whatever jewelry they had left. Ibolya slid her ring into the back of Andy's diaper, hoping the soldiers wouldn't look there.

For the second time in less than two months, Ibolya found herself on another forced march through Budapest. The soldiers led everyone to a stadium, where they were divided by sex, then again into old and young. Any child over a year old was to be left behind. Andy was two years old, and Ibolya watched horrified as soldiers ordered mothers to place their children on the ground and walk away. Ibolya tried to conceal her age by tying a black kerchief over her head, but an attentive soldier shouted at her to put Andy down and join the group of young women. Quaking, she obeyed. Andy screamed until Janka picked him up. Janka then chanced upon a policeman she recognized from her hometown and begged him to help them. He pointed to the line of young people and whispered: "Whatever you do, don't get mixed up in that group. They are going to Auschwitz." The officer then made a show of ordering Janka and Ibolya to join the older group, thus saving them from the gas chamber. Andy would later say that every Holocaust survivor owes their life to the kindness of at least one stranger.

Instead of Auschwitz, the soldiers sent Ibolya, Janka, and Andy to the Budapest ghetto, where they shared a two-bedroom apartment with twenty-seven people. After a week, the fascists barred everyone from leaving the ghetto, even to go get food. Then, on Christmas Day—"Not an important day for Jews," Andy said—his grandfather Henrik knocked on their door.

He'd somehow escaped from the labour camp and returned to Budapest to find his family. Dwindling food stocks tempered the miracle of Henrik's return. He was another mouth to feed.

Although he was only two years old at the time, Andy has three distinct memories of the ghetto. The first was that Katie, the little girl he shared a bed with, had terribly cold feet. Years later, Andy would name his first daughter after this frozen-toed girl. Another was Soviet soldiers entering Budapest on January 18, 1945, and freeing the Jews from the ghetto. Andy remembers one soldier handing him a small roll of Russian rye bread to eat. For Andy, that black roll marked the end of a war in which the Nazis murdered more than half a million Hungarian Jews. Andy wouldn't tell me the third memory, only that it involved his father. "I keep this to myself," he said.

After the war, Ibolya and Andy continued to live with Henrik and Janka. In 1947, a friend of Zolti's named Béla, whose pregnant wife had been murdered at Auschwitz, began to court Ibolya. She eventually accepted his proposal, but neither were in a rush to marry. Ibolya and Béla wanted to escape communist Hungary to Austria, then immigrate to the newly founded state of Israel. Béla fled alone to Vienna in 1948, then sent an escort to Budapest with instructions to smuggle Ibolya and Andy in via Czechoslovakia. Ibolya told Janka of her plans but kept them secret from her father-in-law. According to Andy, Henrik was a "rabid communist" and a high-ranking Hungarian Communist Party functionary. He would not have approved of their escape.

Ibolya and Andy's escort, a young peasant woman, took them and another Hungarian couple to a village near the Czechoslovakian border, where they waited until dark before creeping across. Andy, six years old at the time, walked quietly and bravely alongside the others. But after three hours of walking, he could not continue, so the escort lifted Andy onto her back, where he promptly fell asleep. It was an act of mercy that masked a betrayal: the escort led her charges directly to Czechoslovakian border guards who arrested, robbed, and jailed them. The next morning, the Czechoslovakians delivered Ibolya and Andy to the Hungarian military post, where they were locked in a detention centre.

A small window near the ceiling of their cell allowed in some light. Ibolya leaned a mattress against the wall so she and Andy could climb up and look out. While Andy busied himself counting cars, Ibolya had other plans. She'd written a note and was waiting for someone to pass by so she could throw it down to them. The note asked the recipient to go to the Jewish Congress in Budapest, have them alert Ibolya's in-laws about her incarceration, and send someone to rescue Andy. Ibolya waved the paper outside the window until a young man pushing a bicycle noticed her. The man stopped beneath the window and pretended to fix his bicycle. Then he looked up and waved at Ibolya to toss him the note. He picked it up and rode off. Two days later, Janka arrived to bring Andy home.

Ibolya, though, remained. Her captors transferred her to a city jail, where she was housed with other Jewish dissidents—including the woman who betrayed her at the border. At trial, the court found Ibolya guilty of attempting to leave the country and sentenced her to six months in prison. A lawyer hired by the Jewish Congress appealed the decision, and Ibolya's sentence was reduced to three months. She was freed a few days early, on Stalin's birthday, which Soviet-occupied Hungary celebrated by releasing political prisoners. Ibolya renunited with Andy, Henrik and Janka.

From Vienna, Béla wrote to Ibolya and encouraged her to try escaping again. Ibolya refused. After all she and Andy had endured, she would not risk leaving Hungary without official permission. After the government rejected each of Ibolya's applications for an exit visa, however, Béla grew impatient and went to Israel by himself. They would never marry.

In Budapest, Henrik worked as director of Palatinus Baths, an outdoor swimming centre on Margaret Island in the Danube River. Andy spent much of his youth at the pools and grew into a strong swimmer. He once swam across the Danube River, a dangerous feat that both shocked and infuriated his mother, and hoped to swim for the Hungarian national team. He trained twice a day, five times a week. "With all my heart, I wanted to be an Olympian," Andy said. "In my mind, I still am." He specialized in breaststroke and butterfly, and won a national championship for his age group in 1956 when he was fourteen years old. Earning a spot on Hungary's 1960 or 1964 Olympic team seemed assured.

But politics, and an all too familiar hatred intervened. The year Andy won his championship also saw the beginning of the Hungarian Revolution. Student protests against the government escalated into violence. Molotov cocktails were pitched at Soviet tanks, and soldiers responded with machine-gun fire. Demonstrators raided police stations to steal guns and release prisoners and decapitated a statue of Stalin in the city centre. Budapest's electricity grid went dark and mobs looted stores. Andy didn't join the demonstrators. "I had no reason to protest against anything," he said. "I felt that I didn't have any problems." Besides, the Soviets had rescued his family from the Nazis only eleven years earlier. He could still remember the taste of the black bread the Russian soldier gave him. Why would he quarrel with his own liberators?

As the revolution spun around him, and amid the shouts of "Russians, go home!" and "Freedom for All," Andy read a message spray-painted on a wall: "You Jews don't have to go to Auschwitz. We will kill you right here." Andy considers this moment a turning point. "I was a kid. Living a life," Andy said. "And then because I am a Jew they are going to murder me? Again? That was it. What were we going to do in this wonderful country that hated us so much?"

Ibolya told Henrik that she was taking Andy and leaving Hungary. This time, Henrik nodded his assent. He too had read the graffiti and heard the antisemitic slogans. Henrik saw no future for Jews in Hungary. "He loved me. He let me go," Andy said, emotion cracking his voice. "If my grandfather would've told me to stay, I would've stayed," Andy said. "And though I never, ever discussed it with my mother, I believe she would've left without me."

Andy and Ibolya landed in Halifax in January 1957, after eleven days at sea aboard the MS Berlin. Canada had reconsidered its racist "none is too many" policy concerning Jewish immigrants after the war. Immigration officials welcomed Ibolya and Andy, and the other two hundred Hungarians aboard the MS Berlin, with five Canadian dollars each along with a paper bag containing a toothbrush, towel, and soap. Their first meal was coffee and doughnuts—foreshadowing, perhaps, Andy's taxi driver diet.

Jewish refugees were permitted to go to any Canadian city where they had family. Since Andy and Ibolya had none, immigration officials sent them by train to Winnipeg, where they stepped into the blast of a minus-40-degree windchill. Ibolya found work as a seamstress for twenty-six dollars a week while Andy went to school. Though he was fifteen years old, Andy's lack of English meant he was assigned to a grade six classroom with students three years his junior. He had difficulty making friends, and once came home with bruised cheeks after fighting a boy who called him a "stinky Jew." Ibolya recoiled at Andy's swollen face. He assured her that the other boy looked worse. By the end of the school year, Andy's English had improved along with his social standing. "I was a chick magnet," he told me.

In 1958, Ibolya and Andy moved to Toronto, where Andy attended Central Technical School and became a star on the varsity swim team. Some of his swim records held for a decade. Andy's discipline for swimming didn't extend to his studies, though. His mediocre grades meant he could not attend university, so he apprenticed as a structural steel detailer and obtained his draftsman credentials instead. He worked as a draftsman for six years, but the job never suited him. In 1966, he started driving taxi part-time while working for Toronto's water department. "They had fifty-two people, but only enough work for two. Fifty of us were sitting on our ass doing nothing," Andy said. "I hated it, but that is where I met my wife."

Magdi worked as a bank teller at City Hall. She, too, was the daughter of Hungarian Holocaust survivors, her mother having endured horrific torture and medical experiments at Auschwitz. Andy proposed to Magdi in the fall of 1968 and they married three months later. Knowing how much Andy hated his job, Magdi convinced him to buy a taxi and drive full-time. Seven people loaned Andy the money to buy his licence. He paid them back within a year.

"I enjoyed the job very much," Andy said. "It was good money, and I am easy to engage in conversation. I often quote George Burns: 'Too bad that all the people who know how to run the country are busy driving taxicabs and cutting hair.' They know everything."

"What do you mean they know everything?" I asked.

"Every driver is an opiniated person," Andy said. "You can't be behind the wheel and just sit there and not say word."

A week after our conversation, Andy invited me to St. Peter's Catholic School in Peterborough, where he was telling his family's Holocaust story as part of a lecture series with the Friends of

Simon Wiesenthal Centre for Holocaust Studies. Andy and Ibolya started giving public lectures about their family's experience in 1998. After Ibolya passed in 2006, Andy became a full-time "Holocaust Educator" for the Wiesenthal Centre and now delivers around sixty solo presentations a year.

Andy usually speaks to schoolchildren, but Peterborough's audience would include parents as well. This was the first time he'd addressed a group consisting mainly of adults. He seemed nervous. While he set up his PowerPoint presentation in the library, arriving audience members crowded a table laid with cookies, cupcakes, and slabs of banana bread baked by the school's food studies students. A plastic urn filled with Tim Hortons coffee, naturally, stood beside a tower of paper cups.

The Centre associate who'd driven Andy and me to Peterborough gave a short history lesson on the Holocaust and European antisemitism for the fifty or so audience members. Then Andy stepped up. "Every Holocaust survivor story is a love story," he began. "Love of life, love of family, and love of freedom."

Aside from a *Fiddler on the Roof* reference that didn't quite land with the Catholic teenagers and their parents, Andy's polished lecture had his audience rapt. He showed black-and-white photos of Ibolya as a young woman and his muscular father standing poolside. "I was slated to die because I was the son of two Jews who were madly, passionately, in love with each other," he said. "To the Nazis, I was *lebensunwertes Leben*: a life unworthy of life." Andy told the story of the racetrack, the ghetto, and his early memory of Katie's cold feet. He spoke about liberation and the Russian bread. He showed the audience his mother's wedding ring—"The Ring of Love," he called it—which Ibolya twice hid from the Nazis, first in Andy's coat, then in his diaper. He showed photos of his own children and his grandchildren, too. "This is my revenge on the Nazis," Andy said. "That I became a grandparent."

Near the end of his talk, Andy swapped his tweed blazer for a leather motorcycle vest and talked about "Yidden on Wheels," the Jewish motorcycle club he belongs to whose annual "Ride to Remember" promotes remembrance of the Holocaust. When he rides, Andy keeps the "Ring of Love" in the vest's breast pocket. (His riding gloves wouldn't fit if he wore it on his finger.)

Andy concluded by telling the audience how his Holocaust experience taught him to always fight against bullies. "Inside, I am a lean, mean, fighting machine," he said. "I never took a backwards step." He encouraged his audience to be upstanders rather than bystanders. If there was one lesson to be gleaned from his presentation, this was it.

There are always wars to fight. Bullies to stand up to. Andy had had his revenge on the Nazis. Now he was taking on Uber.

City Council controls how many taxi plates are issued in Toronto. That way, the City balances the growing need of Torontonians for safe and reliable taxi service with taxi drivers' desire to make a decent living. Once issued, plates can be bought and sold on the open market. The market value of the plates grew over time. Taxi companies and individuals bought plates with the understanding they could eventually sell them at a profit or lease them to active drivers once they retired. Everyone regarded a taxi plate as a safe financial investment. "Not only did the City verbally say 'Congratulations! This is your pension' when they issued the plate, the whole premise was that, by limiting the supply of plates, I could make a living," Andy told me on the car ride back to Toronto. He had bought three plates over the course of his cabbie career and rented them to three drivers.

Like other cities across North America, Toronto profited from this taxi license market. From the 1960s until a by-law change in 2016, the municipal government collected a transfer fee ranging from $3,500 to $5,000 every time a plate changed hands. "How do you explain charging so much for a paper transaction? But they did it," Andy said. "The bastards at the City were making a good living out of it." The City charged a fee even if the plates were inherited. In other words, if a driver died and his plates passed to his wife, she had to pay the same fee.

Then Uber arrived. The San Francisco-based tech company's smartphone app allowed almost any driver to treat their car like a taxicab without navigating existing taxi-licensing regulations. Around the world, regular car owners signed and took to city streets en masse as Uber drivers. The public embraced Uber for the most part, and residents of Uber-less cities petitioned their local governments to bring Uber in, especially in cities with expensive or notoriously poor taxi service. Except during so-called "surge" periods of high demand, a ride in an Uber cost less than a typical taxi fare.

Cabbies everywhere cried foul. They'd spent decades adhering to municipal or provincial regulations regarding driver training, insurance, vehicle maintenance, and police checks. In most cities, Uber drivers did not have to adhere to the same standards—if any at all. Uber threatened to pull out of any city that imposed strict regulations, and mobilized potential riders to stage social media protests in support of Uber. The tactics usually worked. In Toronto, for example, Uber drivers remained unregulated for their first three years of operation. When City Council finally imposed rules on Toronto Uber drivers in 2016, they were less stringent than those imposed on traditional taxi drivers.

Cabbies objected to City policies that allowed Uber to circumvent quotas limiting the number of licensed taxis. By mid-November 2019, for example, the City of Toronto had allowed nearly 94,000 Private Transportation Company (PTC) vehicles—mostly Uber and Lyft, another app-based company—to operate on Toronto's streets. Hundreds more PTC drivers signed up every week, resulting in a glut of ride-for-hire vehicles that collapsed demand. Driver earnings plummeted.

Until the late 1990s, Toronto City Hall had limited the number of new drivers who could enter the industry through per capita quotas. The formula called for one car-for-hire for every eight hundred citizens to ensure full-time drivers had an opportunity to make a living while offering acceptable service to customers. According to that ratio, today's Toronto should have a taxi fleet of around 3,200 cars. But City Hall swapped out the per capita formula for a more complicated model about twenty years ago, and the number of licensed taxis ballooned to more than 5,000 by 2020. According to industry insiders, this was already far more than the city needed. Even without Uber.

Now, though, with so many PTCs on the street, Toronto is absurdly overserved. As of February 2020, Toronto had one car-for-hire for every twenty-seven Torontonians. This ratio benefits anyone needing a ride, of course, as wait times are short. An available car is almost always nearby. But drivers don't make much money. On average, traditional taxi drivers lost $39,000 in business during each of the six years Uber has been operating in Toronto. Five hundred and fifty Toronto taxi plates are sitting on shelves because there aren't enough people willing to drive cab. The market value of taxi plates has crumbled. At their peak, a Toronto taxi plate was worth around $380,000. By September 2020, a plate could be bought on Kijiji for $12,000 or less.

Uber isn't making any money, either: not the drivers who must compete with traditional cabbies and each other for fares, and not the company itself. When Uber went public in May 2019, professional investor and analyst Stephen McBride declared investing in Uber "the dumbest thing you can do with your money in 2019." He proved prescient. Uber bled a billion dollars in its first quarter, more than $5 billion in the second, and another $1.1 billion in the third.

Then, in December 2019, Uber released a shocking safety report revealing the company received nearly six thousand reports of sexual assault committed in American Uber vehicles in 2017 and 2018. Among those, 464 were rapes. Uber's chief legal officer found the numbers "jarring and hard to digest." So did investors. Uber's stock value fell by $1.4 billion a few days later, and lost more than a third of its value by the end of the year. Even the company's co-founder and former CEO, Travis Kalanick, abandoned ship. On Christmas Eve, Kalanick announced he'd quit Uber's board of directors and sold all $2.5 billion of his remaining Uber shares.

Perhaps the only entities currently profiting from this mayhem, aside from the remaining entrepreneurs who founded the companies, are the municipal governments who allow PTCs to operate. The City of Toronto will have reaped approximately $75 million in licensing revenues from PTCs by 2020. The City also charged a thirty-cent licencing fee for every PTC ride. From the middle of 2016 to the end of 2019, the City of Toronto collected more than $41.5 million via these charges. In 2020, Toronto's per-ride levies increased to forty-one cents. Many other Uber cities charge similar fees. With revenues like this, it's no wonder so many municipalities are willing to let the traditional taxi industry die at Uber's feet.

Despite Uber's troubles, Andy believes ride-hailing companies will outlive the traditional taxi industry. Many of the old-school cabbies I spoke to figure the industry only has about five years left. For them, staring out the windshield means staring into the abyss. The taxi is less a border than the edge of a cliff.

Even though Andy retired from driving cab in 1980, he continues to act as an advocate for the industry in Toronto. "I felt I wanted to give back because the cab industry was good to me," he said. In 2019, Andy joined a class action lawsuit against the City of Toronto, alleging City officials failed to properly regulate private transportation companies like Uber and destroyed the taxi business in the process. Andy and his fellow plaintiffs sought $1.7 billion in damages, $340,000 for each of Toronto's 5,500 taxi plates.

At the end of 2019, an Ontario judge declined to certify the class action suit and prevented the case from proceeding. The plaintiffs satisfied four out of the five criteria Justice Paul Perell put forward, but they'd failed to include what he considered a legitimate cause of action. "There is no obligation to protect the economic interests of those granted taxi licenses," Justice Perell wrote. "Legislative activities inevitably affect individual citizens; for some the effect is positive, and for others the effect is negative." The *Globe and Mail* published news of the ruling on Christmas Day, and I called Andy the following evening to ask him about this lump of coal in the industry's stocking.

"I was shocked," Andy said. "This is one of those conceited, self-important activist judges who thinks his manure doesn't stink." In January 2018, a different Ontario judge gave plate owners permission to launch an identical class action suit in Ottawa. "This idiot here in Toronto ruled in total opposition to that decision," Andy said. "This judge was something else. I felt like taking a fly-swatter to him." Andy and his fellow plaintiffs appealed the decision and are waiting for a court date.

For Andy, the suit represents a fight against injustice, something he links back to being a Holocaust survivor. "I never started a fight, but neither have I walked from one," he said. A man who does not step back from Nazis will not be cowed by city politicians or a smartphone app. Occasionally, though, Andy's emotions about the subject alchemize into hyperbole. He once wrote an article for the Toronto-based *Taxi News* comparing the plight of Toronto's taxi industry to the Holocaust. The editor, unsurprisingly, declined to print the comparison.

Andy was furious. "What is happening to the taxi industry because of Uber is identical to what happened to the Jews because of the Nazis. It is an extermination of my business," Andy said. "When there was art of historical value, they forced the Jews to sell it to them at prices well below the market value. The City would be forcing me to sell a $300,000 plate for $10,000. Let it sit on the shelf. I am not going to sell it. I will not allow them to rob me. I will tell the judge, when the time comes, that I will stand up and fight."

Andy won't back down in his battle against Uber and his foes at Toronto City Hall. I found his angry-grandpa ferocity both charming and inspiring. But I would meet no anti-Uber pugilist as committed to the cause, and none I would love more, than the Taxi Sheriff of Montreal.

Four

THE BALLAD

OF THE TAXI SHERIFF

THE UBER DRIVER WASN'T SURE WHAT TO DO WHEN THE Lebanese cowboys ambushed him. He'd just arrived at his destination at the Old Port of Montreal when five men clad in cowboy hats, plaid shirts, and bandanas rushed his car and pounded on his window. While the cowboys distracted the driver, his passenger snatched the smartphone from the dashboard bracket and exited the car. He then handed the phone to the posse's leader, Hassan Kattoua, whose authority was made plain by the plastic star on his vest and the toy pistols on his belt. The costumed lawman pocketed the phone and handed the bewildered driver a receipt printed on paper that had been soaked in tea and burned on the edges with a cigarette lighter. The document read:

> We have seized the machine that you are using as a weapon for your outlaw activity that is impoverishing drivers in towns and cities. You will retrieve your weapon as soon as the governor of

the province and/or his minister outlaw and ban the illegal activities you are engaged in and the province returns to the rule of law that it is famous for.

This was the autumn of 2015. Uber had been operating illegally in Montreal for about a year. The city's taxi bureau had issued thousands of dollars in fines and seized more than two hundred cars, but the penalties hardly dissuaded Uber's drivers. Montreal cabbies were furious. "They have turned Quebec into the Wild West," Hassan told a journalist covering his cellphone heist. Hassan turned back to the Uber driver and informed him that if he wanted his phone returned, he needed to take the singed receipt to the Taxi Bureau. After the driver sped away, Hassan pinned a mock "wanted" poster depicting Montreal Uber manager Jean-Nicolas Guillemette, complete with black hat and villain's moustache, to a tree. Then he and his scowling deputies posed for a photo.

Hassan reasoned that when the Uber driver appeared at the Bureau to retrieve his phone, he'd have to admit he'd been driving for Uber and would therefore receive a ticket. But this wasn't enough for Hassan. "I wanted to punish him a little bit more," Hassan told me. He planned to hold onto the phone for three days before bringing it to the Bureau. That way the driver would lose a few days' worth of income. Besides, the delay adhered to the operation's cowboy aesthetic. "It is as if I sent the phone by horseback," Hassan said. "It takes some time."

Montreal's real police were not amused. As soon as the story of his ambush appeared in *Le Journal de Montréal*—under the headline "'Cowboy' taxi drivers steal cellphone from UberX"—the police called Hassan. They ordered him and his accomplices to report to the police station or face arrest. Hassan summoned his posse and told them to suit up. When the four cowboys arrived at the station, dressed again in their cowboy costumes, a local television station was waiting. "I regret not spending a bit more on the outfits," Hassan told me. "They were all from the dollar store. But I did not know we would be on TV."

Police officers crowded the station entrance to watch the spectacle. The rest of Hassan's posse was terrified. They knew they could lose their work permits if they received criminal records. In the end, though, the police didn't charge anyone with anything. They simply scolded the men and demanded Hassan return the stolen phone. "They told me they knew I wasn't a criminal," Hassan said. "But that was the day I became the Taxi Sheriff."

Hassan wasn't wearing his cowboy costume when we met. With his glasses and trim haircut, he resembled an engineering professor more than a Wild West vigilante. As soon as we sat to talk in a downtown Montreal shopping mall, Hassan launched into a rehearsed lecture about the evils of Uber and the injustices perpetrated on Montreal's cabbies by the provincial Transport Commission. He ranted nonstop for nearly ninety minutes about unenforced transport regulations, the corruption of former Quebec premier Philippe Couillard, the shady issuance of airport permits, and so on. Hassan ignored all my attempts to steer the conversation towards his own personal history. Hassan was the driver, after all. Only after telling me everything he thought I should know about Montreal's taxi industry did he share his origin story.

Hassan grew up in Beirut during the Lebanese Civil War. In April 1975, gunmen ambushed a busload of Palestinians in Beirut in apparent retaliation for the attempted assassination of a Maronite Christian Phalangist leader. Clashes between Palestinian-Muslims and Phalangists followed, sparking a civil war that would last fifteen years. Many of Hassan's friends joined the militia groups. So did one of his cousins, who ended up firing at his own house in an attempt to liberate the apartment from occupying gunmen. "Watch out for the windows," the cousin begged his fellow soldiers. "And please don't destroy too many things." No one else in Hassan's family took up arms. His mother wouldn't allow any weapons in the house at all, not even a pellet gun to rid the roof of pigeons.

Hassan fought different sorts of battles. Like Andy Reti, he always stood up to bullies. When a grade-school thug demanded Hassan's bus seat, Hassan wouldn't budge, even after the boy threw Hassan's basket of Easter eggs out the window. Hassan's greatest boyhood victory, though, came at the expense of his fifth-grade Arabic teacher. The man considered himself a fine poet and pressured his students to purchase cassettes of his droning poetry recitations. "Everybody hated him," Hassan said, "but nobody would say anything." Hassan was the only student who refused to buy the cassettes. "I do not like things imposed on me," he said.

Word of ten-year-old Hassan's defiance spread to the school's administration. One afternoon, while Hassan was playing basketball outside his apartment, his mother called to him from their fourth-floor balcony. "Your principal is on the phone and wants to talk to you," she said. Hassan was nervous. He couldn't understand why his eighty-year-old principal, "a strict Palestinian Christian," would want to talk to him outside of school hours. Hassan slowly climbed the stairs to his apartment; the elevator wasn't working due to wartime power shortages. When the principal asked him about his Arabic teacher, Hassan told him about the hard sell of poetry recordings. The principal fired the teacher the next day, and Hassan became a classroom hero.

By the time the war ended in October 1990, between 150,000 and 200,000 people had been killed, most of them civilians. A period of economic crisis followed. Hassan studied electronic engineering after graduating from high school and earned a degree, but had few options. "There was little hope of a better future for a young man like me," Hassan said. "And no place for advancement in a country that relies on who you know rather than what are your qualifications." He decided to apply for immigration to Quebec. His reasons weren't just economic. "To be honest with you, the other sex was completely absent in my life. Up until today, I can frankly tell you that I never held the hand of a woman of my nationality." A lonely and heartsick Hassan figured he'd be an exotic novelty for Canadian women. "I thought Canada is full of blonde women that have not seen dark-haired guys," he said. "Oh boy, was I disappointed that the Italians and Greeks and the Arabs had already set their feet there."

In 1985, Canada shuttered its Beirut embassy due to the war, so Hassan had to take taxis back and forth to the embassy in neighbouring Syria. To prepare for his immigration interview, Hassan studied French and sat for medical exams. When the 1994 Quebec provincial election brought the Parti Québécois to power, and with it the promise of a sovereignty referendum, Hassan worried his immigration hopes were dashed. "The counsellor at the embassy said there was no guarantee my application would be accepted. I went back to Beirut depressed." Two weeks later, though, he received a call from the embassy and an invitation to an interview where he was handed a brochure titled 'Bienvenue au Québec.'

Instead of celebrating, Hassan recalls feeling tremendous anxiety. "Your excitement dies because it is the moment things become serious," Hassan said. "Soon, you will have to leave to the unknown, alone." He had to sell his car and his cherished motorcycle to pay $10,000 for an immigration visa. And he had to leave his parents and two sisters behind. He flew out of Beirut in 1994. "There is a photo of my dad that day. Anyone could see that he was not happy to see his son leave."

In his first letter from Montreal to his mother, Hassan described how the airport bus at Mirabel picked up passengers from the plane, how Canadian toilets flushed automatically, and how "the parking lot at Sears was the size of our neighbourhood in Beirut." He found work at two different tech companies. Both eventually laid him off. A friend recommended Hassan try driving a taxi. Hassan balked at first. "In Lebanon, we looked at driving taxi as an inferior kind of job," Hassan said. "I am educated and didn't want to work as a taxi driver." But the potential for high earnings, flexibility, and job security eventually coaxed him away from the computer screen and behind the wheel.

As an immigrant in Quebec, Hassan felt he had few other options anyway. "I am going to say this very frankly," Hassan said. "In Montreal, certain jobs are reserved for what we call *pure laine*." The term, literally "pure wool," refers to Quebeckers with exclusive French-Canadian ancestry and is often provocatively associated with the notion of racial purity. Hassan believes most well-paying government jobs, everything from police officer to "the people who take the garbage," go to francophone Quebecois first. "Even if you are an Italian and you are born here, and don't have the name 'Silvain,' you have less chance," Hassan said. I can't be sure if this is true, of course. I don't know if structural racism or purity tests determine who gets jobs in Quebec. But I do believe Hassan felt certain careers were beyond his reach as an Arab newcomer to the province. In Montreal, men like Hassan didn't work for the City or the Province. Men like Hassan drove cabs.

Hassan bought a taxi permit in 2003 for $160,000. A bank lent him $100,000, he spent $30,000 of his own savings, and he borrowed the rest from his parents living in Lebanon. "I left them with no money," he said. Hassan worked long hours and made decent money, especially late at night once Montreal's bars closed and the Metro stopped running. He sent money to his parents each month and still had enough left over for the occasional beach vacation in Florida or the Bahamas.

Montreal's taxi business took a hit in the mid-2000s, when the City introduced car- and bicycle-share options, and a new direct bus line to the airport was introduced. The business' lucrative core remained, though. Few Montrealers rode the shared bicycles during winter, most airline travelers would rather take a cab than drag heavy luggage onto a city bus, and late-night drinkers still needed someone to drive them home. "But then Uber came," Hassan said.

The Taxi Sheriff immediately declared war. Hassan's "Great Uber Phone Robbery" was just the first of many operations devised by the Taxi Sheriff. Another involved Hassan adding his own cell number to the listing for Uber Montreal's headquarters on Google Maps (the listing included an address, but no phone number). He did this over and over again, with multiple Google accounts, until Google's algorithm finally accepted the change. Soon afterwards, Hassan's phone rang. Google was calling from San Francisco. "Is this Uber?" Google asked. Hassan assured Google that, yes, they had reached Uber's Montreal office. Google called a few days later to confirm again. This time Hassan was curt. "Stop wasting my time," he told the representative. "I am Uber now." Then he hung up. Google didn't call back.

Hassan used the number to mess with Montreal's outlaw Uber drivers. Any time a driver phoned what they thought was Uber Montreal headquarters—to report a problem with the Uber app, for example—Hassan would impersonate Uber management. He told some drivers that Uber was folding. "I made so many Uber drivers stop working on a busy Friday night thinking the company is closing and they will not get paid for their trips." Other times, Hassan asked drivers for their name, license number, license plate, and other personal information. Then he'd pounce. "This is a stunt," Hassan would announce. "You are stuck now. I have your name. I have your plate. I have your phone number." Hassan told his victims he would send the information to the Taxi Bureau so their cars would be ticketed and towed. He threatened to report drivers to Revenue Canada and to the social assistance department at Emploi-Québec. "Most of them were collecting welfare payments," Hassan explained.

Disgruntled Uber passengers also started phoning Hassan. One man told him that his girlfriend had ordered a Mercedes on Uber Select, a premium service that provides luxury cars at a higher rate, but the driver showed up in a Volkswagen Jetta. Two young women called to complain that their Uber driver kicked them out of the car on a highway in the middle of the night. These calls further angered Hassan. Not only was Uber operating illegally and cutting into the earnings of Montreal's taxi drivers, Hassan said, they were giving lousy service.

Three weeks passed before Uber Canada grew wise to Hassan's scam. They threatened legal action if he didn't stop impersonating Uber. Hassan's cabbie friends told him to be careful, warning him that Uber would sue him "to the Stone Age." Hassan didn't flinch. "Uber is a technology company," he said. "It would be a disgrace for them to make a big fuss and admit a taxi driver hacked their system." He was right. Uber did nothing other than ban Hassan from the Uber app and remove his cell number from Google Maps.

Some of the Sheriff's later operations against Uber lacked the digital elegance of his Google Map hack or the performance artistry of the phone heist. In February 2016, Hassan summoned an Uber vehicle to the Plaza Hotel in downtown Montreal. When the car arrived, Hassan and a crew of co-conspirators pelted the car with eggs and dumped icing sugar over the windshield and rear window. Police charged three men, Hassan among them, with harassment and intimidation. The Uber driver, though operating illegally, wasn't charged with anything. Hassan represented himself in court. "For me, paying $6,000 to a lawyer to defend me over eggs was ridiculous," he said. The trial took three days. In the end, the judge agreed to grant Hassan absolution provided he keep the peace for a year and pay a $500 fine. Hassan said he'd rather go to prison than pay the fine, but a few of Hassan's fellow cabbies, who appreciated his activism, chipped in the money.

The outlaw Uber drivers developed their own scheme to keep working without detection. Taxi Bureau inspectors were tasked with identifying, ticketing, and impounding Uber vehicles, but there were only four of them. Knowing this, Uber drivers sent their members to Taxi Bureau headquarters daily to count how many taxi inspector cars were parked in the lot and then share the information on via a private WhatsApp group. If the scout saw all four cars, it meant no inspectors were on the road and that the drivers could pick up passengers without worrying about being caught. Even Hassan admired the hack.

Montreal's police department was also responsible for ticketing Uber drivers and seizing their cars. Few made this a priority, though, so Hassan devised another operation to shame them into action. To execute it, he needed a new costume. At the time, Montreal police officers had been wearing brightly coloured camouflage pants and red caps instead of their regular uniform as a protest against proposed pension reforms. Hassan purchased a pair of black-and-grey camo pants and a red baseball cap that he emblazoned with a yellow 'X' crossing out the Uber logo. He bought a black coat from Winner's that resembled an officer's jacket and pinned a toy sheriff's badge to his chest. (By then, he'd replaced his plastic star with a silver one.) Though it wasn't a standard police uniform, most Montrealers would take a man so dressed as a protesting officer.

If police weren't going to seek out Uber drivers to ticket, Hassan would deliver them himself. He and an accomplice, an American anti-Uber activist named Larry Frankel, parked their car in front of a police station and called for an Uber. When the car arrived, Hassan turned on his video camera and shouted at officers in a nearby cruiser to ticket him. The driver panicked and sped away. The cruiser switched on its lights and pursued him. Hassan and Larry rushed back to their car and tried to follow, but a second cruiser pulled in front and blocked them, thus foiling their plan to record the police response.

It was at this point Larry noticed that the Uber driver, in his haste, had failed to end the trip on his app. "He was still charging us," Hassan said. Hassan and Larry didn't have to follow the police chase; they could follow the driver themselves using the app. They found him parked nearby and rapped on his window. The driver told Hassan the police officer hadn't ticketed him. The real reason for the police chase, Hassan insists, was to direct the Uber driver away from Hassan's camera.

Two days after the incident, Hassan received a call from the Montreal police demanding he turn himself in. Hassan's stunt had angered the officers, especially his faux police uniform. They charged Hassan with impersonating a police officer, using a badge or uniform article worn by police officers, and intimidating a member of the justice system. Hassan scoffed at the charges. "I didn't act like a police officer. I only brought the car to the police station and asked the police to apply the law. They refused," Hassan said. "Also, I did not wear a police costume because this is not their official uniform. It is a tricky thing, no?" Hassan smirked at this. "Third, I did not intimidate a police officer."

Police fingerprinted Hassan and questioned him for an hour. They confiscated his camouflage pants, his sheriff's star, his anti-Uber cap, and his black coat. The police gave Hassan a nylon jumpsuit to wear—"Like Guantanamo," he said, "only white instead of orange"—then locked him in a jail cell. Later, in a Facebook post, Hassan wrote that the police had humiliated him: "It was not easy to pass eight hours counting the tiles," Hassan wrote, "walking diagonally from side to side, exploring the stainless steel sink for the first time in my life or lying down on a wooden bench using my boots as a pillow." Police eventually pushed Hassan's terms of release through the bars of his cell. He was not to wear clothes similar to police uniforms, he could not interfere with any Uber driver or passenger, and he could not attend any anti-Uber protests. Hassan could either sign the forms or stay in custody until his court appearance two months later—which, coincidentally, fell on his birthday. Hassan signed, even though he considered the terms illegal.

The police would drop all the charges against Hassan, but Hassan nevertheless sued them for treating him like a dangerous criminal. "I want compensation for unjust treatment for putting me in jail for no clean charges," Hassan said. "This affected me greatly. Morally." Hassan initially launched a $35,000 claim against the Montreal Police Service. "But then my lawyer wanted money," Hassan said. "Now I am in a small claims court because I have no one to pay for me."

When police released Hassan from custody, he called a friend to film him leaving the station. In the video, Hassan emerges weary but smiling from the station. He is holding his belt and release papers in his hand and is still wearing his police-issued white "bunny suit," his underwear visible through the thin fabric. Police never returned his clothes, cap, or sheriff's star. In the video, Hassan thanks his supporters for inquiring about his state following his brief incarceration and urges them not to be concerned. "Don't worry guys," he says. "We will win."

They aren't winning. In the fall of 2016, Quebec's transport commission granted Uber permission to operate legally under a year-long pilot project. They renewed the project the following year, and again in 2018. Montreal's traditional cabbies were furious. Like Toronto, Montreal had far more taxis than the population required even before Uber arrived. The commission knew this. Worse, the usual rules didn't apply to Uber drivers. Cabbies needed a licence to operate. Uber drivers didn't. The Province insisted that new Uber drivers submit to police background checks just like taxi drivers, but exempted Uber drivers who'd been working before the pilot project. Cabbies paid higher insurance rates and licensing fees than Uber drivers. They had to dress properly and drive newer cars that they had to keep clean and well maintained. Uber drivers weren't beholden to any of these rules.

Uber's allies in Montreal and in the provincial government argued that the ride service was part of the new "sharing economy" and in high demand. Hassan argues that just because something is popular doesn't mean it is fair. Hassan likes to say that allowing Uber into the market is akin to allowing someone to sell half-price beer out of a cooler on the sidewalk in front of a depanneur—the small and mostly independent neighbourhood stores that sell groceries, snacks, cigarettes, and alcohol. "Imagine you bought a depanneur for $200,000. You have fridges, electricity, employees, taxes. So many things you are paying for," Hassan said. "You go to the dep every day and sit behind the counter. You look outside the window and see that guy stealing your business. Everybody is buying from him and few are walking into your store. But it is legal. You want to kill yourself or kill him."

In October 2016, Hassan turned his depanneur metaphor into another inspired Taxi Sheriff stunt. He fastened a roof light to his cab that read "TAXIPANNEUR" and affixed a decal to the door mocking Transport Minister Philippe Couillard's Uber plan: "Pilot project brought to you by Mister Couillard's 'sharing economy.'" Hassan strapped packages of gum, chocolate bars, and other snacks to the sun visors inside his taxi, stuffed the glove box with bags of potato chips, and installed a cooler bag filled with ice packs, soft drinks, and juice. Then he printed up a menu under a misspelled message in Western typeface reading:

TAXIPANNEUR

WELCOME ABOARD THE FIRST TAXI-CONVINIENCE STORE

IN NORTH AMERICA

The Taxipanneur menu also hinted that beer, wine, and cigarettes would soon be for sale. "I was about to apply online so I could order alcohol," Hassan said. He planned to source cheap cigarettes "from the Indian reserve."

Hassan said his customers would love the Taxipanneur, just like Montrealers loved Uber. "Imagine a client comes in the car and he can buy a smoke without having to stop at the depanneur?" Hassan said. Passengers would appreciate the beer and wine for sale, too, especially late at night. Montreal bylaws forbid depanneurs from selling alcohol after eleven as a way to support the city's bars. "What if I started selling alcohol after 11 o'clock, and screw the bars and screw the depanneurs?" Hassan's printed menu didn't include prices for beer, wine, and cigarettes because he planned to mimic Uber's policy of raising ride fares during busy periods. "I would do 'surge pricing,' too," Hassan said. "I could charge three times the price for alcohol after eleven."

Police shut down Hassan's Taxipanneur as soon as they saw him on the news. Hassan knew they would. That was his point. If Uber's popularity was the primary reason the government allowed it to function, even at the expense of taxi drivers' livelihoods, why should the City protect the dep and bar owners by outlawing Hassan's sure-to-be-popular Taxipanneur?

The Quebec government landed its most devastating blow on the taxi industry in March of 2019, when it tabled Bill 17 to reconfigure ride-for-hire businesses in the province. Under the guise of "levelling the playing field," the Bill required all drivers, traditional cabbies and Uber drivers both, to meet the same standards for licensing, training, and criminal background checks. Taxi drivers could also use a sliding fare scale, like Uber's, with "surge pricing"—meaning passengers would likely end up paying more for their rides. The bill dispensed with quotas and allowed for unlimited cars-for-hire on the road, regardless of demand. Most dramatically, though, the legislation abolished the need for taxi permits entirely. Hassan had drained his parents' savings to buy a permit when he first started driving. His permit had increased in value to $225,000 before Uber arrived. Under the new bill, it would be worthless.

The provincial government allocated $500 million to compensate cabbies for the loss of their permits' value, with an additional $270 million to be raised over the following five or six years through a ninety-cent royalty on every paid ride. An additional $40 million will be given out for "particular needs and cases." In all, Quebeckers will pay $814 million to compensate taxi drivers and tidy Uber's mess. And yet it still won't cover the industry's losses. Quebec's eight thousand permit holders claim their permits have lost $1.3 billion in value since Uber descended on the city. Under the legislation, Hassan wouldn't even recover his original investment, much less the almost quarter million dollars the permit was worth only a few years ago.

In stark contrast to the Taxi Sheriff's lone cowboy operations, Montreal's cabbies demonstrated against Bill 17 en masse in 2019. They staged a daylong strike in March. Hundreds of drivers converged on the National Assembly in Quebec City, while thousands blocked traffic in Montreal. One driver, during a live in-studio interview, said of the Quebec premier, François Legault: "he has no heart. And he took my heart." The man then drew a blade and slashed at his own wrists. He held up his bleeding arms to the camera, but the studio technicians cut away before the grisly scene was televised. An ambulance rushed the man to hospital: his injuries weren't serious and he was soon released, but the incident prompted the cabbies to suspend their demonstrations.

A few months later, posters from Santé Montréal, the city's health department, started appearing on notice boards near taxi stands at the airport and elsewhere. Under a headline reading "Are you experiencing difficulties or distress?" were phone numbers for a 24-hour health-advice line, the Montreal Men's Resource Centre, and Suicide Action Montréal. It's hard to imagine a grimmer, more worrisome symptom of a workforce in peril.

Provincial politicians adopted Bill 17 in October 2019, surprising no one. After years of operating both illegally and under pilot programs, Uber was granted the government's blessing to operate in Quebec. The province's taxi industry swiftly launched three class action lawsuits against the Quebec government and Uber totalling $1.5 billion.

The Taxi Sheriff vows to keep fighting. He has a new Sheriff's badge—a gold-coloured one he fashioned from a belt buckle. He maintains a Facebook page called "Cowboys Contre Uber" whose sepia-toned main photo shows Hassan and three cowboy colleagues from his first heist as the Sheriff. The page includes photos and videos from his various operations, as well as news articles. Occasionally he receives the sort of unconstructive, grammatically fraught advice one expects from an online forum:

> Hassan kattoua—when are you going to commit suicide—you lost a Fortune of money—think about all the vacations and fancy hotels and good shit you Could have bought with the money—you won't ever see that money again-losers like you usually go on shooting rampages and kill people

Hassan always smirked when he described his anti-Uber demonstrations to me. I could tell he enjoyed being the *enfant terrible* of Montreal's taxi industry and a constant burr under Uber's saddle. But Hassan's Wild West bravado and prankster façade fail to conceal his melancholy. He was among the youngest of all the drivers I'd meet, but he was the most weary. "When you first come to the country, it smells of something. Everything was new. Everything was nice," Hassan said. "Now, after all these years, you don't get to enjoy the city you are living in." Hassan shuttles his clients to arts and music festivals he doesn't have time to attend. He lives downtown within walking distance of some of Montreal's most famous nightspots, but lacks the money to enjoy them. "And I'm not in the mood to have fun." On New Years' Eve, while everyone else celebrates with their friends and family, Hassan drives the city's drunks around. He blames the taxi business for the fact he never married. "Do you know how a taxi driver feels when two people are making out in the back of his car? He feels like shit. Especially if he is single," Hassan said. "I should be going out and having fun just like these guys. When everybody is giggling in the back and everyone is happy, you are pissed off. You are sacrificing the best years of your life."

Pushing cab ravages the body as much as it breaks the heart. Hassan complains of stomach pains, back problems, and circulation issues in his legs. His eyes ache from the constant reflection of sun off snow on bright winter days, and the headlights of oncoming cars at night. "Do you know how many people go blind after finishing in this industry?" Hassan asked. "And there are so many heart attacks because drivers work hard hours."

Science bears out Hassan's claims. According to a 2017 occupational health study in the journal *Health Promotion International*, American taxi drivers attributed numerous health concerns to their time behind the wheel. They suffered chronic pain, sleep deprivation, cardiovascular disease, diabetes, kidney disease, and eye problems. A Chicago study revealed that the city's cabbies ate fewer fruits and vegetables and exercised less than the general population. They also smoked more cigarettes and drank more coffee. Researchers in Japan linked the prevalence of lower back pain in taxi drivers to their exposure to high levels of "whole body vibration," the constant rattling that comes with driving. Driving a taxi is physically and psychologically unhealthy, and one of the only jobs where workers are both sedentary and in constant motion.

Of course, Uber cannot be blamed for cabbies' ill health, which long predates its appearance on city streets. The difference is that drivers like Hassan now find reduced reward for these health risks. They work longer hours to earn less and less. "When Uber came, our lives crashed. Not just our jobs. Our lives crashed," Hassan said. He regrets getting into the business in the first place. The money Hassan spent on his taxi license could have been invested elsewhere. "I could've bought a Tim Hortons," he said. "I could've bought a house in Laval for the same money. It would be worth $500,000 now. What did I do? I ruined my life."

I couldn't argue with Hassan. When I consider the intelligence and creativity revealed in his clever activism, I wonder what he might have accomplished had he harnessed those talents elsewhere. More than this, though, I worry for Hassan's safety. In addition to the Montreal cabbie who cut his wrists on camera, eight New York City taxi drivers killed themselves over financial pressures in 2018. I feel afraid for the Sheriff.

Five

DRIVING

WHILE FEMALE

HASSAN'S LONESOME COWBOY SADNESS, WHILE WORRISOME, is hardly unique. "Loneliness has followed me my whole life, everywhere," says Travis Bickle, DeNiro's iconic anti-hero in *Taxi Driver.* "In bars, in cars, sidewalks, stores, everywhere. There's no escape. I'm God's lonely man." Though a taxi driver will serve dozens of people over the course of a shift, driving cab remains a fundamentally solitary occupation. A cabbie interacts with many, but truly engages with few. And, as Hassan revealed, the punishing hours and low-status nature of the job rarely abets romance. In this way, the taxi is another kind of border: that between seclusion and connection.

But solitude hardly defined all the drivers I met, despite the lonely hours they had in common. Outside their taxis, their lives intertwined with the people they loved. These cabbies were hardly God's lonely men. And some weren't men at all.

I first heard of Jass Hothi when my friend Meghan sent a text from Jass' backseat. "Do you want Calgary's only night-shift lady cab driver's contact info?"

"God, yes," I replied.

Meghan sent a phone number along with a photo of a startled-looking cabbie wearing a navy-blue blazer glancing back over her shoulder from the driver's seat. Another message followed: "She is AHMAZING."

Jass was wearing the same blazer, her Checker Cab uniform, and a pair of black-rimmed glasses when we met a few weeks later at a downtown Tim Hortons. She told me she grew up in India's Punjab province alongside two big brothers. Her father granted Jass the same independence he'd allowed his two sons. "My father treated me like a boy," she told me. "He never said 'Don't do that.' He only said 'Go ahead.'"

While Jass' brothers followed their father into the police force, Jass became a swimmer for the Indian national team and the All-India University Team. She specialized in breaststroke, but competed in multiple disciplines. "I played water-polo, even," she said. Jass completed a Bachelor of Arts then earned a diploma as a swimming coach. She eventually landed a coaching job with the National Institute of Sports in the Punjab. I thought of Andy Reti, another breaststroke specialist, and wondered who would win a race between the two of them.

In 1995, the Punjabi-Canadian man whom Jass' parents had arranged for her to marry arrived in India from Edmonton. "We met on Monday. Got married on Wednesday. He went back to Canada on Saturday," Jass said. "He didn't have any interest in India." Jass waited in India for two years until her Canadian passport came through, then boarded a plane to Edmonton. Her husband did not meet her at the airport. When she took a taxi to his house, he told Jass he didn't want to be married to her anymore. "He told me 'Where you want to go, you can go. I don't mind.'" Jass asked him why he married her in the first place. The man shrugged and said his mother wanted him to marry an Indian girl.

Jass left the house and stood outside on the sidewalk with her suitcase in the chill of Edmonton's early spring. "At the time, I don't know where I am going," she said. "I have no family in Edmonton. No friends. I don't even have a jacket." Eventually, out of suspicion or concern, a neighbour called the police. An officer in a cruiser pulled up in front of Jass and asked her something, but she couldn't understand. "No English," she said.

The officer called for an Indian colleague who could speak to Jass. After she explained her situation to him, he asked if she knew anyone at all in Edmonton. The only person Jass had met was her Punjabi seatmate, who'd sat next to her on the flight from Delhi. They'd chatted during the journey and she'd given Jass her phone number. The police officer called the woman and told her about Jass' predicament. The woman then told her uncle, who offered Jass a place to stay. "Her uncle said 'Don't worry. Bring her home.' So she picked me up and took me to her house."

From the kind stranger's house in Edmonton, Jass called her father at his police station in Punjab. She tearfully told him her Canadian husband had abandoned her, and that she wanted to come home. A young police inspector named Amrit had been standing nearby, eavesdropping on the conversation. As Jass' father tried to console her, Amrit tapped him on the shoulder. "I would like to speak with your daughter," he said.

Jass' father was confused. "Why?"

"Because I am in love with her."

Amrit Hothi was born in Jalandhar and had always wanted to be a man in uniform. Amrit's grandfather fought for the British during the Second World War and spent much of the war as a prisoner of the Japanese in a Shanghai POW camp. He used to tell Amrit stories about trading his cigarette rations for whiskey with his fellow prisoners. Amrit's father served in the Indian army, too, and fought against Pakistan. Amrit applied several times to serve in the Indian armed forces. He sat for interviews and completed the entrance exams but was never accepted into its ranks. Joining the police force was the next best thing.

Jass' father handed the phone to Amrit, who introduced himself. ""Yes, I know you," Jass said. She'd seen Amrit with her father many times. He was very tall, and Jass had always found him handsome.

"I want to marry you, if you don't mind," Amrit said.

"Excuse me?"

"I want to marry you."

"But your family's status is much higher than my family," Jass said.

"I don't mind."

"And your education is better than mine." Jass knew that Amrit had a master's degree in economics.

"I don't mind."

"Okay," Jass said. "But you better ask your parents."

Amrit's father called Jass a few days later. He'd approved of the marriage and encouraged her to stay in Canada while they arranged for Amrit's travel. He would send her some money in the meantime. Jass' mother also called and suggested Jass travel south from Edmonton to Calgary, where a "far, far, far relative" was willing to give her a place to stay. Jass lived with this distant cousin for two weeks and found a job sewing upholstery at a furniture factory in an industrial park. Then she rented a basement apartment where she spent nine lonely months waiting for Amrit. "I am sitting inside all the time because I don't know anyone," Jass said. "I don't know how to buy anything. I don't know how to go to store. I don't have a car. My landlord buys grocery for me, and I paid him. Then, Amrit came."

Jass' landlord drove her to the airport to meet Amrit. "At that time, I don't have any words," Jass said. "Just he hugged me. I am so happy. I am crying. He said 'Don't worry. I am here.'" As Jass' landlord organized the wedding, Jass and Amrit consulted with a Punjabi-speaking lawyer about ending Jass' first marriage. Turns out they didn't have to. Her first husband had terminated their Indian marriage in Canada without Jass' knowledge. She was already divorced. "The lawyer said we could get married tomorrow. No problem," Jass said. She and Amrit married a week later, in November 1998. Only Jass' landlord's family and Jass' distant Calgarian relatives attended the wedding. The couple didn't know anybody else.

Amrit had to wait three months for his work permit to come through before he could look for a job. As a lawman, he wasn't willing to break the rules and find illegal work. Unemployment bored him, though. He spent much of his time reading history books in the local library. Jass supported them both. She eventually left the furniture factory and started housekeeping at a Best Western hotel. Jass earned better money at the hotel than she had sewing furniture, but Amrit was appalled: he felt his new wife deserved better than scrubbing filthy hotel toilets and plucking used condoms off the floor. So one day he paid Jass a surprise visit at the hotel. He took her ring of room keys, flung them on her supervisor's desk, and told him Jass would not be coming in again.

Her sudden unemployment concerned Jass, especially since Amrit could not yet work himself. Amrit suggested Jass apply for a job at Tim Hortons, but in her interview the manager said her English skills weren't strong enough. Undeterred, Amrit picked up an application from another Tim Hortons on their way home. Jass was reluctant, but Amrit had a plan. "When you go for your next interview, and they ask you for your name, you say 'My name is Jasmine Hothi. My English is not very good, but if you give me a chance I will try my best. I work hard.'" Amrit and Jass rehearsed those two sentences over and over again at home before the interview. When she delivered the lines to the Tim Hortons manager, he didn't ask a second question. He handed her a uniform and told her to come to work the next day.

The manager gave Jass full-time hours from the start, and she was taking drive-through orders by her third shift. After work, Amrit tutored her in Tim Hortons English. First, he taught her to pronounce "Welcome to Tim Horton's. What can I get you?" Then they studied the Tim Hortons menu like a language phrase book. Together they learned strange Canadian vocabulary like Double-Double, Maple Dip, and Timbit. Jass did not know enough English to hold a regular conversation, but she knew the difference between Old Fashioned Glazed and Sour Cream Glazed.

After seven months, Jass started working twelve-hour shifts from five in the morning to five in the evening. Amrit had received his visa by then, and was putting in double shifts as an airport security guard. He dropped Jass at Tim Hortons each morning at five o'clock, then headed to the airport for his own 5:30 shift. When he finished at 5 pm he picked up Jass and they both went home. They kept up this pace for two years, during which time they had two children, first, in 1999, a daughter they named Amanpreet, then Robin, a son. Amrit named him after cricketer Robin Singh, whom Amrit idolized as a child. Jass cared nothing for cricket and had wanted her son to have a typical Indian name, but Amrit got to the birth certificate first.

Amrit and Jass eventually earned enough to bring Jass' parents to Calgary from India, who watched the children and tended to the house while the couple worked. But Jass hated being away from her children so much. Jass obtained a Class 2 driver's license and took a job driving a school bus. Even though the job paid less than Tim Hortons, she would only have to drive in the mornings and afternoons, and could bring her children on the bus with her. Amrit got his Class 2 at the same time, and found work with an airport shuttle service. In 2000, Jass switched from driving a school bus to driving for "Handibus," the municipal transit service for Calgarians with disabilities. "That was good money," Jass said. "It is a city job."

But Jass was abruptly forced to quit when Amrit's mother suddenly passed away in 2002, Sikh tradition requiring the eldest grandson—Robin, in this case—to ignite the body for cremation. "Without my son, they cannot do the ceremony," Jass said. Amrit left his job as well so the two could travel for the funeral. When they returned two months later, they couldn't get their old jobs back.

Amrit found work dismembering chickens at a poultry-processing plant, while Jass returned to the indignities of hotel housekeeping. But Jass and Amrit would both soon return behind the wheel. One of Jass' co-workers told Jass that her husband made good money delivering pizza for Papa John's. Jass was intrigued, but Amrit didn't like the idea of Jass going to strangers' homes. When she assured him that she wouldn't set foot inside anyone's house, Amrit relented. After a week, Jass was earning between $150 and $200 a day delivering pizza, and so when her manager told her they needed another driver, she convinced Amrit to join her. Eventually, Jass got a second job as a hotel shuttle-bus driver, and Amrit got his airport park-and-ride job back. Jass and Amrit were now both shuttling tourists by day and delivering pizza by night.

As they became familiar with the pizza-delivery game, Jass and Amrit switched from Papa John's to Panago to Pizza 73—each move representing an incremental increase in earnings. By the time they started working at Pizza 73, in 2003, both had quit their shuttle-driving jobs. Their manager loved having a husband-wife driving team. Since their earnings went to the same household, it meant never having to settle squabbles between rival drivers.

When Jass' parents decided to return to India for a year, they offered to take Robin and Amanpreet with them. It was a difficult decision. Neither Jass nor Amrit wanted to be away from their children, but the opportunity would allow them to work even harder, so they agreed. "I missed my kids," Jass said, "but I called them every day."

I wondered when she had time. During their childless year, Jass and Amrit put in exhausting, seventeen-hour shifts delivering pizzas. They also worked as night cleaners at three Calgary restaurants, Jass catching a few minutes' sleep in the passenger seat as Amrit drove them to and from each location in the middle of the night. They kept up this pace even after their family returned from India. Their borderline masochistic efforts paid off. After two years of day-and-night work, they'd saved $65,000—enough for a down payment on a five-bedroom house with a double garage. Two years later, they paid off their entire mortgage. This seemed a miracle to me. Then again, I've never worked that hard. "And you shouldn't," Amrit said. "I was so tired I started to forget things. But every immigrant is like that."

I asked Jass if she and Amrit ever tired of each other during those gruelling workdays. They worked side-by-side for years. She barely understood my question, which perhaps revealed more about my relationship with my now-ex-wife than about her and Amrit's marriage. "My husband is very family," she said. "He is always around us. He is a very good person. A very nice gentleman." Amrit told me that Jass would sometimes compete with him over who would deliver the larger pizza orders, but they worked together well.

In 2006, Amrit suggested they quit delivering pizza altogether. "Now we will do a respectable good job," he said. "You like driving. Why don't you drive a cab?"

The suggestion surprised Jass. "I've never seen a female cab driver," she said.

"So what?" Amrit said. "You can stand first, and the others will make a line behind you."

Female drivers-for-hire have always formed a tiny and exclusive club. The first mention I found of women driving cab dated back to March 1907, when a cohort of female drivers caused a sensation in Paris. The *New York Times* reported that, after a half dozen Parisian women earned their cabbie qualifications, everyone wanted to ride in their horse-drawn taxis. "The Parisians love nothing more than an amusing innovation," the *Times* reported. The new *chauffeuses* rarely went without a fare and earned generous tips. Disgruntled by the perceived intrusion on their turf, some male drivers took to masquerading as women by shaving their moustaches and swapping their coats for capes. The disguises worked, from a distance at least.

But the marvel of Paris' *chauffeuses* wouldn't last long. Nine months later, the *Times* reported that the "petticoated drivers" were disappearing. The number of female cabbies had dwindled from around forty, with at least as many applying for examinations, to "a bare score." One cabbie resigned from this "somewhat turbulent calling" when her fiancé demanded that she choose between him and her profession. Another quit after inheriting a fortune from a wealthy uncle. Others left due to ill health, traffic accidents, or disputes with police and clients. One driver, a countess in her private life, quit at the request of her family, who felt driving cab ill-suited an aristocrat like herself.

The first female cabbies appeared on Canadian streets during the First World War, but hardly in large numbers. According to the *Toronto Star*, labour shortages caused by the war resulted in just one woman, Clara Fennell, becoming a taxi driver in 1919. By 1943, Fennell had apparently been forgotten as Toronto's newspapers christened five newly licensed women—Ella Murray, Phyllis Webb, Esther Burns, Emma Gorrie, and Dorothy Buchanan—as the city's first ever female taxi drivers. The 1931 Canadian Census recorded only twelve women countrywide as "chauffeurs and bus drivers," a category that likely included cabbies. By 1941, the number had increased to a mere forty-two.

Not all Canadian cities welcomed the idea of female cabbies. In 1932, after several Winnipeg taxi firms actively sought applications from women drivers, City Council passed a resolution banning women from taxi driving, declaring cab driving an "unsuitable occupation for young women of good moral character." The Council also worried that driving taxis would "offer greater opportunities for women of loose morals to further ply their trade," and that female cabbies would be stealing jobs from unemployed male drivers who should receive first consideration. A Manitoba provincial judge, however, quashed the resolution.

In Canada, women who drove cabs during the war were considered temporary workers, and, as such, were expected to turn their steering wheels over to returning servicemen after it was over. Sometimes, local governments legislated women out of the driver's seat. In Alberta, veterans were granted first opportunity at any openings in the taxi industry, and city councils in both Halifax and Ottawa tried to impose new rules that eliminated female drivers altogether. The Ottawa measure prompted wartime cabbie Mrs W Baske to write to the editor of the *Ottawa Citizen* in 1947:

> Regarding the ban on women taxicab drivers, when the war began I had to learn to drive a car in order to keep our family taxicab business together. During the six years I have driven over 150,000 miles without an accident and without a fine of

any kind.... The work is made rough and tough often by the taxi-drivers themselves. Many become careless and rude and not dependable and are apt to indulge in too much liquor. But women drivers have never given the police commission, our insurance company or our many customers any trouble.

Female drivers were eventually allowed into the industry, albeit reluctantly. Their numbers rose in the late 1950s, and by the 1970s, female cabbies were relatively more common. Peter Pellier counted Millie McClusky and "The Duchess" among his Mississauga colleagues, and Helen Potrebenko's experiences driving cab in Vancouver during the same era inspired her fabulous 1975 novel, *Taxi!* Late in the book, Potrebenko's fierce protagonist, Shannon, tells a friend:

> ...I like driving cab. Receptionists, sales clerks, waitresses—they all have to look pleasant all the time. I can snarl if I want. There ain't too many women who can do that. Maybe garment workers are allowed to snarl at their sewing machines.

But driving cab is still considered man's work. Female cabbies remain a rarity if not an outright novelty. According to the 2016 Census, of the almost 56,000 Canadians employed as "taxi and limousine drivers and chauffeurs," only about 3,400 were women, or around 6 percent. Anecdotally, even this number seems high. In Toronto, for example, just one hundred of the city's 11,375 licensed taxi drivers, well under 1 percent, are women. Kristine Hubbard, operations manager at Toronto's Beck Taxi, told me that only about five of the more than two thousand cabbies driving for Beck are women. "If I was being generous, we could have ten women who have *ever* driven with Beck," Hubbard said.

Despite the industry's historically lopsided gender ratio, Jass was undeterred. Amrit brought her to the taxi commission and helped her register as a new driver. She filled out the requisite paperwork, then enrolled in the driver-training program. As a former bus driver, she didn't need to upgrade her driver's licence. After she passed the exam and received her taxi license, Amrit brought her to the Checker Cabs office and asked the receptionist if they were hiring. She said yes and asked him for his taxi license. "Not from me," Amrit said. He pointed to Jass. "From her."

The receptionist raised an eyebrow at Jass and summoned her manager. "This is not an easy job," the man warned Jass. "The exam is very hard. You have to pass an English language test, a customer service test, and a city knowledge test." The man took Jass to a room to write the exam. When she emerged a short while later, papers in hand, the manager said. "See? I told you it wasn't easy."

She handed him the exam. "I am done." She aced the test.

Jass started driving for Checker right away. She initially rented a car with a Checker taxi plate from a driver she knew. Then, after a few weeks, she bought her own car from a retiring driver. The other cabbies treated her shabbily at first. Jass said many didn't approve of women working the job, and worried Jass would inspire their own wives and sisters to start driving. Jass, though, wouldn't be pushed around. When a driver pulled his cab in front of hers at a hotel queue, Jass got out and stuck a finger in his face. "I did not come to Calgary to watch the Stampede," she said. "I am here to work. You think I am a female so I am shy? So I don't want to speak up? No. I am not that kind. My nation, my culture, my religion has very strong women. So you respect me, and I will respect you."

Jass reported the offending driver to her manager, who told the man to keep his distance from Jass. "If she parks at the Westin, you are not allowed to go to the Westin. If she parks at the International, you can't go there, either." The manager warned all the other drivers to treat Jass as an equal. She never had another problem.

One day, Jass was standing beside her taxi in front of a downtown hotel. A man emerged from the hotel, saw her jacket and tie, and asked if she was driving the limousine he'd ordered. Jass told him she was just a regular cabbie. After ten minutes, the man's limousine still hadn't arrived, so he asked Jass to take him to the airport. "I am sorry, sir. But I am fourth in the queue. You should take the taxi in the front."

"But I want you to drive me," the man said, and slid into Jass' backseat. According to Checker's rules, if a customer insists on a particular taxi, that driver can jump the line. Jass pulled the car out and headed to the airport.

En route, the man asked "Do you recognize me?"

Jass looked at his face in the rear-view mirror. "No. I am sorry, sir."

"I am a Hollywood star," he said.

Jass looked again. "I am sorry, sir. I am not watching English movies too much."

"You are very honest," the man said.

"If I lied and said I know you, you would ask another question and I won't have the answer," Jass said. "So it is better if I tell the truth."

When they arrived at the airport, the man shook Jass' hand and gave her an American hundred-dollar bill to cover the $33 fare.

I asked Jass if the man ever told her his name. "It was something 'Douglas.' I forget his first name."

"Michael Douglas?"

"I don't know. I don't remember. I don't watch Hollywood movies."

* * *

Fewer than ten women drive cabs in Calgary, and Jass is one of the only ones who drives at night. "I don't know why no womans want to drive at night?" she said.

"Really?" I said. "I can probably tell you why."

Jass smiled. "I know the reasons," she conceded. "I think you just need to be a little bit strong." Jass told me her clients in Calgary are always friendly and respectful to her. Having a female driver is such a novelty for some passengers that they leave her large tips, just like in 1907 Paris. Jass works the lucrative late-night shifts downtown, catering to Calgary's bar and club crowd. She keeps her doors locked and will refuse to open them to drunk men, though she has only done so four or five times in all the years she's been driving. "If it is four young kids, I say no. I say 'take the next one.' I don't even ask where they are going. Doesn't matter. Four young kids always make a mess." Jass would much rather give rides to women. "I try for the girls," she said. "In my culture, I don't like to see womans waiting on the street. I have respect for the womans. If I see womans and men, I say 'girls, come on.' Men can wait ten more minutes."

Amrit got his taxi licence soon after Jass did. "Now it is our family business," Jass said, just like pizza delivery used to be. "We are never late. We are never early. We are always on time." She and Amrit have regular customers who contact them directly. If Jass is unable to pick up a passenger, she'll send Amrit.

Their children are adults now. Both study at the University of Calgary, but still live at home with their parents and Jass' parents. And the family is expanding. When Amanpreet got married, her new husband, who recently immigrated from India and is waiting for his papers, moved in. "My daughter and her husband stay with us because we are helping her," Jass said. "She is studying. In the meantime, she doesn't have to worry about rent or food. But I told her 'If you don't want to study, get out.'"

Jass still finds time to swim once in a while. She remembers the first time she went at her local public rec centre. While her kids splashed in the wading pool, Jass walked to the main pool where three lanes had been roped off for length swimming. As she approached the lane marked "fast," two lifeguards rushed to stop her.

"Excuse me, excuse me. This area is for lane swimming," one said.

Jass frowned. "You think I can't read?"

"You can go over there," the other lifeguard said, pointing to the slow lane.

Jass ignored them, slipped into the fast lane, and started doing her national-team-level breaststroke. The lifeguards went silent. Halfway across the pool, Jass noticed them staring at her. "Don't worry," she called out. "I am not going to drown." Like the passengers in the back of Jass' cab, the lifeguards had no idea who they were dealing with.

Six

THE FAMILY MAN

THIS IS HOW KAREEM YALAHOW REMEMBERS THE DAY HIS wife died: Mary had just given birth to twin girls, their sixth and seventh children and second set of twins. The girls were healthy, but Mary didn't know this. She was unconscious, and in crisis, and she wouldn't stop bleeding. Doctors tried to replace the blood she'd lost. "They used twenty-two units of blood," Kareem told me. They also put her on oxygen and on dialysis. But their heroism failed. Mary's kidneys crashed. Then her lungs. And then her heart.

Kareem was pacing the waiting room when a doctor came to tell him Mary was gone. Shattered, he phoned her parents in Inuvik, and then called friends at his Edmonton mosque, who would arrange Mary's funeral. She wasn't the first wife Kareem had lost. His previous spouse, along with their two children, died years earlier in the anarchy of bombs and bullets in Somalia's civil war. Now he had seven children in Canada to care for, two of them fragile and newly born from Mary's broken body. How would he manage without her?

Then a nurse ran down the hall towards him. "Wait!" he cried. "Mary is alive!"

I arrived in Yellowknife in the late spring. This was my first trip to Canada's north, and as a middle-aged Canadian travel writer, I was aware the trip was absurdly overdue. I'd come too late to view the Northern Lights, but in time for the midnight sunsets that messed with my southerner's rhythm. I was surprised at my inability to adapt. I spent ten days in Yellowknife, and instead of growing accustomed to twenty hours of daylight, I found each night's sleep more elusive than the last.

I'd called ahead to City Cab and asked if I could speak with some of its drivers. General manager Shirley McGrath suggested I hang out at the office on Monday, when drivers came in to pay their stand rent. That way I could meet everybody. When I arrived, the cabbies were lined up in the hallway, waiting their turn to go into the office. I stood beside Shirley's desk and awkwardly introduced myself as each cabbie entered as if I were a one-man receiving line. The cultural diversity of the drivers surprised me. Naively, I expected that almost everyone in this small northern city would be white or Indigenous, but the City Cab's crew of drivers were as diverse as in any other Canadian city I'd visited. I met men from South Asia, the Middle East, and Africa, and grinned at the realization that, in spite of all my travels, the first Zimbabwean I've ever met was a taxi driver in Yellowknife. I wondered how long it had taken these men, who came from places even further south than I did, to grow accustomed to the summer's light, not to mention the winter's cold.

I wouldn't have the chance to ask. The drivers were far less enthusiastic to meet me than I was to meet them. Everyone treated me with bemused kindness, and a few gave me their phone numbers, but no one felt like talking in the end. Kareem, City Cab's vice-president, agreed to meet the following day—mostly, I suspect, out of pity for my failure to convince anyone else. We sat in a dusty conference room down the hall from the dispatch office, and Kareem told me his story.

Kareem was born in Mogadishu, Somalia. His father, Abdirahim, was a career soldier who served Somalia's long-reigning president Siad Barre before retiring and starting a business in the fruit and vegetable trade. Kareem was one of Abdirahim's eighteen children, the youngest of his first wife, and he lived a safe and blessed childhood in a neighbourhood filled with aunts, uncles, and cousins. Kareem and his companions roamed the streets, played soccer in the alleyways, and sat to eat at whoever's home was closest when mealtimes came. No one worried about anything.

Then came the *burbur*, the Somali word for "catastrophe." At the beginning of 1991, paramilitaries ousted Barre from office and dissolved the Somali military. Rival factions fought for whatever scraps of wealth and power the collapsed government left behind. The streets of Mogadishu descended into terror. Guns were everywhere. "Cousins were killing cousins," Kareem said. "It was like the Wild West." The destruction of infrastructure and plundering of food supplies escalated a severe drought into a deadly famine which killed 250,000 Somalis. Between December and March, 1.5 million people fled the country. Eventually, so did Kareem

One night, a gang of thugs dragged Kareem's friend out of a mosque, drove him out of town, shot him, and left him bleeding on the ground. The man somehow survived his wounds and was taken to hospital. Kareem rushed to his bedside. When he heard Kareem's voice, the friend opened his eyes and told him the names of the men who shot him. "That was the last time I knew I was sane," Kareem said. Rage overcame him, and he started to gather a posse of men to avenge the shooting until his family and friends intervened. Someone bought him a one-way ticket to Damascus, via Djibouti, on the last government airline flight to leave Mogadishu. Kareem doesn't know who paid for the ticket. He doesn't even remember boarding the plane. He only knows that if he'd stayed in Somalia he would have ended up a murderer or a corpse.

Kareem's family, though, would not be so lucky. From the safety of his Syrian exile, Kareem learned that a bomb blast had killed his wife and their two children: a one-year-old son and three-year-old daughter. Kareem's father died in the *burbur*, too. So did two of Kareem's sisters. "There was nobody in the country that didn't lose lots of people," Kareem told me. The abundance and facelessness of death in Somalia—a random explosion here, a stray bullet there—meant Kareem had no target for his fury. He felt numb. "I was not in my mind," Kareem said. "I was not awake. I was a zombie walking."

The Somali community in Damascus offered Kareem solace. Then, a cousin who lived in Toronto urged Kareem to seek asylum in Canada. Kareem had worked as an administrative assistant on a United Nations project in Mogadishu, so he was already thoroughly vetted, and Canadian officials processed his application quickly. He arrived in Toronto, then moved to Edmonton, where he found work fabricating tubing for oil-drilling operations. Kareem started driving taxi in 1993, after the factory laid him off, and he met a fellow Somali at the Edmonton mosque he attended who was starting a cab company in Inuvik and needed drivers. Kareem followed him north.

It was there, in the Inuvik taxi dispatch office, that Kareem met Mary Apsimik.

One night in Aklavik, sometime during the 1960s, William Apsimik prayed for a wife. God delivered. According to a story William was fond of telling, a plane arrived the following morning from Alaska. Pastor Don Violet stepped out of the plane, looked down at William, who attended his Pentecostal ministry, and said "William! I heard your prayer. You want a wife? I've got one for you."

"You heard my prayer to God?" William asked, suspicious.

"Yes. I have a wife for you."

The wife was a sixteen-year-old girl named Eva. Her mother, an Inuk drum dancer from Barrow, had contracted tuberculosis. They'd both flown to Aklavik for her treatment. Lest he seem ungrateful for God's swift answer to his prayers, William proposed to Eva. She wasn't sure she wanted to marry him. "I am here in Aklavik for only two more days," William told her. "Then I have to go back to Tuk." William lived in Tuktoyaktuk, where he herded reindeer. "So you have two days to decide if you want to marry me or not." Eva agreed to marry William, and he returned to Tuk and his reindeer buoyed by their engagement.

With her mother in the hospital and her fiancé in Tuk, Eva had no one to take care of her, so Pastor Violet sent her to Inuvik Indian Residential School. By the time William came back to marry her, the cruel institution had robbed Eva of her language. During their more than sixty-year marriage, William never stopped trying to speak to Eva in Inuvialuktun, but she always refused to answer. She never forgot the punishment those words bore. Eva is in her eighties now, and she still doesn't dare speak the language of her people.

William and Eva moved to Tuktoyaktuk after they married. The couple appears in an obscure 1977 book called *God's Fire on Ice*, which recounts author and missionary Kayy Gordon's time with the Inuit and includes an incident that strangely mirrors Mary's near-death experience. In the book, "Eskimo Christians" tell Gordon a story about how Eva had suffered a miscarriage and started to hemorrhage. As she lay bleeding on a wooden bunk covered with reindeer skins, far from medical help, her Christian friends gathered around her to pray. "With a faith that refused to be defeated, this little band of true believers besought God to touch Eva with His wonderful healing virtue," Gordon writes. Eva's bleeding stopped. Heat returned to her hands and feet, and "the blueness around her lips began to leave."

Miscarriages and miracles notwithstanding, William and Eva would have ten children together. Their daughter Mary was born in Inuvik, and was raised under her father's strict Pentecostalism. "She was fed the Bible as breakfast, lunch, and dinner," Kareem said. The family lived in several northern communities before moving to Inuvik, where Mary would end up working at the same taxi company as Kareem.

I told Kareem I would like to speak to Mary. "I can ask her," he said, "even though I know she is very shy." A little while later, he sent a message saying "Mary is fine to talk with you but wants short time. She is not talkative like me." When I arrived at their house a few days later, Mary had prepared a pot of hot tea and a tray of fresh bannock made from her mother's recipe. She smiled at me from beneath a floral-patterned hijab. The three of us sat down at the kitchen table and I asked Mary about the first time she met Kareem.

"It wasn't love at first sight," she said softly. Mary was in a common-law relationship at the time, and had brought her two-year-old daughter with her to the office. Kareem started playing with the girl as soon as he saw her. "That's what I liked about him," Mary said. "He was so good with children."

An affection grew slowly between Kareem and Mary after her relationship ended. Mary's father had never met a Muslim before, and was suspicious of Kareem's faith. Kareem recalls William's eyes growing wide as Kareem explained the beliefs Muslims and Christians shared. William was surprised that Kareem knew of Noah, John the Baptist, Isaac, and Abraham. And that Muslims believed in both the holiness of Jesus Christ and his eventual return. "He thought we believed in some kind of fire god with horns," Kareem said. "When he got to know me, he relaxed."

Then, at the beginning of 1997, Kareem got into trouble. He was among twenty-two people charged in the largest financial scam in Northwest Territories history. According to regional telecommunications company NorthwesTel, callers in Inuvik and Yellowknife had obtained a code that allowed them to bypass the company's billing system, thus allowing them free access to long-distance calls valued at $11 million. Eighteen months passed before the company finally grew wise. Kareem claimed that Inuvik's Somali, Sudanese, and other immigrant communities were simply exploiting a "glitch" in the system. A judge would eventually dismiss nearly all the charges, but the risk of a criminal record spooked Kareem and many of his fellow cabbies. They could lose their taxi licenses in Inuvik if the courts convicted them.

Kareem decided to flee to Yellowknife, and he wanted Mary to join him. First, though, she had to agree to a list of conditions tied to Kareem's beliefs. While he did not insist that Mary convert to Islam, he did want her to follow some of the rules of the faith. She had to promise not drink alcohol, for example, and Kareem insisted they get married before living together. Mary found this hard to accept. Like her mother before her, she balked at the thought of marriage. Her father, though, approved of Kareem and Mary eventually agreed.

In 1997, they moved to Yellowknife, and their first child, Adam, was born. Two more children followed in the next three years. Then, in 2004, Mary became pregnant with twins, a boy and a girl. Her Yellowknife obstetrician considered her pregnancy high-risk, and sent Mary to an Edmonton hospital during her second trimester so she could be more closely monitored. During that time, Kareem drove himself and their three young children back and forth from Yellowknife to Edmonton, fifteen hours in each direction, to visit Mary in hospital whenever he could.

During one of these visits, a doctor told Kareem that a fetal MRI showed severe brain abnormalities in the male twin. Doctors warned Kareem that, even if the child survived to term, which they deemed unlikely, he would always be a burden. The comment infuriated Kareem. "A child is a gift from the Creator," he scolded the doctor. "And a gift can never be a burden. Never say the word 'burden' to me again."

Mary delivered the twins four months premature. Both survived, even though one weighed only two pounds, and the other even less. The fragile infants faced long stays in the hospital before going home, and Kareem despaired leaving them. He decided to move the entire family to Edmonton as the twins gained strength.

When Kareem had first lived in Edmonton, more than a decade earlier, he used the language skills he gained working with the UN to assist other newly arrived Somalis. He connected many to immigration and social agencies, for example, and helped his friends navigate the taxi-licensing system to become cabbies. Now, with Kareem's family in need, the Edmonton Somali community returned the kindness. Kareem's Somali friends found a house for the family to rent, paid their damage deposit, and filled the fridge with food. A restaurant owner agreed to run an open tab for the Yalahows. They could come for three meals a day if they wanted, and the community at large would cover their bills. The feeling of community Kareem grew up with in pre-war Mogadishu had been transferred across the world to Edmonton.

The twins stayed in hospital for nine months. A second scan on the little boy, whom they named Bilal, showed the same brain abnormalities as the fetal scan. Once again, doctors warned Kareem and Mary that Bilal's prognosis was poor. "The doctor said he will never move. He will just sit on a bed. And he will never talk," Kareem said. The news crushed him. "You won't believe how much I cried. Like a little baby. I prayed every night. Please God help me. I can't sacrifice all my time to this one child and neglect the rest."

But Bilal thrived. Despite a nearly imperceptible cognitive delay and some stiffness in one of his legs and hands, he otherwise progressed like any healthy child. When Bilal turned three, Kareem brought him to a specialist. The doctor looked down at the boy and asked Kareem "Is this Bilal Yalahow?" Kareem nodded. "No. I am not talking about this child," the specialist said, staring at Bilal's health records. "There must be a mistake. I am talking about your other child. The one who is bedridden."

"We have no child in bed," Kareem said.

The doctor reached out his hand to Bilal. Bilal shook it. The doctor held up his other hand. Bilal high-fived it. Bilal walked when the doctor asked him to walk and jumped when he asked him to jump. At the end of the examination, the astonished doctor told Kareem, "This case is closed. You never have to come see me again. Whatever you are doing, keep doing it." Bilal is a teenager now. He plays basketball, and, with Kareem's guidance, has memorized the Koran.

The Yalahow family stayed in Edmonton. Both Mary and Kareem went back to school. Mary wanted to upgrade some of her high-school marks so she could earn a certificate in office administration. Kareem took advantage of a government education program for new immigrants in order to upgrade his English skills and earn a high-school diploma—no one recognized the certificate from his Somali school. He also completed a two-year program in graphic communications at a tech school while driving an airport taxi van.

Each weekday morning, Kareem dropped Mary off at her classes, brought his two youngest children to daycare, two others to kindergarten, and the three remaining to their school bus stop. Then he would go to his own classes. At the end of the day, Kareem picked everyone up and dropped them off at home, then drove to Edmonton's distant airport to take his place at the back of the taxi queue. He could usually rely on three hours passing before his cab inched forward to the front of the line. He'd spend his first three-hour wait napping. Then, after driving his fare into town and returning to the back of the airport taxi line, he'd spend his next three-hour wait doing his homework. Two or three such round trips provided just enough income for Kareem to support his family. He usually returned home around midnight, often finding Mary doing her own homework on the kitchen table. "We lived like this for two years," Kareem said.

In 2009, Mary became pregnant with her second set of twins. "That is when things turned ugly," Kareem said. That's when Mary died. And when she came back.

Mary remained in a coma after she'd been revived, and doctors prepared Kareem for the worst. They told him she'd likely suffered brain damage when her heart stopped. "The doctor told me even if she comes back, she will never move," Kareem said. But he'd heard such dire predictions before, with Bilal, and wasn't ready to take the doctors at their word.

Nine days passed before Mary came out of her coma. "Where are my girls?" she asked, her eyes bright. Kareem showed her a photo of the twins, and told Mary their names: Asmaa and Leila. She smiled. "All this time I wanted to name a girl Leila. I had two girls before, but it was not time for Leila yet. That's the name I really liked. When he told me Leila, I was so happy."

Kareem had never pressured Mary to convert to Islam, but he did speak to her about the faith from time to time and read to her from the Koran. And she was a willing pupil. "When I heard the Koran, sometimes I would almost cry," Mary said. "The reading of it just touched me. It felt soothing. I knew there was meaning to it." Still, she hadn't wanted to embrace Islam just for her husband's sake; she'd wanted to make the decision for herself. Her near-death was the sign she needed. "God gave me the time to learn Islam," Mary said. "That's when I knew I had to start learning. He gave me another chance." She formally converted and started to wear a hijab. "Islam touched my heart," she said.

Mary's heart, though, remained weak, even months after her near-fatal delivery. The powerful medication her doctors prescribed debilitated her. Her duties as the mother of seven children left her with little time to rest her body. Then Kareem's mother called from Somalia: she would care for all Kareem and Mary's children in her home for as long as they needed. Kareem sold his taxi van for $20,000, just enough to cover the airfare for his enormous family. Mary's doctor declared her healthy enough to travel, and they all flew to Hargeisa, capital of the self-declared breakaway state of Somaliland, where Kareem's mother had a house. Somaliland might not officially exist according to international law, but Hargeisa was free of the violence and crime that plagued Mogadishu. Kareem's mother's house was a sanctuary, both from distant memories of war and from the pressures born of Mary's health emergency. After a lengthy visit, Kareem and Mary flew back to Canada, leaving their children behind.

I thought of Jass and Amrit, who'd also decided to leave their children in the care of their parents overseas. Of all the sacrifices taxi drivers make for their loved ones—leaving the familiar comforts of their homelands, trading professional careers for driving cab, enduring Canada's cold winter welcome—choosing to live apart from their own children must be the hardest.

Kareem and Mary moved to Yellowknife. Living without their children weighed heavily on them. Mary eased her sadness by visiting her friends and family and spending time with their children. "I was borrowing other kids," Mary joked. "That's what kept me from going insane." Kareem and Mary made trips back and forth to Somaliland whenever they could, sometimes for six months at a stretch. Occasionally, on their way back from Somalia, they'd steal some time to take short European vacations. Mary had never travelled outside Alberta and the Northwest Territories her entire life. Most of the time, though, Kareem and Mary worked. Kareem found a job in a diamond mine before driving cab again, and Mary worked both as a taxi dispatcher and hotel housekeeper. They lived alone in Yellowknife for seven years before they finally brought their children home.

On a Friday afternoon in Yellowknife, cabs representing all three of the city's taxi companies monopolized the parking spaces around the Centre Square Mall. As I waited for Kareem in a second-floor hallway just outside the Yellowknife Public Library, about sixty men, many of them cabbies, slipped off their shoes, silenced their cell phones, and entered the library meeting room that hosts Friday prayers for the city's Muslims. Some wore long grey or tan *jalabiyas*. A few of the worshippers used the hallway water fountain for their pre-prayer ablutions and left tiny puddles on the floor beneath notices for "Celebrity Storytime" and the library's annual Lego donation drive.

Yellowknife's Muslim community, about three hundred strong, is building a new mosque. In the meantime, the library accommodates their Friday worship. On the other days of the week, the community holds prayers in a strip mall next to a vape shop behind the City Cab offices. Kareem had shown me the spot a few days earlier. He told me the sign on the door, which simply read "Temporary Musalla," was designed to deflect unwanted attention from potential Islamophobes. Most non-Muslims don't know "musalla" is another word for mosque.

Kareem was scheduled to give the sermon on this particular Friday, and I'd wanted to listen in, but one of the men told me he'd fallen ill that morning. Nothing serious, he assured. In Kareem's place, a Palestinian named Rami Kassem would take the pulpit. I knew Rami. He used to be a taxi driver, too, and now co-owns the Javaroma coffee shop. Rami was born in Beirut's Shatila refugee camp. He was a child when his family barely escaped the brutal massacre that occurred in the camp in 1982 and left at least 1,400 people dead. Every taxi driver has a story.

Another Muslim cabbie missing from prayers that Friday was Ahmed Mahamud Ali. Just after 3:30 am on a November morning in 2018, Ahmed had picked up eighteen-year-old Elias Schiller from a downtown apartment building and driven him home. The two men argued over the fare in front of Schiller's house. Their fight escalated. Ahmed shoved Schiller and ran from his cab. Schiller chased Ahmed down, beat him about the head and neck, and left him unconscious and bleeding on a public street. Schiller went home and consulted with his father, James. Twenty-five minutes later, the Schillers pulled a comatose Ahmed by his head into his taxi's backseat, drove him to the hospital parking lot, and left him with the engine running. The elder Schiller then called the hospital from a payphone, and said in a disguised voice that an injured person in a taxi outside required medical attention. Police found Ahmed's body in his taxi. Emergency doctors pronounced him dead.

Police used information from City Cab's dispatch office to learn the location of Ahmed's last fare. They visited the Schiller's house the next morning and found Ahmed's blood on the street, even though James Schiller had shovelled snow over it the night before in an attempt to hide the evidence.

Everyone in Yellowknife's taxi and Muslim communities adored the man they called "Uncle Ahmed." His death shook them. "He is very much missed," Kareem told me. "He could come to a place where everyone was gloomy, and just light a fire and make everybody laugh. He had that talent." A month after his murder, a procession of ninety cabbies tied black ribbons to their antennas and drove in a slow procession down Franklin Street in Ahmed's honour.

Kareem came from the same part of Somalia as Ahmed and had arrived in Canada at around the same time. Kareem suspects they might even be distant cousins. Ahmed grew up in the Somali countryside, then moved to Mogadishu when he was a young man. From there he spent a few years in Saudi Arabia before immigrating to Canada. Ahmed never stayed in any one place long enough to find a wife and start a family. He felt he'd become too old to marry. "Once you pass forty, marriage becomes blurred in your mind," Kareem said. Even though Ahmed had no children of his own, he used his taxicab earnings to support thirty-five orphaned children in Somalia. This reminded me of Michael Kamara in Halifax. Both were men of meagre means supporting children in Africa who had even less.

The Yellowknife RCMP charged both Elias and James Schiller with second-degree murder. Kareem had met Elias when he was a child, and Elias' mother, a well-known Yellowknife singer, is related to Mary. Kareem knew Elias was a troubled young man, but the homicide charge still surprised him. "You know someone as a child," Kareem said. "And all of a sudden he is a murderer." James Schiller's own criminal history included impaired driving, assaulting a peace officer, and an almost comically bungled drug deal. In 2009, Schiller sent two Ziplock bags of weed in a package labelled "meat" from Yellowknife to Ulukhaktok via a parcel-delivery company but put his own name and return address on the waybill and left his fingerprints all over the baggies.

In October 2019, Elias pled guilty to manslaughter and his father to being an accessory to aggravated assault. The court sentenced Elias to four years in prison, and James to six months. Kareem appeared on the local CBC news after the sentencing to speak on behalf of Yellowknife's taxi drivers. "We came up to the one conclusion," Kareem said. "Uncle Ahmed is dead. We cannot bring him back. We might as well go ahead and forgive what happened, and forgive them, Elias and his dad." Kareem told the CBC that Ali's family wanted "Ahmed's blood to become a bridge to cross to each other, and forgive each other, and handshake each other, and open a new chapter of our life."

Ahmed wasn't the last Yellowknife cabbie to be assaulted. Only six months after his murder, police arrested another two men, brothers this time, who allegedly beat up a taxi driver and stole his phone. A witness overheard one brother say to the other, "just shoot him." Both men already had assault and theft convictions on their records. In 2017, the younger brother spent fifteen minutes punching, kicking, and choking the woman babysitting his girl-friend's daughter. He served fifteen months in prison for the attack.

Violence has long been recognized as an occupational hazard for taxi drivers. As early as 1932, a taxi industry advisory committee in Toronto suggested adding glass partitions between passengers and drivers to act as a "deterrent to the driver being assaulted by passengers and vice-versa." The committee didn't think tourists would appreciate the partitions, however, so they weren't installed.

Attacks against taxi drivers started to increase in the 1950s and throughout the 1960s. The shooting of Toronto cabbie Larry

Botrie in 1968 was the first in a wave of crime against taxi drivers. In the two years after his murder, police responded to twenty assaults on cab drivers. The violence peaked in the 1980s, a decade that saw five drivers murdered in Toronto, including three killings within three months in 1988. Toronto drivers suffered frequent physical and sexual assaults, armed robberies, and unlawful confinement when thieves locked them in the trunks of stolen cabs. Two Ontario cabbies were stabbed to death in separate incidents within three days of each other around the 2000 New Year. One, Baljinder Singh Rai, was the uncle of federal NDP leader Jagmeet Singh. A 2012 Statistics Canada report revealed that taxi drivers are murdered on the job at a higher rate than workers of any other legal profession. Even police officers are killed less often.

However, none of these statistics shook me as much as scrolling through the Canadian Taxi Driver Homicide project. The remarkable online database includes the names, photos, and stories of the 215 Canadian taxi drivers who've been murdered since the end of the First World War. The first victim in the database, Carmine Lapello, was stabbed fifteen times in the back with a stiletto knife in Toronto in 1917. His murder remains unsolved. The last driver on the list is Balvir Singh Toor, a ten-year cabbie and father of three who was stabbed to death in Winnipeg in March 2020. Uncle Ahmed's name sits fourth from the top.

The dangers of driving cab inspired Parliament to amend the Criminal Code in 2015 to encourage courts, when sentencing defendants found guilty of assault, to consider it an "aggravating circumstance" if the victim were a taxi driver or public transit operator. In other words, an assault on a cabbie should be considered a more serious offence than on a non-driver when sentencing. At a hearing for a 2018 cabbie assault case, a Manitoba judge told the court that the Canadian Criminal Code should formally recognize taxi drivers as vulnerable, akin to emergency workers.

"The justice system has to set an example that taxi drivers are off limits," she said. "Taxi drivers provide a public service."

During my year among the cabbies, I read news reports about drivers being assaulted every few weeks. In the last eight months of 2019 alone, passengers physically attacked cabbies in Kitchener, Thunder Bay and Saskatoon. In Hamilton, a man and a woman teamed up to assault their driver after quarrelling over the fare, and a Toronto man tried to choke his driver with a seat belt before stealing his wallet. (In many cities, cabbies are exempt from local seatbelt laws as a precaution against this type of strangulation.) Knife-wielding passengers robbed cabbies in Saskatoon, Surrey, and Lethbridge. In the latter case, two women walked out of a 7-Eleven with their faces covered, entered a taxi, and threatened the driver with a six-inch hunting knife. When the driver tried to escape, his attackers slashed at his face. The cabbie finally managed to flee on foot, his face bleeding, while the two women drove away in his car. I can only imagine how many assaults go unreported.

I asked Mary if she worries about Kareem when he's driving cab. She said that she prays for God to watch over him. "Sometimes it is hard," she said. "Sometimes you wonder." But she and Kareem cannot let such fears intrude on their lives or livelihoods. "We have bills to pay," Mary said. "We have a big family." Adam is twenty years old now and studies at Aurora College in Yellowknife. Their youngest, twins Leila and Asmaa, are ten. Kareem says they all miss their time in Hargeisa—the weather was better there and grandma spoiled them—but that they do love living in the north. This might be the only thing his children have in common. Kareem marvels at how different each of them is. One has a crew of skateboarding buddies, while another focuses on her schoolwork and has few friends at all. One never leaves the house, while another is always out. "The only time you see him at home is when he is changing clothes, taking a shower, or sleeping."

All seven of Mary and Kareem's children still live at home. I joked with Mary that they'll need to get rid of some of them soon. She laughed. "Not just yet. Not ready just yet. I don't want them to go. Even when they are old enough. I am not ready to let them go yet."

Seven

THE CHARMED LIFE OF ALEX SELIGA

ALEX SELIGA IS IN HIS SIXTIES, BUT MOVES LIKE A GAZELLE. He's tall and fit, and I struggled to keep up with him as he led me through the Royal Glenora Club in Edmonton's River Valley. Alex didn't seem like someone who lived on fast food and spent his days seated behind a steering wheel. If many cab drivers suffer from poor nutrition and a lack of exercise, Alex is an exception.

Alex paused at the front desk to flirt with the young receptionist and ask whether anyone was looking for a tennis partner later that afternoon. I followed him past an arena and swimming pool to a second-floor cafeteria overlooking the club's seven courts. Tennis plays an outsized role in Alex's story, so the location felt apt.

As Alex recounted his fascinating biography for me, I quickly realized how deeply his life intertwines with that of his daughter, Iva. So much of Alex's history is Iva's, too. Their relationship, though frayed and fraught at times, is what defines Alex. If

Kareem Yalahow's life is in part a love story about a husband and wife, Alex's is a love story between a father and daughter.

In 1979, Alex lost his job at the Skoda automobile factory in Bratislava, Czechoslovakia, after complaining to his wife, Dasha, about life under the socialist regime. "How come we have nothing and they're telling us this is the best country and the best system in the world?" Alex asked her. "Your brother-in-law in Switzerland is nothing special, and he can travel anywhere, and he's got cars, and everything." A co-worker overheard Alex slagging the government and informed the factory overseers, who fired him.

Frustrated and jobless, Alex devised a scheme to escape Czechoslovakia. He applied for permission for his family to travel to Yugoslavia. From there, he planned to apply for transit visas from the Austrian embassy, then request political asylum once he crossed the border—something Dasha's not-so-special brother-in-law had already managed. Officials approved Alex's exit visa but would not give permission to Dasha and Iva. Restrictions like these, forcing travellers to leave family behind to ensure they returned, were common behind the Iron Curtain. Undeterred, Alex told Dasha to examine the handwritten transit visa in his passport and copy it onto her and Iva's passports. "She's got really good handwriting," Alex said.

Dasha doubted her amateur forgery would pass inspection and fully expected to be sent back once they reached the Czechoslovakian border. As her mother wrapped pieces of roast chicken in foil for their journey, Dasha assured her they would be back soon. She was wrong. Alex managed to drive his family in their battered Skoda 1000 through Hungary and Romania, then into Yugoslavia, a near thousand-kilometre journey, with Dasha's sham visas getting them past every checkpoint and border crossing. This sort of unlikely success has become a recurring theme in Alex's story. His entire life has been a series of comically ill-conceived ideas ultimately redeemed by his good luck and natural charm.

The escape plan briefly faltered in Yugoslavia, when Alex couldn't find the Austrian embassy, something he blames his "idiot" brother-in-law for. "The guy told me the embassy was in Zagreb, but it was somewhere else," Alex said. They left Zagreb and drove to the Adriatic coast, where Alex steered the car aboard a ferry destined for a resort island called Lošinj. Alex can't recall why he did this. The diversion made little sense: landing on Lošinj did not advance their mission. Perhaps Alex was looking for a quiet place to consider his next move. If so, Lošinj was a poor choice. The family couldn't afford to stay in the island hotels with the few Yugoslav dinars the Czechoslovakian government had given Alex for his trip. A campground caretaker offered the family a free campsite after Alex claimed he had a tent in the trunk. He didn't. Then Alex drove the Skoda over a rock and cracked the car's differential. The family was now stranded in an island campground with a busted car, no tools to fix it, and nowhere to sleep.

Fellow campers took pity on the Seligas. They cared for the family for a week and helped Alex fix the Skoda. A kind Slovenian man could tell what Alex was up to. "You are trying to escape, aren't you?" he whispered as he and Alex slathered epoxy on the Skoda's gear train. The man gave Alex two options to reach Western Europe. The first was to travel over the eastern Alps into Italy, a choice Alex rejected on culinary grounds. "I don't like macaroni," he told me, then quickly apologized in case he'd offended my Italian sensibilities. Instead, he chose the second option: to travel north and cross into Austria. The family returned to the mainland and drove the glued-together Skoda to the Maribor border post, where a Yugoslavian soldier stopped Alex and examined his documents. Even though Alex had Czechoslovakian plates on his car and no visas allowing him to leave Soviet Eastern Europe, the border guard let Alex cross. His good luck had held.

The Austrians on the other side of the border were less sympathetic. They locked the family in a prison cell overnight. Alex remained outwardly cheerful for Iva's sake, but he felt afraid. "When you escape, you expect to be free," Alex said. "To be free from the persecution of the communists. You expect a good life. But now we were in prison. I didn't know how long we were going to be in there."

Iva doesn't remember much from her night in the Austrian prison. She was only three years old, after all. She doesn't remember the guard removing the laces from their shoes before locking them up. And she doesn't recall her father demanding more than a bowl of white rice for her breakfast. "This is not enough food for a child," he shouted to the guard, who responded by pouring a glass of milk into the bowl.

But Iva does remember the bars on the windows, and how her father made their brief incarceration feel like an adventure. When I met her a few months after talking to Alex, at an Edmonton Starbucks, she told me, "My dad was always clever, whatever we did. My dad was that kind of guy."

Their jailers interrogated Alex after breakfast. When they were satisfied he wasn't a Soviet spy, they released the family and directed them to the famed Traiskirchen refugee camp. Austria first opened Traiskirchen in 1956, after converting the former military cadet school into a shelter for refugees fleeing the Hungarian Revolution—the same revolution that chased Andy and Ibolya Reti out of Budapest. Alex, Dasha, and Iva were among five thousand refugees from thirty-five countries who passed through Traiskirchen in 1979. Most, like the Seligas, came from communist Eastern Europe. Alex's weary Skoda looked right at home alongside the dilapidated East German Trabants and Soviet-made Fiats in the camp's parking lot.

Traiskirchen also took in those escaping uprisings in Africa and the Middle East, as well as political refugees fleeing right-wing dictatorships in Latin America. The camp didn't treat all guests equally, though, and Eastern Europeans like the Seligas often had better luck than their African and Arab neighbours finding work outside the camp. A nearby hotel hired Alex to do gardening work during the day while Iva played with a little Polish boy she'd befriended. Later, Alex trained as a machinist at a camp workshop.

When a Slovakian-Canadian visited the camp to recruit Slovak-speaking workers for his factory, Alex promptly signed up. After six months at Traiskirchen, the family left and immigrated to Toronto. Alex worked long hours for minimum wage for three months before moving the family to Edmonton, where a Slovakian friend owned a machine shop. He earned enough to make a down payment on a $90,000 house and paid off his entire mortgage within five years—another immigrant mortgage miracle that reminded me of Jass and Amrit. Alex also paid for a presidential pardon from the Czechoslovakian government through their embassy in Ottawa.

During Iva's early years in Canada, she was definitely a daddy's girl. Alex took her everywhere. Iva recalls Alex knocking on Iva's bedroom door after his car broke down during a snowstorm. "Come on, Iva. You have to help me out." Alex borrowed Dasha's car and he and Iva drove to where Alex's car had stalled. He linked the two cars together with a length of chain. Then he put his car in neutral and sat nine-year-old Iva behind the steering wheel. "I am going to tow you," he said. "You have to drive the car. Just turn the steering wheel and follow me." He advised her to gently press the brake pedal whenever she saw his brake lights go on.

Iva didn't understand the danger of what she was doing. Like their night in the Austrian prison cell, this was just another adventure with dad. "He was so much fun," Iva said. "He taught me not to fear anything."

Alex lost his job in 1981, after he took an unapproved seven-week vacation to visit family in Bratislava. He soon found another machine shop job, but he also conceived a scheme: he would turn his nine-year-old daughter into a tennis champion and earn lucrative prize money. Even if Iva never became a star, she could still make high wages as a tennis pro. Alex would be her coach and trainer. A more typical parent might push their child into law or medicine, careers with a more realistic and well-trodden path to wealth, especially in Canada. But Alex wasn't typical. And he didn't come from the West. In communist Czechoslovakia, a doctor earned no more than a mechanic. One of the only ways to get rich in Soviet Eastern Europe was by becoming a successful professional athlete. To Alex, his plan made perfect sense.

What made less sense was the fact that neither Iva nor Alex had ever played tennis. And that Iva had no interest in learning. None of this mattered to Alex, though. He was the father. He knew best, even if he really didn't know anything about tennis at all.

The first step in Alex's grand plan, oddly, was to sign Iva up for taekwondo lessons. He believed martial arts would strengthen Iva's legs to prepare her for tennis. At her first taekwondo competition, organizers accidentally registered Iva, whose full name, "Ivitzia," is more commonly a boys' name, in the boys' division. Her hair was also cut short. "My dad cut my hair because he was so cheap," Iva explained. She won the boys' tournament. And in her subsequent competitions, she so dominated the other girls that organizers registered her in the boys' division by default. Iva was a bona fide badass who once broke her own hand in a competition and who had earned a black belt by the time she turned ten. Despite her success, Iva never enjoyed taekwondo. "I just wanted to play with dolls," she said.

While Iva kicked the boys and made them cry, Alex began his own tennis education. He enrolled in a coaching certification clinic at an Edmonton tennis club. He watched hours of tennis training videos. "If he is intrigued with something, he will study it," Iva said. "He will learn it. He will smell it. He will watch it. He has no qualms studying for hours on end something that interests him." Alex also consulted with Milan Kelesi, a Slovakian-Canadian who'd coached his own daughter, "Hurricane" Helen Kelesi, to the thirteenth spot on the Women's Tennis Association rankings. Milan was from Bratislava and was happy to give his fellow Slovak some coaching advice.

Once Alex felt he and Iva were both ready, he pulled Iva out of the dojang and pushed her onto the tennis court. Alex quit his machine shop job and started driving a taxi in order to work around the strict training schedule he'd designed for Iva. They practised together every morning for two hours at Edmonton's Royal Glenora Club before Iva went to school, then for another two hours after school. Alex worked with her the entire time, putting in as many hours on the court as his reluctant protégée.

Off-court, Alex focused on Iva's intellectual development. He played backgammon with her at dinner time to sharpen her brain. "Unless *Three's Company* was on," Iva said. "Dad loved Jack Tripper." Alex even kept an electronic chess board on the back of the toilet "so even when you were on the shitter, you were learning." During summer vacations, Alex insisted Iva complete a set of difficult math equations he'd concocted before he allowed her to play with her friends. If Iva made a mistake, he would add another two equations. She couldn't leave the house until she got everything right.

Alex brought Iva to Slovakia for most of the summer to train. He hired Slovakian coaches and studied their techniques. Alex's natural charms endeared him to the elite sporting community that frequented Bratislava's tennis clubs. On one trip, Alex pitted Iva against the daughter of a member of Slovakia's national men's soccer team. Iva lost the first match but won the second. The following summer, when Iva was fourteen, Alex ran into hockey legend Petr Šťastný, the NHL's second-highest scorer in the 1980s behind Wayne Gretzky. After they chatted for a few minutes, Šťastný hired Iva to coach his teenaged daughter. "She had braces," Iva remembers of her Slovakian charge. "And the other Slovakian kids didn't know what they were." Afterwards, Alex brought Iva to Oilers games whenever Šťastný's New Jersey Devils were in town. Alex would bang on the plexiglass during warm-up to get Petr's attention. This embarrassed Iva, but Šťastný always skated over to say hello.

Alex's coaching regimen, though unorthodox, paid off. Iva was a winner. She competed at nationals three times, was ranked nationally for a while, and earned a sponsorship deal from racket-maker Wilson. At one national championship in Toronto, Iva played so well against the country's top-ranked player that the latter's coach offered to train Iva in Quebec. She declined. Alex always believed in her abilities, and together they trained as hard as anyone. Iva still wonders what, if anything, separated her from Canada's best players.

Maybe Alex did. Despite Iva's success, she only enjoyed tennis when her father wasn't around. "He was kind of an asshole," she said. The Soviet-era coaching style Alex learned from Kelesi employed humiliation and punishment as motivational tools. During matches, Alex sarcastically praised Iva's errors from the sidelines. "He would start clapping when I made a mistake," Iva said. "If I hit the net he would yell 'Oh, beautiful!'" After a poor performance, Alex would force her to run lines. Alex believed the taunts and abuse would infuriate Iva into playing better.

It didn't. Looking back, Alex recognizes his error. "I was pushing her and pushing her," he said. "That is a stupid thing. I didn't know any better." Alex's coaching style didn't endear him to Royal Glenora Club members, either, who would shout at him from the stands to ease up on his daughter. Alex didn't care. When Glenora's head tennis coach scolded Alex for the abuse, Alex glibly pointed out that Iva was winning more matches than his own kids were. The club coach tried to get Alex banned from the club, but a ten-member jury voted to allow him to stay.

Iva had had enough of her father's tennis court cruelty by the time she reached her mid-teens. She'd had enough of her father in general. Alex and Dasha were going through a vicious divorce and Iva sided with her mother. The break-up was also an opportunity to be free of her father's iron-fisted training regime. She remembers their last day together on the tennis court. Iva had told her father many times that she wanted to quit tennis. "He would shrug it off and we would come back the next day," Iva said. This time, though, Alex just gave up. Iva had never seen him so resigned. After they walked off the court, Iva didn't know what to do. "My whole life had been me and my dad," Iva said. "Me and my dad and tennis."

Alex quit the Royal Glenora. He paid off Dasha for the house, and she and Iva moved out. Iva wouldn't speak to her father again for almost thirty years.

In 1992, Alex's nephew in Slovakia called to tell him that his new bride had five single friends who might be interested in marrying a Canadian man. Alex flew to Bratislava. He started dating one of the five, a law student named Mira twenty-one years his junior.

Alex also reconnected with two childhood friends, both of whom now drove taxis, like Alex. During his two months carousing with Mira and his blue-collar buddies, Alex started to realize the folly of his lifelong fixation with status. Ever since driving his Skoda out of Bratislava, all Alex had ever wanted was something to boast about. He had long idealized men with money and felt insecure in their presence. This insecurity fuelled his ill-fated scheme with Iva. Alex knew he'd never be as rich as the men he'd met at the Royal Glenora, but he'd believed the prestige and wealth his daughter could earn as a tennis star would transform him into a big shot by association.

Alex's taxi-driving Bratislavan buddies made him realize he could be fulfilled regardless of wealth and station. The men were working-class scoundrels. "Unbelievable cheaters and liars," Alex said with affection. They didn't earn much money, but they were happy. And women adored them. Alex believes Mira fell for him after watching him interact with his rowdy friends. "People don't want some uptight asshole to brag about something," Alex said. "They just want a good time, and someone to make them feel good about themselves. That really changed my life."

Mira followed Alex back to Edmonton and registered at the University of Alberta. Since she didn't have an undergraduate degree, the U of A's law school wouldn't admit her, so she enrolled in an accounting program instead. Mira's foreign-student tuition was expensive, and Alex didn't know how he was going to pay her fees on his cabbie's income. He asked his passengers for advice. One suggested Alex marry Mira so she would only have to pay regular Canadian tuition. So he did. Many people, Iva among them, questioned Mira's intentions and doubted that the marriage would last. They were wrong. Mira and Alex have been married for more than thirty years.

Alex renewed his membership at the Royal Glenora Club shortly after he and Mira married. He'd learned to love tennis during his time as Iva's coach and longed to get back on the court. Training with Iva had made Alex an excellent player himself, and he won a men's singles gold medal in the 60+ division at the 2013 World Masters Games in Turin. Four years later, in New Zealand, he won bronze in the 65+ division singles and silver in the 60+ doubles. He remains one of the Royal Glenora's, and Canada's, best senior players.

Medals aside, Alex values the camaraderie tennis offers. He joined a group of older tennis players who called themselves the "Froth Blowers" because they always went out for beers after their matches. Alex isn't a drinker, but he would sit for hours listening to their stories and drinking lemonade. "They were lawyers, doctors, and that kind of stuff," Alex said. "But nobody talks about money." Alex rarely joined the conversations at first. "I was shy," he said. "And they were big shots." Alex's charisma quickly earned him the affection and respect of these powerful men, despite the economic divide. "I can see I am equal with them," Alex said. "I am not just a taxi driver."

In a way, Alex started living, by proxy, the privileged life he'd long desired. He infiltrated the frontier of class and wealth. Alex's well-heeled friends invite him and Mira into their luxurious homes, and often pick up the tab when they eat out. For a time, Alex's doubles partner was Dr Raj Sherman, former leader of the Alberta Liberal Party—though Alex's politics reside well to the right of Sherman's. Another of Alex's "billionaire" friends once flew him to Palm Springs in his private jet to watch a tennis tournament. "He always tells me I have a better life than he does," Alex said. Alex returns the favours when he can, often in the form of free taxi rides to and from Edmonton's distant airport. "I want to give something back to the person who gives to me or is nice to me. This taxi thing is what I can do."

Despite Alex's friendships within his community at Glenora, he remained estranged from Iva. Alex and Mira had a daughter,

Sasha, who would end up one of Iva's good friends despite their age gap. For years, Iva would drive to Alex and Mira's house to pick up Sasha and never talk to her father at all. Sasha urged Iva to reconcile with their father. Iva always told her she would reach out to him when she was ready.

Then, over a year and a half, a storm of tragedy raged over the family. A brutal car accident left Dasha's new husband in a vegetative state. Iva's best friend died. So did her father-in-law. And Sasha's long-time boyfriend killed himself. "All that taught me life is precious," Iva said. "Then Dad got stabbed."

In April 2018, a man named Brady Alook and a female friend flagged down Alex's cab and asked him to drive them to the Edmonton Remand Centre, where the woman's boyfriend was locked up. Once Alex dropped her off, Alook asked Alex to bring him to an ATM so he could withdraw cash for the fare. Alook returned from the bank empty-handed, but told Alex that if he drove him to a particular hotel, he'd be able to get the money there. "He told me he was a drug dealer," Alex said. "I said you don't have to tell me anything. It's okay. Just get me the money."

Alex had a pleasant conversation with Alook. "He told me I was the best taxi driver he ever had," Alex said. But their chumminess ended when they arrived at the hotel and Alex insisted Alook leave his backpack in the car as collateral while he fetched the money. "Whatever the hell you do, I don't care," Alex said. "But there is $65 on the meter. Leave something here." Alook refused. Alex insisted he wouldn't let him leave the cab. They argued until Alex lost his patience and called his dispatcher, who suggested Alex drive Alook to the police. "I didn't want to go," Alex said, "but I thought this might scare him a little bit, so he'd give me some collateral or something." Alex started to drive, slowly, towards the nearby police station.

Then Alex saw a quick flash in his rear-view mirror. He instinctively ducked his head as Alook slashed at him with a hunting knife he'd drawn from his bag. Alook just missed Alex's neck, plunging the tip of the blade into the soft flesh below Alex's right ear instead. Alook jumped into the front seat to try again for Alex's throat. And in that moment, Alook learned he'd attacked the wrong taxi driver. Alex, in addition to everything else, is trained in full-contact Kyokushin karate. "Vladimir Putin does the same style," Alex told me.

Years earlier, Alex had met Mac Mierzejewski, a fellow cabbie and Kyokushin sensei, who used to spar for prize money in underground fight clubs in the UK. At Mierzejewski's invitation, Alex joined a Polish cultural club, where, for three years, he, Mierzejewski, and a group of Edmontonian Poles practiced for two hours, three times a week. Alex competed in the national Kyokushin championships three times. Except for Mierzejewski himself, no Edmonton cabbie is more prepared for a taxi knife fight than Alex.

As they struggled—and as Alex continued, somehow, to drive—Alook jabbed the knife into Alex's ribcage. Instead of panicking, Alex took advantage of Alook's closeness and slammed his forehead into Alook's. The headbutt dazed Alook, and he lowered his knife. Alex, with one hand still on the steering wheel, grabbed and twisted Alook's wrist and forced him to drop the knife, a maneuver Mierzejewski had taught him. Disarmed and desperate, Alook bit down on Alex's hand and wrist. Alex stomped on the brakes and finally stopped the cab. "Then I go back to headbutting," he said.

Two passersby noticed the struggle in the taxi and rushed to help, but their heroics were short-lived. "They open the doors, and they see the knife. Then they closed the door and took off," Alex said. Alex, bleeding, slipped out of the car and started kicking Alook from outside the driver's side door. "Once I was free, I could really do some damage," Alex said. "I could finish this guy off." Alook slid over into the driver's seat and tried to start the car again hoping to drive away. But Alex's taxi was a hybrid with no ignition key and Alook couldn't restart the engine. A crowd gathered. Alex remembers a woman with glasses eventually pulling him back as police showed up.

The police towed Alex's car away for evidence, and EMS took him to hospital. Emergency-room doctors spent four hours sewing up the inch-deep gash on the side of Alex's face, several deep cuts on his hand, and a stab wound in his side that nearly punctured his lung. They also treated bite marks on Alex's arms. After Alex returned home, he cleaned up, then he and Mira went out for Thai food.

Alex went to the police station the following day to record a statement and reclaim his taxi. The police charged Alex for the impound, which seemed to have angered him more than the attack itself. When he returned home, Alex discovered that the police had left all Alook's possessions in the back seat, including his crack pipe and a stash of crack cocaine. When Alex brought the pipe and drugs back to the station, one of the officers asked Alex what he would like to say to the men who saved his life. Alex had no idea who they were talking about. No one saved his life. Alex didn't want to appear disrespectful though, so he told the police he was thankful for their help.

Six months later, one of Alex's tennis buddies showed him an article in the *Edmonton Journal*. The Royal Canadian Humane Association had honoured Alex's supposed rescuers—the men who opened, then shut, the taxi door during the attack—the bronze medal for bravery. The men claimed they'd returned to Alex's car after phoning 911, disarmed Alook, tossed his knife into the trees, then helped drag Alook out of the car. The award gobsmacked Alex. "This is a lie!" he told me. Still, Alex doesn't much care. I suspect Global News' description of him as "an elderly driver" rankled more than any misplaced heroism and unearned medals.

Alook nearly hacked off one of Alex's fingers during the attack. The strength in his hand has not fully returned and Alex cannot play as much tennis as he used to. But in the wake of the stabbing, Alex regained his relationship with Iva. "I could've lost him. I would have never thanked him for making me the strong woman that I am. That's exactly what he wanted," Iva said. "In that way, he was successful with me. I didn't become the tennis player he wanted me to be, but I am sure not one to be shit upon." Iva saw her father for the first time in twenty-seven years on Christmas Day in 2018. Now they talk every couple of days and see each other on weekends. "All of us are together. My kids are there. It feels great. Feels right."

Iva marvels at how little her father has changed physically. Alex thanks his young wife for his own youthfulness, but Iva credits his constant activity. Alex is nearly seventy years old, but he never sits down. He plays tennis. He goes to boot camps and does yoga and Zumba. He plays pickle ball. He flirts with the women at the Royal Glenora, and jokes and laughs constantly. "Our walls were shaking while he was playing Uno," Iva said. "He's insane. He could probably build a boat."

Traces of Alex's desire to ingratiate himself with his wealthy friends remain. "I still have to figure out how to not be affected by what people think of me," he recently told Iva. Most of the time, though, Alex's love of life beams out of him. "I am happy every day like it is Christmas. I work with tennis club millionaires and doctors and lawyers and whatever. They are envious of me and what I have."

"That's what he is," Iva said. "People are intrigued by him. They wonder: how is this guy so happy?"

Eight

WHAT DO WE DO WITH A RUSSIAN SAILOR?

SERGEY CHUDINOV NEVER WANTED TO COME TO CANADA. And he doesn't want to stay.

I met Sergey at a generic, all-you-can-eat sushi restaurant on St. John's historic Water Street. He had startlingly blue eyes and a bent boxer's nose. Sergey's Russian-accented voice rumbled out low and quiet, and I had to lean forward to hear him properly. Sergey and I grew up on the opposite sides of the Iron Curtain. I was born in Canada in 1973; Sergey in the Soviet republic of Byelorussia in 1967. Were it not for the site of our rendezvous, our meeting would've felt Cold War conspiratorial.

When Sergey's father died in 1971, his mother raised their seven children on her own. According to Sergey, Soviet socialism made this possible. "Kids were looked after," he said. He told me how every school in the Soviet Union had a dental office, and government-assigned dentists would travel from school to school to clean students' teeth and fill their cavities. The government also assigned pediatricians to make emergency house calls to any home with children under six years old. The state paid for Sergey and his siblings' swimming and cross-country ski lessons. He wrestled and rock climbed on the government ruble.

At the time, all young men owed the USSR at least two years of military service, but the government permitted students to finish their education before being drafted. Sergey joined after he finished a post-secondary certificate in fishery technology. The military assigned Sergey to a paratrooper division, which Sergey considered lucky. He feared his maritime experience would land him in the navy: sailors served for three years while soldiers and airmen served only two.

The Red Army sent Sergey to Afghanistan, where the USSR had been fighting insurgent groups since first marching troops into Kabul on Christmas Eve in 1979. But by the time Sergey arrived on the battlefield, in 1987, the Soviets had little need for paratroopers. The previous year, the American government had equipped the *mujahedeen*, invariably described as "ragtag" by Western media, with shoulder-mounted Stinger missile launchers that enabled them to take down Russian aircraft. Photos of *mujahedeen* soldiers firing Stingers from their shoulders became iconic images of the conflict. Military scholars still argue whether or not the Stingers changed the course of the war, but they did put paratroopers like Sergey out of work. "Basically, at that point, we lost the air over Afghanistan," Sergey said. "We only flew aircraft in rare cases. There was no solution to the Stinger."

Instead of leaping out of the sky, Sergey fought relatively small ground battles against Sunni and Shiite *mujahedeen* and fighters from around the region. "Uzbeks, Turkmen, Pakistani, even Chinese. All the Arabic countries. All were fighting against the USSR unofficially," Sergey said. His enemies also included mercenaries and followers of a young Saudi named Osama bin Laden. "A lot of interesting characters." Buoyed by $2 billion the

CIA funnelled to the Sunni *mujahedeen*, these characters eventually drove out the mighty Red Army in 1989.

Sergey spoke little about his combat experience. Afghan culture interested him more than warfare. He praised the cultural training he and his Red Army comrades received. "Every soldier had to keep a little brochure with them at all times," Sergey said. "The brochure started with these words: 'You will be deployed in a friendly country and among a friendly population. As a soldier of an international cause, you have to follow their cultural rules.'" This booklet advised soldiers on local customs and traditions. "It told us what we shouldn't do, and what would happen if we crossed the line," Sergey said. Red Army policy prohibited soldiers from entering the women's area of a private home, for example, even during a search. And a soldier who stopped a single woman on the street could face an immediate court martial.

When an Afghan soldier invited Sergey to his home for dinner, one of Sergey's comrades briefed him on Afghan customs beforehand. "Anything you compliment your host has to give to you," Sergey said. "Even if it is the last thing in the house. If you see a sword hanging on the wall, and you say 'Wow, what a beautiful sword you have here,' he would have to give it to you." Sergey learned the complicated etiquette required to refuse an Afghan's generosity without causing offense, and discovered that he, as a dinner guest, would be always offered the best pieces of meat. These cultural quirks and complexities fascinated Sergey, and that fascination, in turn, endeared him to me. He seemed more traveller than warrior.

Sergey spoke of his time in Afghanistan with more affection than I'd expected from a former soldier describing a war his country lost. His recollection of the conflict countered what I'd learned in history classes and bad Hollywood movies; namely, that the Soviet invasion was "Russia's Vietnam," and a failed exercise in communist imperialism. Sergey, though, considered the USSR's action in Afghanistan justified. He still does. "I never failed to believe," he said. Most Canadians don't understand how a country can send young men into war against their will, Sergey told me, but Russians saw things differently. "I remember growing up, in my childhood, we grew up with the mentality that we have to fight for our country. That was the way the system worked. Maybe it is cultural. In Russia we say 'don't ask what you country has done for you. Ask yourself what you've done for your country.'"

"That's not a Russian saying," I told Sergey. "JFK said that."

"Oh, that's right," Sergey said, grinning at his error. "But in Russia, that saying is quite a good description of our culture." According to Sergey's rosy view of his country's history, Russians have always valued community good over personal benefit. "Russian people have never been individual," he claimed. "Of course there are exceptions, but the majority feel this way. And it is still the same." He believes that fighting for a common cause inoculated Soviet soldiers in Afghanistan from Post-Traumatic Stress Disorder—that soldiers suffer PTSD when they don't have faith in the righteousness of their mission. "I don't know many guys who have PTSD," Sergey said. "Actually, I don't know any." He suggested that this paucity of post-war trauma proves the war's virtue.

This idea troubled me. I didn't believe Sergey was lying—why would he?—but I had a hard time accepting his narrative of the virtuous Soviet soldier fighting a war so ethical it left no marks on anyone's conscience. Sergey's respect for Afghan culture may have been sincere, but it wasn't universally shared. Not all Sergey's comrades followed the rules laid out in those army-issue pamphlets. According to a 1985 report by the United Nations Human Rights Commission, Soviet soldiers massacred civilians, bombed hospitals, and maimed children with booby-trapped toys. And more than fourteen thousand Soviet troops died in the

Afghan battlefields. Fifty-three-thousand returned home with broken bodies. At least some of these men returned with broken psyches, too.

Whatever trauma Sergey experienced came after his seven-month tour in Afghanistan, not during. "When I came home to civilian life in 1989, I couldn't believe what had happened to the country." Mikhail Gorbachev had instituted his program of reforms called *perestroika*. The word means "restructuring," but Sergey considers the program more of a demolition. Gorbachev's decentralization of the economy created a vacuum that was quickly filled by organized crime. Decorated soldiers returning from Afghanistan were advised to keep their service a secret lest they be recruited into the gangs that now ran everything. "The honour of having served your country was put aside," Sergey said. "Now you had to hide that honour."

Sergey quickly found work as a fisherman. This kept him away from the corruption that darkened Russia's big cities. "For me it was easy," he said. "At least I could hide at sea for nine months of the year. But a lot of guys, after a few years of civilian life, they were cracked." Some of Sergey's military comrades joined gangs. Others became policemen: essentially gangsters with badges and government paycheques, Sergey said. He earned decent wages as a fisherman, and didn't need to engage in anything illegal. Aside from smuggling the occasional crate of Russian vodka into Norway, Sergey obeyed the law. His virtue didn't impress his girl-friend, however. Sergey told me she refused his marriage proposal because she'd rather he became a proper criminal like everyone else than spend so much time away from home.

Under the weight of corruption, the Soviet-era factories closed and the economy tanked. "Think about it. I left home in 1987 when the USSR was a stable, strong country with a solid ideology. Suddenly, in only two years, the country was fall-ing apart."

"And we cheered for this in Canada," I said.

"I know. Lots of stereotypes about the USSR made people in the West cheer for that. But they did not know the details. Canadians are not stupid. They just lack information." Gorbachev's economic changes failed to bring prosperity. Then, according to Sergey, Gorbachev left. "After finishing his term, he lives in a villa in Germany. He has property there. He never came back."

This is not true. Between 2006 and 2016, Gorbachev owned a lakeside villa in Bavaria, and purchased an apartment in Berlin for his daughter, but he always lived in Russia. Fake history notwithstanding, his belief that Gorbachev abandoned the country he helped demolish aligns with Sergey's nostalgia for his Soviet childhood. While we in the West celebrated "Gorby" by hanging a Nobel Peace prize around his neck, handing him honorary degrees, inviting him to socialize with heads of state, and hiring him for Pizza Hut commercials like some sort of Cold War mascot, Sergey mourned. "If we are talking about stress or trauma, this is what traumatized me," Sergey said. "The country became a potato field."

Until I spoke to Sergey, I'd never felt even the smallest amount of empathy for those who "lost" the Cold War; the Soviet Union's fall had always represented a black-and-white victory of good over evil. Those who'd long suffered under socialist tyranny were freed. They could now be like us, and should feel grateful for it. And then there were people like Sergey who felt shattered. Scholars can debate which economic system better serves a given populace, but no one can argue with Sergey's broken heart.

In the winter of 1996, Sergey was working on a Ukrainian fishing boat off Canada's East Coast when the company that owned the boat abruptly folded. In debt to creditors and suppliers and with no cargo to pay its debts, the company simply abandoned the ship and stranded Sergey and the rest of the Russian crew in Newfoundland. The Russian and Ukrainian embassies in Ottawa refused to pay for their transit back to Russia. "I was stuck," Sergey said.

Just as my generation harboured negative stereotypes of Russia—fuelled by Hollywood, the nuclear arms race, and the demonization of communists by our politicians—Sergey had been taught to hate the West. "I grew up with the impression that nobody cares about anyone else in this part of the world," Sergey said. "Not like in the USSR. I thought you had to have a job in order to be looked after by doctors here. Not like in the USSR. My impression about Canada was not positive. When I came here, I was worried." All he wanted to do was earn enough money to return to Russia.

Sergey applied for refugee status, even though he knew his claim would be rejected. "I was just buying time," he said. He sold hot dogs out of a cart near the George Street pubs in St. John's. He rented a basement apartment with the $50 he made every week, and lived on instant noodles like a typical Canadian undergrad. Sergey managed to save $300 to buy a car. "It was junk," he said. "But that junk made me able to deliver pizza." He worked for a restaurant run by a pair of kind Lebanese Christians who eventually offered Sergey an interest-free loan to buy a better car. Just like Jass and Amrit in Calgary, Sergey would eventually leave the pizza job and start driving a taxi.

Around this time, Sergey got into what he called "a simple fight" with two Russian brothers, one of whom was a fellow crew member from Sergey's stranded fishing boat. Sergey was reluctant to share many details about the incident, only that police charged him with two counts of assault and two counts of assault with a weapon. Sergey had a knife on him at the time. Police would later add a conspiracy charge after the brothers claimed Sergey had been contracted by a Ukrainian gangster. "They told a story that some sort of mafia hired me to go after them. Like I am a hitman," Sergey said. "A hitman who eats hot dogs and those freaking noodles!"

Sergey understood the brothers' scheme. Both men faced deportation from Canada. They reasoned Canadian officials would not send them home if they suspected the Ukrainian mob wanted them dead. So the brothers instigated the fight with Sergey and concocted the hit-job story to persuade an appellate court to let them stay in Canada. The brothers also knew that even if they failed to convince the court of their likely murder in Ukraine, the case would delay their eventual deportation for at least a couple of years. Like Sergey with his refugee claim, the brothers were buying time.

Sergey's legal aid lawyer told him he faced eight to ten years in prison for the assaults. "The lawyer didn't even look at me," Sergey said. "He just picked at his yellow fingernails." Sergey scrounged up $160 for a consultation with a private lawyer who agreed to take the case, but was hardly more optimistic. After the preliminary hearing, the lawyer turned to Sergey and told him he'd probably be sentenced to seven years. When Sergey finally stood trial almost two years later, the conspiracy and weapons charges were dropped, but he was found guilty of the assaults.

Oddly, the judge allowed Sergey to return home before sentencing. "My lawyer couldn't believe it," Sergey said. "I had no family in St. John's. I was found guilty of assault. And still the judge let me go. It was a good sign my sentence would be light." Sure enough, Sergey received no prison time. Instead, the judge sentenced him to twelve months' house arrest and 120 hours of community service. His probation officer landed Sergey a gig at a local Baptist church, where he worked with children, an unlikely job for a man convicted of assault. Clearly, Sergey was not considered dangerous.

By the time Sergey was convicted, the Canadian government had partially lifted the moratorium on cod fishing in Newfoundland imposed in 1992. Workers like Sergey, who were already familiar with fishing equipment, were suddenly in demand. A fishing company owner who'd heard about Sergey from television news reports about his trial offered him a full-time job as a netmaker. He gave Sergey a generous wage, a uniform, a truck and a huge 1990s-era cellular phone. "It was a luxury at the time," Sergey said. Eventually, the company hired Sergey as a proper fisherman and he now spends weeks at a time on the boats, just as he did after his tour in Afghanistan. He continues to drive cab when he's on land.

Sergey met and married Olga in 2002. "If you ask her where she is from, she will say Russia. If you ask her what part, she will say Ukraine. In her mind, Ukraine is still part of Russia. Furthermore, she is from Crimea." In 2014, Olga's entire Crimean family voted to leave Ukraine and join the Russian Federation in a referendum most of the international community considered illegal. Olga and Sergey had two sons together, but have since separated. Olga and the boys live in Ontario now, but Sergey sees them often and remains close to Olga. "We are still connected," he said. "I don't even know why we separated. We couldn't live in the same house, I guess." Olga didn't enjoy life in Newfoundland anyway. "Too cold. Too cloudy," Sergey said.

After nearly twenty-five years in Canada, Sergey is still homesick for Russia. "I like this country," Sergey said. "My children were born here. This country let me meet my wife. But somewhere in the back of my head I am still Russian. A lot of people, when they immigrate, say that they hate the place where they are from. I don't have that hate." One of Sergey's friends asked him who he would support if a war broke out between Canada and Russia. "I had to really think," he said. Sergey decided that if Russia invaded Canada, he would support the Canadians. "I would protect my children from Russia," he said. "But if Canada invaded Russia, I would fly back home to fight."

"But when Canada plays Russia in hockey, who do you cheer for?" I asked.

"Sweden," he said.

Sergey told me he'll move back to Russia eventually. And to Siberia, no less. "I just feel like it is a good place for retirement." His brother lives in southern Siberia. He hikes and hunts in the woods there, and even though he's more than twenty years older than Sergey, they look the same age. Sergey credits his brother's enduring youth to his Siberian life.

There is also a woman there, another Olga, whom Sergey met online. This Olga worked as an army nurse during the Soviet-Afghan War, and Sergey claims he saw her working in a military hospital when he was a soldier, but that she didn't remember him. "There were hundreds of men," he shrugged, "and only her." After the war, Olga worked in Yemen, then in Eastern Ukraine, before moving to southern Siberia. She hopes to open a clinic there, and an orphanage for children with disabilities. Sergey wants to join her. I asked Sergey if he and Olga were romantically involved. He reddened. "We are grown over that age," he said. "We are not at the Balzac age. At the same time, we have a lot of things in common. Things in the past."

In the meantime, Sergey will continue splitting his time between fishing boat and taxi cab. Driving taxi up and down St. John's steep hills grants Sergey access to the "pulse of the city," he said. Sergey recalls driving a pair of out-of-town business-men to their hotel from the airport. "A couple of big shots here for a conference." He eavesdropped as the men started talking about the inner workings of their respective companies. After a while, Sergey figured out which companies the men worked for, and that the information he was privy to as their cabbie could be valuable to someone investing in stocks. "It was pretty much insider information," Sergey said. The men had no idea Sergey was listening. "In cases like that, people look at the cab driver as part of the cab," Sergey said. "If I ever became a stockbroker, I would definitely hire a few cabbies. I'll buy their taxi licences for them, and put them in certain places where businessmen hang out. Certain restaurants at lunch time."

Driving taxi also gives Sergey the opportunity to challenge stereotypes his passengers might have about Russia. "I feel like I can do it by making conversation." Clients ask him about vodka and about the cold weather in Siberia. Canadians seem obsessed with places where the weather might be even colder. "They don't know that in southern Russia we grow watermelons," Sergey said. Lately, though, everyone wants to talk about politics, especially about Vladimir Putin. While Sergey said he is "not a big fan" of the Russian president, he is quick to defend him. "There are no angels in politics," he said. For all his thuggery, Putin ended the war with the Chechens, kicked the oligarchs out of the Russian parliament, and restored salaries to police. "One of the guys I served with in Afghanistan was on the SWAT team. He didn't get paid for six months. He just got food rations. Putin found a way to improve that." Russians spent ten years so worried about violent crime they wouldn't leave their homes. They don't feel that way anymore. According to Sergey, what Russians may have lost in democracy, they've gained in a strong leader who can protect them. "In general, people are like sheep," Sergey said. "Many of them need to be guided."

I was just as surprised to hear Putin described as anything but a cruel strongman as I was to hear Sergey speak about life in the Soviet Union with wistful fondness. Some of the other cabbies I met expressed a yearning for the homes they'd left before coming to Canada. Michael Kamara missed the food in Sierra Leone and the tight relationships he shared with his neighbours. Andy Reti missed the success he found in the swimming pools of his Hungarian youth. Kareem Yalahow spoke lovingly of his childhood neighbourhood in Mogadishu. And almost everyone preferred the weather in the places they came from.

None, though, spoke of their homelands with Sergey's nostalgic affection. The Russia Sergey remembers was a place where everyone took care of each other. Where soldiers were virtuous and wars just. Where strongmen acted in the citizens' best interest. It's a Russia that hardly resembles the troubled place I grew up reading about. I wondered if Sergey's idealized Russia ever really existed.

Then again, isn't my inborn conception of Canada almost as rosy? I'm not so naive as to think of Canada as some maple-dipped Valhalla, and I know the challenges immigrants face. Financial pressures. Language barriers. Racism. I learned these things as much from the cabbies as from anyone. But I'd always imagined life was better here than just about anywhere else. I was raised to love this place, and I swallowed our national storyline: that the only thing luckier than ending up in Canada is being born here in the first place.

Part of me wondered if Sergey's praise of Mother Russia was a thinly veiled critique of Canada. Sergey never wanted to come here. This land never represented sanctuary and opportunity for him as it did for many of the other drivers I'd meet. Nor would Sergey's Canada ever resemble the flawed but beloved country I believed in. I'd be arrogant to dismiss his nostalgia for his birthplace as misguided or illogical while clinging to my own. When Sergey claims he'd rather be in Siberia, he's only saying he'd rather be home.

Nine

THE WOMEN OF IKWE

IN MAY 2015, A HALIFAX POLICE OFFICER FOUND AN INTOXI-cated young woman passed out in the back of a taxi wearing only a tank top. Her driver, Bassam Al-Rawi, was between her legs, her underwear in his hands. Police charged him with sexual assault, but in 2017 Judge Gregory Lenehan acquitted him after finding no evidence of a lack of consent. "Clearly, a drunk can consent," Lenehan said. His remarks outraged many, but a retrial judge upheld the acquittal.

Al-Rawi moved to Germany with his family after the trial, but had to return to Canada in 2020 to face a second charge. He was accused of raping another intoxicated passenger, this time in his Halifax apartment in 2012, while she pretended to be unconscious. The victim reported the assault right away, but police didn't charge Al-Rawi. She came forward again in 2017 after Al-Rawi's first acquittal. Nova Scotia's supreme court found

Al-Rawi guilty of sexual assault and sentenced him to two years in prison. He filed an appeal in January 2021.

Al-Rawi's are two of the most high-profile cases of sexual assault by taxi drivers. Nearly every other month or so seems to bring reports of a cabbie fondling or propositioning a female client. Or worse. In 2017, a fourteen-year-old girl in Happy Valley-Goose Bay accused a driver of sexually assaulting her, then threatening to kill her if she told anyone. In June 2018, an Alberta court convicted a Calgary driver for sexually assaulting a drunk passenger during the Calgary Stampede. A Toronto cabbie was arrested for sexual assault in November 2018, and a Kitchener driver received a ninety-day prison sentence in August 2018 for sliding his hand under a passenger's dress. The West Vancouver Police arrested a sixty-year-old cabbie in January 2019, after a woman complained he'd grabbed her genitals and forced her hand onto his crotch. Not all the victims were women. A Yellowknife cabbie was charged with the sexual assault of a sixteen-year-old boy in April 2019. And these are just the incidents that made the news.

The cases spooked many of the drivers I'd meet. No one told me they disbelieved the accusers or rejected their claims, but they felt vulnerable to similar allegations. Michael Kamara said he was grateful for the camera in his taxi because the footage could defend him against false charges of misconduct. I wondered if his anxiety was rational, so I reached out to John Duffy, publisher of *Taxi News.* "False accusations do happen," Duffy said. "But I have no way of knowing how many false allegations are filed, investigated by police and dismissed." Taxi drivers don't like to talk about such incidents, especially to people like me. "At the very least, they are embarrassing," Duffy said. At worst, such allegations might spur women to question the safety of taxis in general, which would be bad for business. "There is the attitude of the public thinking 'Where there is smoke there is fire,'" Duffy said.

Nowhere is the smoke so thick as in Winnipeg, where many women, especially Indigenous women, fear taking taxis. CTV News reported that between January 2015 and the end of February 2016, fifteen women, Indigenous and non-Indigenous both, reported being sexually assaulted at the hands of Winnipeg taxi drivers. In the fall of 2016, a cabbie pled guilty to sexually assaulting a seventeen-year-old girl in the back of his cab. Then, that November, a nineteen-year-old Indigenous woman woke up in bed with a man she didn't know. She, too, had been sexually assaulted, and the last thing she remembered was her taxi driver bringing her to a parking lot, putting her into a car that wasn't a cab along with two other men, and someone offering her something to smoke. And these are just the assaults. Many of the city's Indigenous women have a story about harassment at the hands of drivers, most commonly about cabbies proposing "another way to pay." In February 2016, a First Nations woman filed a complaint with police claiming her driver had offered to refund her ten-dollar fare if she had sex with him. Most such "offers" go unreported.

In 2016, this scourge of abuse prompted the Southern Chiefs' Organization, which represents thirty-four southern First Nation communities in Manitoba, to create the position of taxicab complaint community advocate. The advocate would act as a liaison between taxi companies and Winnipeg's First Nations communities with the aim of making Indigenous women and children feel safe using the city's taxi services. The Southern Chiefs also produce taxicab safety brochures in six languages, including Cree and Ojibwe, which inform passengers of their rights and how to make complaints. The brochures provide safety tips, too. Passengers should always sit in the back seat, for example, and make sure the door has a handle on the inside. Passengers should also note the cab company's name and the cab number—though when CBC host Rosanna Deerchild photographed her taxi's cab number, the driver tried to kick her out in the middle of the street. The advocate's efforts didn't stop the cruelty. Indigenous women continued to complain about harassment, rudeness, racial discrimination, and unwanted sexual advances at the hands of Winnipeg's cabbies. Some of the incidents are truly horrifying. A seventy-seven-year-old Indigenous woman named Illa Garson, for example, broke her collarbone and dislocated her shoulder in the winter of 2017 when she jumped from a taxi out of fear her driver was abducting her. Garson rolled across the road and into a snow-bank. "I was screaming and nobody heard me," she told the CBC. "I phoned my daughter and told her I was lying on the ground."

In the summer of 2018, dancer and choreographer Angela Gladue noticed she was being followed by a strange man along Winnipeg's Portage Avenue. When she jumped in a cab and asked the cabbie to start driving, he responded with, "You got any money?" Gladue told him she did, but that he needed to start driving because she was being chased and was scared. "Give me ten dollars," he said. The cabbie wouldn't budge, even when the man chasing Gladue caught up and started pacing next to the cab.

Gladue had grown up hearing her mother's stories about the violence suffered by First Nations women, and the hundreds who have disappeared or have been killed since the 1960s. She donates her time as both a choreographer and beadwork artist to raise funds to help causes related to missing and murdered Indigenous women and girls, an epidemic known by the acronym MMIWG and which a national inquiry declared a genocide in 2019. Gladue was acutely aware of the sort of danger she might have been in and tried to explain this to her cabbie, but she could not compel him to drive.

With her pursuer still outside the cab, Gladue exited the car and ran to another taxi. She explained to the driver what had happened. He told her to walk. Gladue started crying. "Please give me a ride," she begged. "My life is in danger." The driver relented and drove her the four blocks to her hotel. Gladue gave him ten dollars. "I just felt disposable," she said. When she tried to report the incident to the taxi company, the supervisor's email inbox was full.

During my year among the cabbies, I would come to see most taxi drivers as inherently good. Some were crude or boastful. Others had life stories edged with violence or other such darkness. But the more time I spent with the drivers, the more I liked and admired them. In Winnipeg, though, cabbies were the villains in almost all the stories I heard. And they didn't want to talk to me. I reached out to Winnipeg's taxi companies a half dozen times hoping to arrange conversations with drivers. I wanted to give them a chance to address their reputation. None responded.

Nearly every troubling news item I read about Winnipeg's taxi industry also mentioned Ikwe Safe Rides, a non-profit ride-share service that matches volunteer female drivers with women needing a ride. Ikwe, which means "woman" in Ojibwe, is intended to give Winnipeg's women, especially Indigenous women, an alternative to frightening taxi rides. If cabbies were the villains in Winnipeg, the women of Ikwe were the heroes. And if the cabbies didn't want to talk to me, I would talk to the women of Ikwe.

Anishinaabe artist and community activist Jackie Traverse founded Ikwe Safe Rides in 2016. The idea was simple: women who needed a ride could sign up as Ikwe members and post requests on a dedicated Facebook page. Women with a vehicle and some spare time then offered to pick them up. Within the first few days of the launch, about a dozen women volunteered to be Ikwe drivers. After four months, more than ten thousand women had registered as members. Traverse eventually left Ikwe, but in the hands of a crew of volunteer administrators, Ikwe continued to grow, and now boasts more than eighteen thousand members. Nearly a third of Winnipeg's Indigenous, Inuit, and Métis women have signed on, making up 80 percent of Ikwe's total membership. By the summer of 2019, Ikwe's fifty-four volunteer drivers had given more than seventy-five thousand rides.

I met with Christine Brouzes, Ikwe's co-director, at her home in Winnipeg. While Douglas, Christine's border-collie-husky cross, laid his head between my legs and begged for my attention, Christine described her history with Ikwe. Christine became involved with the organization soon after the MMIWG National Roundtable came to Winnipeg in 2016. Christine, herself a Métis woman, moderated a group discussion between twelve people whose families had lost members to the crisis. She listened as these traumatized people shared their stories with the rest of the group. The experience shook her. "I am a social worker. I always see the good side of everything. There is a silver lining to every cloud," she said, but she couldn't see the value in compelling people to recount such nightmares. "If anything, I felt I was harming those people by making them repeat their stories again."

After the two-day session ended, Christine wondered how she could contribute to the lives of Indigenous women outside of the MMIWG roundtable structure. "I always feel that to make a change in the world, you change one small thing. You don't know how it will grow. Like a pebble in the water sort of thing." Then Christine met a woman who drove for Ikwe Safe Rides. "She told me 'We are trying to help women not become murdered and missing.'" Christine signed on as one of Ikwe's first drivers, but soon shifted to an administrative role where she helps recruit new volunteers, manages current drivers, and acts as Ikwe's unofficial spokesperson.

Christine also vets new members. In order to join the Ikwe community and book rides, potential members must first issue a formal request to Ikwe's Facebook group. Members must be at least eighteen years old and identify as female. (Later, and for journalistic purposes only, Christine would allow me to join the page. As far as I know, I still have the honour of being Ikwe's only male member.) Potential members must also have a profile photo that's a reasonable likeness. No photos of celebrities, pets, or babies, however adorable.

"Then we look at their Facebook profile and snoop a little bit," Christine said. "We snoop a lot, actually." Christine and other site administrators scroll through old photos and posts of would-be members in search of anything that indicates criminal activity. Drug dealers and shoplifters often use their Facebook pages as a marketplace for goods and services, and Christine must stay abreast of the everchanging lingo of petty crime. "Jib" is crystal meth. "Perks" means Percocet. "Killer Fish" is crack cocaine. HMU stands for "Hit Me Up" and IBM is "Inbox me." "Booster available" means the poster is a professional shoplifter. "You can message a booster 'I would like some steaks and a pair of size 8 Nike shoes' and they will go steal it for you," Christine said. Suspected criminals are not allowed into the Ikwe group. Christine doesn't want her drivers ending up as unwitting couriers for thieves and drug dealers. Those who evade Ikwe's benevolent cyber-stalking are usually found out soon enough. "The drivers are a chatty, social bunch," Christine said.

If an approved member needs a ride, she'll post a request on the Ikwe Facebook page with information about her current location, destination, the time she needs picking up, and number of other passengers. Ikwe allows men to accompany female members. Women ride with their sons, husbands, and boyfriends all the time—Ikwe is a popular service for Winnipeg date nights—but men can never outnumber women in an Ikwe vehicle.

Members also indicate how much they're willing to pay for the ride. Ikwe operates as a registered charity rather than a taxi company, and cannot legally charge fares. Instead, Ikwe encourages members to make a donation to the driver. Their Facebook page recommends donations comparable to city taxi fares, or a little less. One of the first things Christine explains to potential drivers during their training session is that driving for Ikwe isn't a part-time job. Ikwe is not Uber. Volunteer drivers can make decent money if they put in long hours, but those earnings rarely cover the cost of gas and maintenance over time. "If you are looking to make extra money to pay the rent, then you are in the wrong place," Christine said. "That is not the kind of driver we want to add anyway. We want to add people who are kind and helpful and want to support their community."

Occasionally, a member cannot afford to pay at all. Ikwe's drivers usually give these women rides nevertheless. And drivers never expect donations for emergency rides, such as trips to the hospital for non-life-threatening medical problems. Christine recalls picking up a member who was in labour. "She comes out of the house, moaning and groaning," Christine said. "She's all by herself. Has no money. Came out with no bag or nothing." Christine brought her to the hospital, walked her into the emergency room, and helped her check in. "It's the kindness we want to give," she said. "So we don't just drop the person off at the hospital and wish her well." Christine believes this is one of the advantages of using a Facebook page instead of a ride-sharing app or taxi dispatch. "You can post 'Somebody help! My water just broke! Come get me!'" To date, Ikwe's drivers have delivered twenty-one pregnant women to their deliveries. "We have twenty-one Ikwe babies," Christine said.

Because Winnipeg is the closest large city to Nunavut, Inuit from remote northern communities often travel there for medical services. Many of these patients and their families sign up as Ikwe members. "When they come here, often they are in culture shock," Christine said. "The Inuit don't identify as being part of the Indigenous culture here in the south. They are often quite shy. They hear about what happens in taxis and they are afraid." These northern travellers, though, feel comfortable with Ikwe's drivers. Instead of cowering in their hotel rooms between doctor appointments, they request rides to the movies or to go shopping—things they can't do in the tiny communities from which they've come.

Christine has no way of knowing whether the women of Ikwe have saved any lives since the service began. "What if a woman posts on the site: 'Please help me. My grandpa is in the hospital and is very sick. I just want to visit him'? If we didn't give her a ride, she would walk there. And maybe she would get scooped off the sidewalk. Who knows?" In January 2020, Ikwe volunteer driver Bessie Johnson spotted a woman about to jump off Winnipeg's Louise Bridge into the icy Red River. Johnson stopped her car, bounded across the bridge traffic and helped coax the woman to safety. "If it would have been a second later, she would have been gone," Johnson later told a reporter.

Such heroics aren't Ikwe's primary goal. "I quickly realized that Ikwe was about spreading kindness. Being good to each other. And being helpful," Christine said. "Our members just want to get to where they are going. I can do that."

Chery Lee drives a white Pontiac Trans Sport van with pink trim, pink hubcaps, and a fuzzy pink dashboard cover. A "Barbie" decal adorns the sliding rear door, and the bumper sticker on the hatch warns IF YOU CAN READ THIS I'M ALREADY FILLING OUT THE INSURANCE CLAIM. Two other large decals on the side doors, which depict a black feather on a rainbow background, read "Ikwe Safe Rides: Women Helping Women." Chery started driving for Ikwe in 2016, just a few months after the service began, and now acts as both a nighttime driver and administrator.

I met Chery in the parking lot of a twenty-four-hour Tim Hortons in Winnipeg's North End—Ikwe's informal nighttime headquarters. It was after eleven on a warm July evening. Chery had parked her "Barbie Van" near the far end of the lot and was sipping a monstrous six-shot iced cappuccino. I asked about her van's décor. "Some of the other drivers call me Barbie because my hair is dyed blonde, and sometimes I do things that are not smart," she admitted. Once, she poured transmission fluid into her gas tank because the bottle said it improved fuel economy.

Chery was expecting a busy night. It was "Child Tax Day," when the provincial government mails out monthly child-benefit cheques. Members would want rides to bingo halls or to "socials"—the pre-wedding fundraiser parties unique to Manitoba. Other members would want to visit the twenty-four-hour Wal-Mart to buy groceries. I asked Chery why anyone would go on a grocery run in the middle of the night. She explained that some of their members who struggle with gambling and addiction issues, recognizing their problems, rush to spend their benefit cheques on necessities before their less-productive impulses tempt them elsewhere.

A red Dodge Ram pickup rumbled into the lot and parked beside the Barbie van. Debbs, another Ikwe driver, stepped out and said hello to Chery. Debbs, known affectionately by her Ikwe colleagues as "The One Who Yells," told me about some of the young women she frequently drives around. "A lot of these girls are like my kids," Debbs said. "Quite a few of them call me 'Mom,' maybe because I am always giving them heck. I get mad when I see they have hickies." As we talked, a striped cat jumped through the driver's side window and onto Chery's pink-fuzzed dash. The cat hangs around the Tim Hortons parking lot, just like the Ikwe drivers do. They consider him their unofficial mascot and call him "Timmy" since they don't know his real name.

Timmy and the Ikwe drivers are just one element of this particular Tim Hortons' odd nocturnal environment. Bob the streetcleaner usually shows up around three in the morning. "He knows all the Ikwe ladies," Chery said. So does another man who comes to the lot late at night to sell T-shirts, ballcaps, and other random items. Chery figures he's trying to support a drug habit. "I bought a plastic Iron Man mask from him once. I gave it to Debbs."

Off-duty drivers from Winnipeg's traditional taxi companies also socialize in the parking lot, but they only started coming here once they learned this was Ikwe's favoured haunt. Winnipeg's regular cabbies aren't fans of Ikwe. "I can tell when they are talking about us," Chery said. "Even though I don't understand their language, I can hear the word 'Ikwe.'"

Racial undertones complicate the Ikwe-cabbie battle. No other city I visited had a taxi industry as ethnically homogenous. In 2017, MLA Mohinder Saran told the Manitoba legislature that the province's taxi industry was 90 percent "East Indian," and, according to Christine, Winnipeg's taxi drivers are overwhelmingly Punjabi. Because of these demographics, many felt the cabbies' behaviour towards Indigenous women reflected badly on Punjabi men in general. To suggest that all Punjabis inherently hate First Nations people is, of course, racist itself. None of the women I spoke to made such a claim, but a few wondered whether or not the cabbies' behaviour had something to do with their culture.

The idea made me uncomfortable. As much as I admired the Ikwe drivers I met, and as much as I believed the stories they told, I simply couldn't swallow the suggestion that Punjabi men are innately racist or misogynist. I couldn't imagine Amrit Hothi in Calgary engaging in such behaviour. At the same time, if Winnipeg's drivers have a reputation of contempt for Indigenous women, and if nearly all these drivers are Punjabi, I could understand the source of the stereotype. The fact that no one from Winnipeg's taxi industry agreed to speak about the accusations hardly helped. I couldn't understand why drivers would reject an opportunity to defend themselves. I wanted to hear their side of the story.

Christine said cabbies occasionally accuse the Ikwe drivers of giving them a bad name, or making up the stories of abuse. Taxi drivers resent claims that they treat Indigenous women unfairly, in spite of all the anecdotes and news reports. They complain, too, that Ikwe steals their business while not having to pay for regular taxi licenses and other fees. Fair enough. If I sympathized with the Taxi Sheriff and his Montreal cabbie-colleagues in their struggles against Uber, which I do, then I could understand the frustrations of Winnipeg drivers who'd lost clients to Ikwe. But Ikwe isn't a giant tech company. They're a community of women responding to a problem. They're women helping women, as Chery's decal states.

And the cabbies' response to Ikwe hardly engenders sympathy. In an immature act of vehicular passive aggression, taxi drivers often triple-park their cabs at the end of the Tim's parking lot where Ikwe ladies like to hang out. Other times they snarl insults at the Ikwe drivers, flip their middle fingers, or pound their fists on the sides of Ikwe cars. Some Ikwe volunteers opt not to attach the Ikwe decal to their vehicles to avoid such confrontations. One night, a crew of cabbies teamed up to box-in Chery's car in a Wal-Mart parking lot. "As soon as one cab driver would leave, another one would pull up and do the same thing," Chery said. I wondered if these taxi drivers realized that their acts of petty intimidation against Ikwe didn't help their cause, that they only solidify their reputation as bullies. They didn't seem to understand that if women in Winnipeg felt safe in taxi cabs, Ikwe wouldn't have to exist at all.

Allegiances in this particular war occasionally shift. Chery pointed to one driver leaning against his Pontiac sedan. A few weeks earlier, he and his wife had been arguing in the Tim's parking lot. The wife stormed off, furious, and, in full view of her seething husband and his fellow cabbies, marched up to Chery and asked for a ride home. "It was definitely a spite-ride 'cause all of them saw her get into my vehicle," Chery said.

In the Barbie van, the woman told Chery her husband and the other cab drivers were trying to run them out of the parking lot. "She was mad at him, so of course she was going to tell me everything," Chery said. The woman told Chery she supported what the Ikwe drivers were doing, even though they were stealing business from her husband and taking food away from her kids. "But she wasn't saying it in a rude way," Chery said. "She was super nice." When Chery dropped the woman at her house, she handed Chery a donation and told her "This is from my husband."

Chery first heard about Ikwe after another such mutiny. In 2016, a taxi driver friend told Chery he planned on quitting the business because he'd had enough of his fellow cabbies' behaviour. "He hated his co-workers," Chery said. "He was getting a bad rep because of everyone else." Chery's friend told her he hoped Ikwe would put the traditional taxi companies out of business. Chery signed up that same day.

As a night driver and administrator, Chery usually starts her shift at four or five in the afternoon and works until six in the morning. "Literally, I wake up. I start driving. I go home. Go to sleep. Wake up. Start driving." She only gives about a half dozen rides herself each night. Most of her hours are spent quarterbacking the Ikwe Facebook page and matching drivers with ride requests. Ikwe briefly considered developing their own app instead of relying on Facebook, but doing so would be costly and would require a skilled technician to maintain. Facebook offers everything Ikwe needs for free and its business tools allow

Ikwe to monitor user statistics and count every ride. Facebook Messenger also has a GPS function that volunteers can switch on when they drive to sketchier neighbourhoods so other volunteers know exactly where they are at all times. Ikwe also operates a private Facebook page where potential members can sign up, and another for current drivers, who use it to schedule their volunteer shifts, and to share information about traffic problems, road closures and, occasionally, members who misbehave.

Chery monitors all of this on her phone as she holds court at the Tim Hortons while simultaneously chatting with Ikwe's other night drivers. "I take care of everyone," she said. "I make sure everyone is okay." Drivers quickly learn to recognize ride requests that seem suspicious. A booking from a member who claims not to know her destination raises red flags. So do requests for multiple stops at residential addresses, a sign that the member is dealing drugs. Ikwe drivers employ a kind of gallows humour about these dangers. Debbs told me Ikwe always sends Chery to pick up rides in rough neighbourhoods because they figure no one would want to carjack the Barbie van. And they use code words on the Facebook page. If a driver posts the word "pineapple," they're really saying "I'm worried. Someone follow me." "Fruit salad" means "Call the police."

Even experienced drivers like Chery and Debbs have gotten into trouble. Three men dragged Debbs out of her Dodge one night, beat her up, and drove off with her truck. Chery once picked up two women who pulled a knife and ordered her to bring them to a house for what Chery figured was a drug deal. One woman went inside the house while the other stayed with Chery in her van. Chery coolly suggested they both step out and have a cigarette. As soon as the woman left the van, Chery locked the doors and sped off. A bag of pills was left in Chery's back seat. Chery gave another ride before driving to the police station to make a report and hand over the drugs. The police and Ikwe management both scolded Chery for not going directly to the station, but the ride Chery picked up turned out to be a psychologist and Chery received free trauma counselling for her frightening ordeal.

Chery's origin story is as colorful as her van. She grew up in the Winnipeg suburb of Transcona. "Nobody goes there unless they were born there," Chery said. Her father, Robert F Lee, ran a private investigation business before he retired to build and sell yurts. Now he's the prolific, self-published writer of more than a dozen books. His oeuvre, which ranges widely, includes a series of guidebooks on "minimal living," a collection of fairy tales, a sci-fi novel, a book of short stories, a collection of strange anecdotes on bachelorhood, and a memoir of his PI days called *Wild People I Have Known*. According to Lee's webpage, the latter recounts his "experiences with dozens of murderers, rapists and other violent criminals during his more than twenty years in law enforcement and working as a private investigator." In his author photo, Lee bears a glorious white handlebar mustache worthy of Hulk Hogan.

Chery's mother worked as a collection agent. When I suggested that a PI and a collection agent must have made a good match, Chery disagreed. "They divorced," she said. "My family's a little bit weird." Chery ran away when she was sixteen to be with her twenty-eight-year-old boyfriend. "That's normal in Winnipeg," Chery said. "I wasn't a bad kid. I just wanted to be with my older boyfriend. I didn't talk to my parents again until I got pregnant." Chery and her boyfriend had a daughter they named Paradise, but the boyfriend didn't stick around. Chery eventually married his boss. "Yeah, a little bit of a soap opera." They've since separated.

Many Ikwe drivers find a feeling of kinship with their fellow volunteers that's lacking in their regular lives. Some don't have

many friends, or run with what Chery calls the "wrong crowd."
"If you're in the North End, a lot of times you are going to be
hanging out with people that are doing drugs," Chery said. "And
you can be the nicest person ever. Hang out here, and then two
years later you're addicted to something. It's just because of who
you surround yourself with. And people kinda get into your head.
And people here are pushy." Ikwe offers its drivers membership
in a community of women devoted to one another's well-being.
"They come to us, and they meet a whole new crew of people,"
Chery said. "They learn how good women can be to each other."

This leads to a sort of benign addiction. Chery and Christine
both told me about volunteers who end up as "Ikwe addicts."
Helping out their fellow women in Winnipeg gives them a rush.
The camaraderie and altruism is intoxicating. Nearly all the Ikwe
drivers I spoke to gained a unique personal benefit from driving.
Driving helped Chery overcome her shyness, for example. She
recalled a breakfast meeting a few years ago with the other Ikwe
drivers. "All they did was say my name and I bawled my eyes out.
I'm that shy," Chery said. She admitted, too, that she was terrified
to talk to me, even though Christine assured her I was "a super-
nice guy." "If you met me two years ago, I wouldn't sit here and
talk to you at all."

Chery started to overcome her shyness by talking to the
women she drove around. "I actually had to force myself at first,"
she said. It took six months before her conversations with passengers felt natural. "I usually start by saying 'How was your day?'
Usually you can get a feel of whether they want to talk or not.
About half my rides are silent rides because I don't know what
to say next." Fortunately, many late-night ride requests came
from regulars, and Chery felt more comfortable with them. One
member called for a ride home from her boyfriend's house almost
every night. Another member, the mother of small children who
couldn't leave them alone at night, requested coffee-and-doughnut

deliveries instead of rides. Still another wanted nightly trips to 7-Eleven for Slurpees.

One of Chery's most memorable regulars was Turtle, a young woman from Nunavut. Turtle was pregnant with twins, and spent the final month of her pregnancy in Winnipeg waiting for her babies to be born. When Turtle went into labour, terrified and alone, she messaged Chery for a ride to the hospital. Chery picked Turtle up from where she was staying and drove her to the emergency room. "There is nothing like picking up a woman who is in labour that cannot afford the $500 for an ambulance," Chery said. "And it's not like it's dangerous to pick somebody up who's in labour. The worst that can happen is you end up with a wet seat."

Later that same day, though not much later, Turtle messaged Chery for another ride. "Just me. No baby," she wrote. Turns out Turtle's labour was false, and now she needed a ride home from the hospital. Over the course of a month, Turtle called Chery six times for emergency rides to the hospital. Each time was a false alarm. "It became a running joke," Chery said. "She kinda apologized over and over again." Chery wasn't driving on the day Turtle finally gave birth. "I got her all six times that she was in false labour, and then somebody else got her when she was actually in labour."

"That hardly seems fair," I said. "She should've named one of those babies Chery."

"The world doesn't need another Chery," she said. I'm not sure I agree.

Ikwe held a volunteer-appreciation picnic in June 2018 for drivers and their families, who gathered in Vimy Ridge Park on what Christine called the "nicer part" of Portage Avenue, Winnipeg's main drag. The women brought food to share. They brought their kids and dogs. "Then we heard a ka-bang," Christine said. "And

I saw a body fly through the air." A Dodge minivan had collided with a motorcycle on Portage. The van's driver and a passenger fled on foot, leaving their battered vehicle and the injured rider on the street.

Christine marshalled the group into action. She stood up on a folding chair and assigned someone to call 911. She tasked someone else to stay in the park with the children while she fetched a medical kit from her car and rushed to the accident scene with the other Ikwe drivers. The motorcyclist, a forty-year-old father named Matthew Cave, lay on the road, unmoving. "I knew he was dead because he was grey," Christine said. A horrific wound on his torso wasn't bleeding, Christine said. "His heart wasn't pumping when he hit the ground. There wasn't even a drop of blood."

Christine handed out latex gloves from the first-aid kit. She and two other Ikwe drivers cut off the man's helmet and clothes and performed CPR until the paramedics arrived to bring him to the hospital. "We got his blood pumping," Christine said. "His head and shoulders were pink. If he was to live, he would've been a paraplegic, but he didn't live."

Once the paramedics took Cave away, the Ikwe drivers returned to the park. They were shaken. Some were crying. Christine felt she needed to do something. "Let's come together for a second here," she began. "We all just went through something. Let's have a prayer right now. Be silent if you like. Hold hands if you like." Christine bowed her head and "blathered on to God." She prayed for everyone to be calm, and to return home safely. She asked god to watch over the man's family and gave thanks for the paramedics. When she finished her prayer, a few of the women echoed her "amen." Others didn't. Then they all went home.

Many of the women were rattled by the experience, and Christine needed someone to talk to. Her own husband was "very not touchy-feely." So on the night of the accident, Christine visited the women who'd performed chest compressions on Cave. An Indigenous driver reached out to Christine the following day and asked if she could perform a tobacco ceremony for her. Christine agreed, even though the ceremony wasn't part of her own "generic Christian" tradition.

Police told the media what the Ikwe volunteers already knew: Cave had died. "A lot of cops hang out at the Tim's parking lot. We've made friends with them and we have ways of finding out information before anyone else does," Christine said. On the CBC, Ikwe volunteer Heather Traverse called upon the minivan driver to come forward and clear his conscience. Police arrested a suspect the following spring.

I would hear about the Vimy Ridge Park accident several times during my meeting with the Ikwe women. Even though the accident occurred outside the Ikwe context of drivers and riders, the tragedy was a significant chapter in Ikwe's story. Cave's accident and death had bonded the women even closer together. First they rallied to help him, then they huddled to help each other.

I visited Vimy Ridge Park a year after the accident to meet Ikwe driver Jackie Hartog. We sat on a picnic table while her youngest daughters, Jaelene and Jada, played with their friends in the splash pad.

Jackie comes from Lundar, Manitoba, about an hour's drive northwest of Winnipeg. She left home when she was seventeen and moved to the city. "I just wanted to get away from home," Jackie said. "I had a great upbringing, but I grew up in a small town. I wanted to get out and experience things." She enrolled in an accounting program after high school, but her post-secondary career lasted only three months. "I was drunk all the time," Jackie admitted. She'd fallen in love with a much older man soon after arriving in Winnipeg. "He plied me with alcohol, something I never had access to at home," Jackie said. "I grew up a really, really good girl." She quit school and moved in with her boyfriend. Then he started to hit her. The boyfriend also demanded she stop drinking because he thought it would cause her to cheat on him. He sabotaged her lifeguard job out of the same paranoid fear. "The pool would phone to tell me my shifts, and he wouldn't give me the message because he didn't want me to go to work in a place where other men would see me in a bathing suit."

Within a year of their relationship, Jackie was pregnant. "I got stuck. You know how the story goes." She gave birth to a daughter, Jennifer, and they both lived with Jackie's boyfriend and his abuse for six years. Jackie warned him, "I'm a big girl. If you hurt me, that's one thing. But if you hurt our daughter, I'm gone." He did, so they left. "I am not saying it is a good thing he hurt her, but it is a good thing he hurt her. So we could go."

But Jackie's liberation from her abusive boyfriend also meant she was free to resume drinking. She drank hard for nearly a decade until she got pregnant again from a different partner. "That's when I realized I had a drinking problem," she said. Jackie struggled to remain sober during her pregnancy. She could resist the bottle during the week, but would binge through her weekends. When she was in her sixth month, her obstetrician warned her that if she didn't stop drinking he would ensure Child Services was present at her bedside in the delivery room to take her baby away. Jackie finally quit. Thankfully, her daughter Jessica showed no signs of fetal alcohol syndrome.

Jackie stayed sober this time. She and Jessica's father had another daughter, Jaelene, and when they broke up Jackie had a fourth daughter, Jada. "My littlest one is 'Treaty,'" Jackie said. Jada's father is Indigenous, and Jada plays for the Anishinaabe Pride Basketball Club, where players learn basketball skills as well as values based on First Nations traditions. "It is very important for our children to grow up knowing their culture," Jackie said, even though she pokes good-natured fun at Jada. "I am always teasing her that I am going to make her start jigging, if that's her thing," she said, referring to a Métis folk dance. "And I tease her about her bannock butt. Jada doesn't really have a bannock butt, but I tease her about it."

When Jessica was born, Jackie went on social assistance. Her case worker encouraged her to enroll in a program that trains single mothers to be educational assistants. "I went to school for a year pretty much because they told me to," Jackie said. "Thank god. I am good at what I do. Really good." Jackie has worked one-on-one with inner-city kids with behavioural issues ever since. She prefers working with the boys, even though they tend to have "bigger behaviours." "A boy will punch me and the next day he will sit on my lap and call me 'Mom,'" Jackie said. "A girl will punch me, and then the next day she'll punch me again. And the next day call me a bitch. And the next day punch me. Finally she will forget why she is fighting with me and we can start."

Jackie also spent a year working part-time as a custodian at a shelter for women who'd been abused by their partners. Once her regular work was finished, Jackie would sit and chat with the women, or play with the children in the daycare. Her time in the shelter revealed to Jackie the widespread abuse of women and children in Winnipeg. She vowed that once she'd retired from her educational assistant job, she'd devote herself to helping women in her community.

But when Jackie heard about Ikwe, she decided not to wait until retirement. She signed on and quickly became one of Ikwe's busiest drivers. In her two years with the organization, Jackie gave over two thousand rides. Her fellow volunteers called her "Ridehog" instead of Hartog because of her quick-draw replies to ride requests. Jackie is another Ikwe addict. She drives nearly every day, and volunteers for both day and night shifts. "They tell me I should pick one or the other, but I don't want to," Jackie said. "I like driving whenever. And I have insomnia. I don't sleep well anyways. I might as well drive." She pointed to Jada splashing in the wading pool. "I can't wait to put this one to bed later so I can go out and do some more driving."

Just as Ikwe enabled Chery to confront her shyness, Ikwe gave Jackie something personal, too: rare social time with adults. "All day I work with kids," Jackie said. "When I come home, I got my own kids. So all the time I am talking, talking, talking to kids. Selfishly, I go and do an Ikwe ride just so I can talk to an adult. To have some grown-up conversation." Sometimes, Jackie will write on the Ikwe Facebook page that she's "in the mood for conversation." This always attracts ride requests. "Members want to talk." Often, Jackie's passengers want to talk about their terrible experiences in the city's taxi cabs. "They are in my car for a reason," Jackie said. "Every single one of them has a story about these cab drivers and things that have happened to them. I've cried because of some of the stories these women have told me."

I reached out to Jessica, Jackie's second daughter, who used to ride along on Jackie's Ikwe volunteer shifts and eavesdrop on these stories. When she turned eighteen and started driving for Ikwe herself, Jessica started hearing the stories firsthand. On one occasion, she drove a member to a retreat centre twenty minutes out of town. When they arrived, the lady asked Jessica how she made it there so quickly—the same trip had taken an hour the last time. Jackie jokingly asked Jessica if Chery had been her previous driver—Chery's Ikwe colleagues tease her relentlessly for driving slowly. Turns out it was a cab driver who stretched a twenty-minute drive into an hour, then charged $72 for a ride that Jessica accepted a $20 donation for.

One night in the fall of 2017, Jessica spotted a young First Nations woman she recognized from rides with her mom. "She waved me down hardcore," Jessica said. The woman, who'd just gotten out of a taxi, ran to Jessica's car, bawling. She'd paid what she thought was a flat rate up front, but midway through the ride the driver demanded more. The woman argued and asked to be let out. The driver said no, and locked the doors. "He wouldn't let her out," Jessica said. "So she jumped out of the frickin' window. Her legs were all scraped up." The traumatized woman was a friend of Jackie's, so Jessica called her mother to come meet them. Jessica and Jackie comforted the woman for three hours in Jackie's van.

Jackie encouraged Jessica to volunteer for Ikwe, but worried about her driving late at night. Jackie replied to several calls from women who'd just been beaten up by their partners and needed someone to rescue them. These requests always frightened Jackie. "If a woman is not in a safe place and I go pick her up, then it is quite possible that I am not in a safe place either," Jackie said. She doesn't want her daughter on these sorts of calls. "Jessica is eighteen," Jackie said. "I don't want her to see the things that I have seen."

Five months after our meeting in Vimy Ridge Park. Jackie Hartog died of a brain aneurysm. Her passing was shocking and sudden. She'd been out driving just the night before. I cannot imagine the impact of Jackie's death on her four daughters, but Ikwe's Facebook page hinted at what Jackie meant to the Ikwe community. When Christine announced Jackie's passing on the page, hundreds of members wrote messages of condolences:

> I would always prefer rides with her because we laughed the whole ride & gave me a lot of heartfelt talks.

> She was an amazing lady and I'll always remember the time she kept apologizing 'cause her van smelled like pickles.

The last time she drove me home we sang "Bohemian Rhapsody" together.

She was so nice. I had three kids and a bunch of bags. I was so stressed she made me laugh and feel so comfortable. Even my niece who didn't know how to talk was babbling away with her.

You were a beautiful kind lady. I'm truly blessed I got a ride from you.

When I called Jessica the following fall, she was still driving for Ikwe. At twenty years old, Jessica and her roommate Bethany were the youngest Ikwe drivers by at least a decade. "So I have a lot of special rules on me," Jessica said. During late-night shifts, Jessica must always have a "buddy driver" with her, usually Bethany, and they are forbidden from driving any men at all. Jessica cannot be alone in the Tim's parking lot either, and must constantly share her location on the Facebook volunteer-group-chat page. "They treat me like a baby," Jessica laughed. She's unsure if her training wheels will ever come off.

When Jackie died, about a hundred of her regulars sent messages of condolence to Jessica. "A lot of people who were my mom's regulars are my regulars now," Jessica said, although some purposely avoid riding with Jessica because she looks so much like her mother. Jessica understands. She appreciates this sombre solidarity. Like all the women I spoke to in Winnipeg, Jessica values her relationships with the other Ikwe drivers more than anything else. "We have a lot of fun hanging out," Jessica said. "We dance in the Tim's parking lot." The women of Ikwe grant Jessica some solace in her grief. "They are a second family to me," she said. "Having that makes me feel so much better."

As I flew home from Winnipeg, I thought about how charity is so often framed as "helping out the less fortunate." Those of us who "have" give to those who "have not." It's a structure built on good intentions, but it also suggests an economic imbalance. When I offer to serve food at a homeless shelter, say, or when someone sponsors a refugee child, the giver and receiver rarely belong to the same socio-economic group.

Ikwe Safe Rides suffers no such imbalance. The volunteer drivers seem to lead the same modest and often difficult lives as the members they drive around. They've endured the challenges of single-motherhood. Alcoholism. Domestic abuse. I met no one who had an easy life. The only things the drivers possess that their passengers don't are a functioning vehicle and some spare time. Maybe this is why Ikwe's drivers love this work so much. In addition to their high goals of protecting women, they're serving their own sisters. No borders stand between them.

Ten

THE BULLY

OF BAGHDAD

MOHAMMED "MO" ABDUL JALIL PICKED ME UP FROM MY
hotel in a dark blue BMW 7 Series sedan. I wouldn't have noticed
the model of the car, but Mo mentioned it twice. When I told
him I'd come to Halifax to talk to taxi drivers, he asked if I also
wanted to meet with "losers." I assumed he meant cabbies who
didn't drive luxury sedans. I suggested we talk at a nearby coffee
shop or, since we were in Halifax, at a famous donair place nearby.
Mo silently rejected this idea and drove instead to a downtown
restaurant. He parked the car under a "No Parking" sign, and I
followed him inside.

The restaurant was on-trend but uninspired—the sort of place
where the music is too loud and the women much younger than
the men they're with. Still, after meeting so many cabbies in the
nation's Tim Hortons, I welcomed the change. Mo was a regular here and made a show of flirting with the hostesses and pok-
ing good-natured fun at the servers he knew by name. I watched

as they returned his greetings with stiff-smiled tolerance rather than genuine affection, a look I recognized from my years bartending and waiting tables. Everyone in the industry knows customers like Mo.

We sat at the bar and ordered eighteen-dollar hamburgers. Mo barely touched his. By the time I reached Halifax, I'd learned there are two types of taxi drivers: those who refuse to talk, and those who won't stop talking. Mo clearly resided in the latter camp, and his burger grew cold as he told me his story.

Mo was twelve years old the first time the bombs fell over Baghdad. It was September 23, 1980, his little brother Ahmed's birthday. The explosions frightened Ahmed to tears, but Mo rushed up to the roof to watch the bursts of flame until his father screamed at him to get inside. "In a very stupid way it was like fireworks for me," Mo said.

The explosions rattled the house for four hours. Thankfully, Mo's father had anticipated the assault, and had taped up the windows the day before, right after Saddam Hussein marched his troops, rumbled his tanks, and flew his Russian-made fighter jets across the border into Iran. The Iranians retaliated with a sustained bombing of Iraq's airfields and military bases. According to Iraqi officials, and to Mo, Saddam's military shot down sixty-seven Iranian fighter jets that day, though most historians consider this an exaggeration.

Mo's family lived in a middle-class Baghdadi neighbourhood Mo described as idyllic. "Across from us there is an older lady from Turkmenistan," Mo said. "Right beside her, a guy named Ibrahim from Pakistan. His wife was Turkish. Right beside him is a Muslim Kurdish family." All the neighbourhood kids played together, regardless of their faith or background. "We were kids. We were playing. We were happy." Nobody's parents cared who their children played with, as long as they weren't learning to curse or smoke cigarettes. "It was a perfect model of Iraq. You are what you are. Nobody gives a shit."

The war drew wider and darker lines between Baghdad's diverse families. The war darkened Mo and his brother, too. Television newscasts constantly flashed gruesome images into the Jalils' kitchen. "They showed us dead, burned, and chopped bodies. As we were eating dinner. We grew up with that," Mo said. "We were mutated." When one of Ahmed's friends was literally frightened to death by a missile striking near his home, Mo and Ahmed thought him a coward. "Now I cry about that kid," Mo said. "But at the time, we were laughing at him."

Despite the mutations of war, Mo considered his childhood "over-sheltered." His father worked as a school district supervisor and Mo attended good schools. Mo's social status rose in his midteens thanks to his mother's job at Iraqi Airways. A pilot friend flew the London-Baghdad route, and Mo used to get him to bring Brylcreem and jean jackets from London, and a switchblade comb like the one he'd seen in the movie *Grease*. The friend also used to deliver a recording of the BBC's "Top of the Pops" broadcast to a Baghdad radio station every Friday. "But he would bring it to us first, on Thursday night," Mo said. He and his friends would stay up all night recording the songs before the pilot delivered the master tape to the radio station. "We had all the latest music before Iraqi FM." Mo wasn't wealthy, but he was cool.

He was also huge. Mo had sealed his tough-guy reputation when he was in grade one, after he pounded a grade sixer in a schoolyard fight. By the time he reached his mid-teens, Mo was over six feet tall and weighed more than two hundred pounds. I would learn that much of Mo's life story was propelled by the fact that he was always the biggest, toughest guy in the room.

Mo's father, a national-level wrestling coach who coached Iraq's wrestling team in the 1960 summer Olympics, decided his unruly and privileged son would benefit from the sport. He assigned Mo to the strictest wrestling coach he knew, Coach Qassam. "He was one of my father's toughest motherfuckers," Mo said. Coach Qassam wouldn't tolerate any laziness from his athletes, and wielded a stick to ensure as much at wrestling practice. "If he says do fifty push-ups and you do forty-nine-and-a-half, he will break that stick over your back," Mo said. "My father realized I needed that kind of discipline. Secretly, I loved it."

Mo excelled under Coach Qassam and won the 1985 Arab Championships in the 100 kg division after only two years in the sport. He showed me a photo on his phone of his team posing with a framed portrait of Saddam Hussein. "I was beating veteran wrestlers in record time," he said. "But it got into my head. I became an arrogant fuck." He also became a bully. Mo was particularly cruel to the school's "pretty boys": those who dressed in suit jackets and ties to impress the girls. He'd push them around, beat them up, and pour Pepsi into their pockets when they weren't looking. "I was such an asshole," Mo admitted.

The Iraqi army drafted Mo after his eighteenth birthday, in 1986. He showed up late for his draft date, and his superiors punished him by making him run, do squats, and crawl in the mud. Officers locked all the new recruits into their barracks on that first night. "They handed us two buckets, one for piss and one for shit." In the morning, everyone was marched onto a bus. None of the new soldiers knew where they were going. The bus drove for three hours before stopping on the highway, where officers divided the soldiers into three groups and ordered them onto military trucks. All three trucks drove off the highway and towards the Iranian border. "There were some palm trees. They were burned and chopped," Mo remembers. "We started to hear some bombing. And then we were in the middle of it."

The soldiers climbed out of the trucks and lined up in front of a colonel for their assignments. Mo was sent to the first unit.

"The colonel singled me out because I was the biggest and because I had the longest moustache," he said. "It was the fashion at the time." Another officer handed Mo a chemical mask he didn't know how to use, an AK-47 he'd never fired, and ammunition he didn't know how to load. He didn't even know how to salute properly. The officer then pointed to a trench and told Mo to follow it. At six-foot-three, Mo stood taller than the trench was deep, and his head and shoulders were exposed as he walked. He followed the trench for two kilometres until he reached some other soldiers.

"Then I started to hear bees," Mo said. "They were going by me. Buzzing above me, behind me, in front of me." A soldier shouted at Mo to get down. "Those bees were not bees," Mo said. "They were bullets. If that sniper was any good, I would've been dead. That was my second day in the military."

Mo's unit occupied a valley between an Iraqi-occupied hill and an Iranian-occupied mountain. Hundreds of landmines seeded the no man's land just beyond the barbed-wire coils edging Mo's trench. Tripwires were rigged to ignite buried drums of napalm, or to detonate vicious "bounding mines" that jumped a metre into the air before exploding. The area was so dangerous and so isolated that Mo's superiors considered his unit expendable. "Every night, we were recorded as losses," Mo said. "In the morning, they would count us and put us back in."

The soldiers fighting in Mo's unit came from all over Iraq, including small villages in the far reaches of the country. Mo's urban, middle-class upbringing meant he'd never been exposed to rural Iraqis before. "I had culture shock," he said. He met Iraqis with strange rural names—Arabic equivalents to "Cletus and Billy Bob," Mo said. They were far more superstitious and religious than the Baghdadis he grew up with. Many wouldn't spend any of their army stipend before offering the money to their village imam back home, as required by their Shiite faith.

Mo equated their religious devotion with gullibility and naiveté. "They're true believers in that bullshit," Mo said. He spoke with patronizing affection. "Deep inside I sympathized with them because they didn't know any better. They live in marshes. They raise water-buffalo. They fuck mules," Mo said. "But they are pure, nice people." Still, none of this mattered in the trenches. The Iranian bombs didn't distinguish rural from urban, rich from poor, believer from skeptic. "Everybody cared for everybody. Everybody hurt when someone was lost," Mo said. The horrors of trench warfare, unseen since the First World War, united them. So did death. Mo saw dead bodies for the first time when an officer ordered him to empty the pockets of two killed Iraqi soldiers who lay in the back of a truck. "That will scar you," he said. "No matter how much you say you are tough."

Mo once came close to being killed himself. He'd recently returned from home leave and was handing out cookies to his fellow soldiers. "When you come back, you don't come empty-handed," he said. "Your buddies have been sitting for a month eating army food. You bring them a treat." It was Mo's night to fetch water for the camp, but since he was busy divvying out baked goods, one of the other soldiers offered to take his turn fetching water. He never returned. The soldier was hit with an Iranian 60mm mortar shell three minutes after he left Mo's tent. "You can hear the 80mm shells coming. You can hear the 120mm shells coming. But you don't hear the 60mm coming," Mo said. "That was supposed to be me. That was my turn."

Mo's unit faced nearly constant bombing from Iranian positions, and soldiers learned that a particularly heavy day of bombing signalled a nighttime ground assault. "The Iranians used to throw waves of people at us," Mo said. "Those gullible rural people." When the Iranian infantry advanced, Mo blindly fired his rifle over his head and above the top of the trench. He occasionally hurled a grenade if he felt the enemy was getting close.

"You peek every now and then," he said. "You don't have time to think. All you have to know is that you're shooting, you are shooting and shooting until you are done shooting." People often ask Mo if he killed anyone. "Yes, I did. But it is not like in the movies. It is not like Brad Pitt shooting at the Germans," Mo said. "There is no background music. Nothing in slow motion. Nothing in black and white. I have no words for it. Only chaos. Survival. Adrenaline."

Despite this chaos, Mo claims he never felt afraid during the war. The bombs and constant threat of death became part of his daily life, as mundane as making tea and smoking cigarettes. A night without bombing was so rare as to be disconcerting. "When it was quiet, we'd yell at the Iranians: 'Come on guys! Send us a couple of bombs so we can sleep!' I became something different than I was before."

"What did you become?" I asked.

"I became a bit of an animal."

Because of his wrestler's physique and enthusiasm for combat, Mo's superiors pulled him out of the trenches to train for a special unit. The training lasted forty-five days and combined a sadistic regimen of physical endurance with hand-to-hand combat and target practice that Mo excelled at. For their final test before graduation, soldiers were forced to stare into the sun for three minutes before being pushed into a dark room where five men armed with broomsticks were waiting. "They beat the hell out of you, and you have to come out with a stick," Mo said. "If you don't, they keep beating you until an ambulance comes to get you." Mo was the fastest to emerge from the room with a broomstick.

Mo returned to his unit after graduation, but the war ended before his special skills were needed. The ceasefire came without warning at noon on August 8, 1988. "We celebrated," Mo said. "Everybody was shooting in the air." After eight years of brutal war,

Iran and Iraq ended up with the same borders as before the war. A million soldiers were killed, an entire generation of young men wasted, and neither side had anything to show for it but graveyards.

The restaurant hostess, Tasha, interrupted Mo's story to tell him a parking officer had ticketed his BMW and called for a tow truck. Mo faux-scolded her—"You could've defended me!"—then bounded out of the lounge to move his car. When he returned, he ordered two lattes for us and told me about his second war. For Iraqis of Mo's generation, just two years divided the end of one conflict and the beginning of the next.

Mo's Iran-Iraq War story began with bees. His Gulf War story begins with a fly. In August 1990, he was working a soft desk job at an army intelligence unit when Saddam Hussein invaded Kuwait. During a morning inspection, an errant fly flew into Mo's nose. Mo swatted at his face. The inspecting officer hollered at Mo: "Why did you move?"

"A fly went up my nose," Mo responded.

"You are a soldier at attention!" the officer said. "You don't move even if a snake crawls up your leg! Run to the end of the training grounds and back!"

Mo ran his punishment lap but returned grinning. His smile infuriated the officer, who ordered him to run another lap. When he finished, still smiling, the officer demanded Mo complete the base obstacle course twice while carrying his rifle and wearing a gas mask. Then he made him crawl on his belly with his hands behind his back. Mo smiled through all of it.

"What the fuck are you smiling about?" the officer yelled.

"This is good morning exercise," Mo quipped. "I am happy."

"I'll show you exercise," the officer said, and ordered Mo to swim through a fetid swamp behind the mess hall.

"I am not going to swim in the swamp," Mo said.

The officer's eyes widened. "Why not?"

"You've already punished me for my mistake. And a little bit more."

"Are you going to teach me how to be an officer?"

"I think somebody should."

Enraged, the officer lifted his swagger stick over his head, but before he could strike, Mo grabbed his neck and threw him to the ground. "I didn't think of his rank. I didn't think of shit," Mo said. "I took him by the throat and put him down. Boom." In that moment, Mo realized the brutal sessions of combat training he endured during the Iran-Iraq War had left him with what he calls "a tic." He never used these skills against his Iranian enemies, but the potential for sudden, reflexive violence had been tattooed on Mo's psyche. Until that day with the officer, Mo had no idea what he was capable of. Such a reflex encased in a man with Mo's training and muscle made him dangerous.

Mo left the officer on the ground and marched past the stunned soldiers to the barracks jail. He knew he would face a court martial for assaulting a superior officer, but a colleague advised him of a possible way out. If Mo wrote a patriotic plea to the head of intelligence and volunteered to be sent to the war's front line, he could delay his court martial. Mo composed a long, florid letter full of the sort of flag-waving slogans he'd read in government newspapers. He gushed about how he'd be honoured to fight for his country and the glory of the Ba'ath Party on the battlefields of Kuwait.

Mo's mock patriotism so impressed the head of intelligence that he offered Mo his choice of assignments. Mo chose Unit 118, a surveillance and communication division of Iraq's famed Republican Guard. After the invasion, the unit occupied a farm across the Kuwait border, in Al Mutla. The post was perfect. Mo figured he wouldn't just avoid his pending court martial while serving with the 118, he'd avoid actual combat, too.

Still, Mo felt he had to establish himself at the top of the unit's informal hierarchy. And so as soon as he arrived at the base in Kuwait, he sought out its fiercest drill sergeant. "If you beat him up within a week, nobody will fuck with you again," Mo said. He coaxed the drill sergeant into the barracks with another box of cookies from home. Then he locked the door behind him and pummelled the drill sergeant until his superiors, responding to the drill sergeant's screams, climbed through the windows to his rescue. Mo was sent to the unit jail, as he knew he would be, but he'd also successfully claimed his role as the unit's alpha.

Mo was sitting in his jail cell at the beginning of Operation Desert Storm in 1991. The UN Security Council had given Saddam Hussein until January 15 to leave Kuwait. Hussein refused and declared Kuwait a province of Iraq. The next day, the American-led coalition launched a sustained aerial bombardment of Iraqi forces. Mo's hope for a cushy non-combat posting proved a miscalculation. After quickly destroying Iraq's air force and anti-aircraft facilities, the coalition turned its guns on the Republican Guard's intelligence and communication facilities. "We were targeted like a motherfucker," Mo said.

When the air-raid siren went off at the Unit 118 base, everyone panicked. Mo's guard fled the prison and Mo broke out of his cell. When I asked him how he did this, he just said "I was a mule." Mo joined his fellow soldiers as they cowered under the shock and awe of American carpet bombing. The coalition forces had received erroneous intelligence reporting that Iraqi troops were hiding in reinforced concrete shelters. "It was a joke," Mo said. The structures sheltering Unit 118 were built on soft sand and were fragile enough to be kicked over by a soldier's boot. Mo dug himself a two-metre-deep hole, laid his sleeping bag inside, covered it with a plastic tarp, then added a layer of discarded car bumpers as reinforcement. The intensity of the bombing made fetching food a near-suicidal mission. Eventually, a soldier dared to sprint across the field to the kitchen. The helmet half-filled with dry rice and a bit of salt he returned with would have to feed eight men.

"Then the Americans brought the *Missouri*," Mo said. "And that is why I fucking love 'If I Could Turn Back Time.'"

The USS *Missouri*, a battleship aptly nicknamed "Big Mo," anchored off the Kuwaiti coastline. The *Missouri* had served in the Pacific theatre during the Second World War, and the Japanese signed their surrender documents on its deck, but by the time of the Gulf War the battleship had become more famous as the set for a music video. In 1989, a body-stockinged Cher sang "If I Could Turn Back Time" while frolicking on the *Missouri*'s deck in front of blissed-out sailors. During the performance, Cher dons a sailor's cap for a verse and straddles the battleship's 16-inch cannons. About a year and a half later, those same Cher-anointed guns were firing at Mo. "It is a very special song for me," Mo said. I couldn't tell if he was joking.

The *Missouri*'s ordnance left craters wide and deep enough to hold three tanks, according to Mo. He and his fellow soldiers had never seen anything like this before, and Mo said it was the only time he ever feared for his life. The unit needed to escape, and the only road that led out of Al Mutla, Highway 80, stretched north to the Iraq border and onward to Basra. The highway was less than half a kilometre from Mo's base, and the unit could see Iraqi vehicles withdrawing. But coalition forces continued to bomb the retreating troops, picking off fleeing vehicles as if they were ducks on a pond.

Unit 118 waited out the bombing until a blessed foggy morning offered cover and a chance to escape. The soldiers sped out of Al Mutla at four in the morning, "before the Americans woke up," Mo said. They reached Highway 80 and raced towards the border. The unit spent about an hour on what became known as the "Highway of Death" before crossing into the relative safety of Basra. Burned out or abandoned Iraqi army vehicles were scattered all along the road. There were stolen civilian vehicles, too, many filled with stolen booty, both military and banal. Looted televisions, baby strollers, and plastic-wrapped dress shirts were crammed into trunks alongside grenade launchers. A *Los Angeles Times* reporter described "sacks of silk and lace tablecloths and a box of silver spoons" spilling from "a red pickup loaded with AK-47 rifles."

But what Mo remembers most is the charred corpses. "We drove over bodies," he said. They were everywhere. In the sand. On the tarmac. Some twisted out of car windows. He described the blackened bodies as "crispy." Many consider the massacre of withdrawing soldiers and fleeing civilians on Highway 80 a war crime.

Iraq remained under a state of emergency after the war, and Mo's military service continued. He returned to a ravaged Baghdad and his previous job with the intelligence department. Mo had evaded his court martial for assaulting his superior officer by volunteering for the 118, but the charges still hung over him. He needed a new plan. Mo learned that the Iraqi military offered pardons for soldiers who had deserted their posts during the Gulf War as long as they turned themselves in for reassignment. He hadn't deserted the 118; the unit fled Kuwait only after Saddam had declared a withdrawal. But Mo surrendered anyway, and "confessed" to deserting a military unit he'd never been a part of. He reasoned that thousands of soldiers would confess to desertion, and since the military bureaucracy used paper documents rather than computers, it would take a long time to uncover his lie.

This was just the first move in Mo's long game to avoid prosecution. After copping to a desertion he did not commit, from a unit he never served, Mo asked to be transferred as far away from Baghdad—and the military court—as possible. Then he used his desk job to construct an obstacle course of paperwork between him and his court martial. Mo's clerical job granted him access to payroll information, personnel files, transfer orders, and furlough requests. He was always among the first to read inter-unit correspondence. Whenever a message came from the military court trying to track Mo down, Mo would bury the file. And when a position at distant base opened up, Mo would request another transfer. Each time he changed units, he added another layer of documentation to hide behind. "The paper trail became longer and more complicated," Mo said. He lost himself in military bureaucracy for two years, changing units three times, before the military court finally tracked him down through his salary records. "They found me through the accountants," Mo said, reminding me a little of Al Capone.

In April 1993, Iraq's military court found Mo guilty of assaulting a higher-ranking officer and sentenced him to a year in military prison. He arrived at the facility with about forty other court-marshalled soldiers. After the new inmates were processed, guards led them all into a large room, where they asserted their authority by making an example out of the biggest new inmate. This, of course, was Mo. With no warning, a guard struck Mo in the middle of his back with a copper cable as thick as a soda can. Mo's body went numb. This ended up being a morbid blessing, because when four other guards circled round and started whipping him with cables, Mo felt nothing. "You are supposed to be crying and screaming and pleading. But I just stood there" Mo said. They beat him until they were out of breath, then dragged him to his cell.

Mo spent a full year in a prison that smelled of sweat and piss and always felt cold. Violence and torture were common. Mo witnessed officers beating the soles of inmates' feet with broomsticks or electrocuting them by tying them to cell bars wired to a wind-up army phone and dousing them with water. One man died that way. Mo got into the occasional brawl himself—mostly with snitches or to defend new inmates from being raped. For the most part, though, Mo behaved himself in prison. "I didn't have a gang. I didn't do drugs. I didn't gamble. I didn't fuck boys. I didn't look for trouble." Because of his size, and the beating he silently endured on his arrival, the other inmates left Mo alone.

Elsewhere in Iraq, inflation surged under UN sanctions. The same package of cigarettes Mo bought for six Iraqi dinars before his first day of prison cost 120 dinars on the day of his release. "My parents were in a miserable state," Mo said. They had retired by then, and their combined monthly pension wasn't enough to feed them. Mo needed a job. He found work in the Persian rug market as a dealer and a middleman shuttling between desperate sellers and wealthy buyers. He worked hard, built a reliable clientele, and made decent money. He also got married to Suad, an English literature student at the University of Baghdad. "I was not a student, but I used to mingle there," Mo said. "There were no nightclubs anymore, so the university was the best place to meet girls."

After two years of selling carpets, Mo was bored. Iraq's fluctuating currency rate scrambled the economy and the country's politics started to darken. "Saddam was losing his grip," Mo said. "We were all chickens living in Saddam's backyard. This guy gets fed today. This guy doesn't. This guy gets executed. This guy gets fried." He and Suad decided to move to Jordan, where her family lived. Her father promised Mo a job. Mo told the Iraqi authorities they were travelling to Amman to purchase carpets, but they had no intention of returning to Iraq.

Not long after arriving at his in-laws' home, Mo could tell something was wrong. Nobody mentioned the job his father-in-law had promised, and the warmth of their original welcome grew cold. A week later, Mo's father-in-law asked Mo how much it would cost to divorce his daughter. He wanted to pay Mo to go away. Mo realized the job offer had been a ruse to bring Suad out of Iraq. Under Iraqi law, a woman under fifty years old could not leave Iraq without the supervision of a brother, father, or husband. "I was her ticket out," Mo said. "I didn't know that. Neither did she."

Mo and Suad moved out of her parents' house. "She was pleading and crying," Mo said. "But we stuck to each other." Mo found a construction job, but for all his toughness Mo couldn't handle the physical work. "I'd never worked as a labourer my whole life," Mo said. "I had the softest hands." His three Egyptian co-workers pitied the enormous-but-useless Iraqi on their crew and picked up his slack when he fell behind.

One day, while eating shawarma from a street vendor on lunch break, one of the Egyptians noticed an ad on the newspaper his sandwich had been wrapped in. He handed the greasy paper to Mo. "Aren't you a good artist?," he asked. Mo had been drawing ever since he was two years old. Sometimes he'd stay up to finish a drawing after his parents had gone to sleep and would still be working on it when they woke up the next morning. He'd applied for illustration jobs in Amman before, but no one would hire him. "I looked like a thug," he said.

The shawarma ad was from a children's magazine looking for illustrators. Mo was among fifty artists who applied and among five the magazine hired. He drew cartoons instructing children how to wash their hands properly and safely cross the street. The gig padded Mo's portfolio and boosted his confidence. He landed another gig with a prominent ad agency, one that had previously rejected him, to draw storyboards for a toothpaste commercial. Mo's work started to attract the attention of creative directors at agencies around Amman and he was suddenly in demand. He raised his rates accordingly, and he and Suad moved out of their basement suite, furnished with two mattresses and a hot plate, and into a proper two-bedroom suite. "I became well-to-do," Mo said. "Comfortable. I could afford dinners out. Taxis. Clothes. Cologne. All the luxuries."

Still, their life in Amman was not secure. Their visas had long expired and both were living in Jordan illegally. Mo worked off-book and was paid in cash. This put him at the mercy of unscrupulous employers who could easily stiff him, knowing he had no legal recourse. He and Suad decided to emigrate to Canada. They landed in Halifax in 1999, Suad continuing her English studies at Dalhousie University and Mo enrolling at the Nova Scotia College of Art and Design.

NSCAD disappointed Mo. He felt his fellow students' work didn't deserve the praise it received. "Everybody strokes everybody," Mo said, "So when it is their turn, everyone will come and stroke them." And Mo didn't fit in with the conceptual artists and "washed out hippies" he shared a classroom with. "I was scary looking," he said. A group of film studies students cast Mo and two other men as extras in their graduation film project. Mo remembers lining up for his turn in the makeup chair. The first man was cast as a scrawny, pill-popping drug addict, so the makeup artist darkened his eyes, added pockmarks to his face, and sent him on set. The second extra was cast as a gang leader. Makeup drew on a few facial scars and sent him off. Mo would play a bruising bodyguard and hitman. When he sat in the makeup chair, the artist put her brushes down. "You're fine," she said. "I can't make you look any worse."

I reached out to Renée Forrestall, the artist who taught Mo the anatomy of the human figure during his time at NSCAD. She was one of the few teachers Mo admired. Nearly twenty years had passed since Forrestall taught Mo, but she remembered him. "I would say Mohammed was very earnest. Very keen," Forrestall said. "His work was a bit brute. He had a coarse, expressionistic style." Most of his drawings were of manly superhero figures.

"He liked to draw muscular he-men. That was his thing," she said. This didn't surprise me at all. Mo was essentially drawing himself. Forrestall recognized that Mo was suffering from trauma. "He didn't really know it, I don't think," she said. "He told me confidentially he had ill effects from the war." Mo never detailed his experiences to Forrestall, but she could tell his memories burdened him. "He had a hard time with some of the things in class and would have to leave once in a while," Forrestall said. At the end of the semester, Forrestall planned to bring her students to the gross anatomy lab to do drawings of real human cadavers. Mo asked Forrestall to be excused. After all he'd been through in Iraq, Mo couldn't bear to be in a room full of dead bodies.

"I think it might have been a time of real transition for him," Forrestall said of Mo's time at NSCAD. "He was very mature and was facing all these frivolous children poncing around in art college with nothing else to do. I could see where he might be a little cynical about that. And judgemental. And maybe rightly so. Who am I do say? A lot of the kids are annoying." Forrestall remembers Mo looking around the room with a sweeping motion of his arm and joking to her "during the *fatwa*, you will be one of the only ones to be okay."

I felt sorry for Mo. Not much worked out for him during his first decade in Canada. "I had culture shock," Mo said "The West is not all *Footloose* and *Saturday Night Fever* and *Grease* and all those movies. It is not like that. People work hard here." After Mo left NSCAD, he found a job at a prominent marketing agency, but quarrelled with his bosses and didn't last long. He then manned the door at a nightclub for a couple of years before working in a pizzeria. Then he and Suad divorced. Their parting was civil. "I helped her move. I took care of her. Went out for dinners and movies. We laughed with each other. We wondered why we didn't do this when we were married." Suad eventually remarried and moved to Mississauga. Mo still sends her texts on her birthday.

Things got better for Mo in 2005 after he started dating Rosalyn, "a white girl from Dartmouth." Mo moved into her house in a posh Halifax suburb, and the couple would go on long drives into the countryside together. Rosalyn even inspired an unlikely hockey fandom in Mo. Back in Baghdad, nightly sportscasts would often end with a montage of hockey fights, but Mo had never seen an actual game. In 2005, Rosalyn took Mo to see a Quebec Major Junior League playoff game between Rimouski Océanic, led by a young Sidney Crosby, and the Halifax Mooseheads. Mo was enthralled even before the puck dropped. "The national anthem. The last verse when the seats start shaking. The roar. 'This is Mooooose Country!' Even now I get the chills," Mo said.

Mo showed me several photos of himself posing with the Stanley Cup on his phone. I was gobsmacked. He made me vow not to write how he managed multiple audiences with Canada's most beloved trophy. I can only say that each time Sidney Crosby brought the Stanley Cup from Pittsburgh to celebrate with his family and friends in Nova Scotia, Mo was there. Mo Jalil, Iraqi wrestling champion and soldier for Saddam, has drunk champagne from the Stanley Cup three times—once more than Bobby Orr.

Thanks to Rosalyn, Mo started to finally appreciate the beauty and "simplicity" of his life in Halifax. "She is like my soulmate," Mo said. "Who would've thought we'd find ourselves on the other side of the world?" After listening to Mo's coarse words about so many people in his life, I was startled to hear him speak of Rosalyn with such tenderness.

But the solace Mo found with Rosalyn soon sparked its opposite. Mo remembers sitting on Rosalyn's deck one afternoon watching a swan on the waters of Bedford Basin. The scene was so idyllic as to be a Halifax cliché. But then a plane flew overhead and Mo's knees buckled. "Immediately I felt I was back in Kuwait," Mo said. He suddenly feared the American cluster bombs that always followed the sound of a plane. "By the time you heard the plane engine, it was too late," Mo said.

Mo knew he'd been traumatized by the wars he'd fought in. He was aware of it enough to opt out of the gross anatomy class, after all. But he'd never suffered this sort of flashback before. Mo believes that the relatively banal challenges of school, work, and divorce that he'd faced over the previous few years distracted him from a deeper crack in his psyche. Now that those pressures were easing, his wartime memories had space to surface. And they've continued. Ever since that first flashback, Mo's mind occasionally returns to the tortures he witnessed in prison, to the horrid food he ate in the trenches of the Iran-Iraq War, to his brother's friend who died of fear. "It hits me at the happiest of times. This heaviness. It ruins my best moments," Mo said. "I relive the whole thing as if it is happening. The sound. The smell. All that shit. I feel it. I live it." A doctor diagnosed Mo with PTSD, and he takes medication now to ward off the panic.

The drugs, though, haven't cured Mo of his "tic": the violent reflex grafted onto him in the trenches and army bases of Iraq, the impulse that landed him in an Iraqi military prison, followed him to Canada. In 2005, Mo inserted himself in an argument between a fellow pizzeria employee and another man. When the man told Mo to "fuck off," Mo went blank. The next thing he remembers is holding the man by the ears and smashing his face into the ground. The crack of the man's nose breaking had snapped Mo out of his rage like a gruesome alarm clock. Police arrested Mo and charged him with assault. He eventually settled out of court.

Mo began driving for Yellow Taxi in 2014. He started in a Chevy Impala with a taxi license, referred to as a "roof light" in Halifax, that he rented from another cabbie. Mo worked fourteen-hour days at first. "I used to sleep in the car," Mo said. "And chug coffee after coffee." He bought a second car, a Maxima, then an Infiniti. Then his BMW. Mo amassed a miniature fleet of vehicles, which he rented to other cabbies. Since roof lights can't be transferred in Halifax, Mo leased them for his drivers from other owners.

According to Mo, the other drivers and management at Yellow Taxi started to envy his success. I suspect, too, that Mo's bosses, like his military superiors, found him combative and insolent. His managers started urging the roof light owners who leased to Mo to lease to somebody else. When one of these roof light owners broke his lease contract, Mo sued him and Yellow Taxi's general manager in small claims court. The court awarded Mo damages, but the decision hardly flattered him. The court adjudicator described Mo as "difficult," and wrote that he "displayed an overbearing character." The roof light owner told police that Mo had threatened his life, though nothing came of the allegation.

Mo quit Yellow Taxi soon after and started driving for himself. He didn't want to keep relying on "grocery ladies and drunken kids and dumbasses" for fares. He wanted to cater to a higher class of clientele. His first high-rolling regular was a local businessman who used to invite Mo into his house for cigars before getting Mo to drive him downtown. He enjoyed listening to Mo's stories and introduced Mo to his wealthy friends. "Those hundred-thousand-dollar guys with company credit cards started to introduce me to legit millionaires. And the million-dollar guys introduced me to the hundred-million-dollar guys." Many members of Halifax's moneyed class soon had Mo's number in their cell phones.

At first, Mo simply acted as their favoured driver. These men-and-women-of-means preferred Mo's pristine BMW 7 Series to riding in a regular cab. Soon, though, Mo evolved from driver to personal concierge. Not only would his clients hire Mo to fetch their colleagues and business contacts from the airport, they also gave him their credit cards to pay for their high-end dinners and hotel suites. One of Mo's patrons once called him from his vacation in Italy: he needed Mo to take care of a visiting engineer who was coming to Halifax for meetings. Mo picked the engineer up from the airport, drove him everywhere he needed to go during his stay, and made his dinner reservations before returning him to the airport for his flight home, paying for everything with his client's credit card.

Another client once phoned Mo from a party aboard his yacht. He wanted to move the party to his home, so he sent Mo to buy two cases of wine and two cases of beer and bring them to his house in advance of their return. Not only did Mo have the man's credit card in his wallet, he also knew the security code at his mansion. This same client once flew Mo to Austin, Texas, for another party. "He has a castle," Mo said. The host went to bed at midnight, leaving Mo to watch over his guests. "He had four bars in the house, with bottles of Louis XIII cognac," Mo said. "That costs five hundred dollars an ounce. Someone has to keep an eye on things."

Mo keeps an eye on his clients, too. Some tend to lose control when they drink, so they hire Mo as their chaperone. Mo joins them at nightclubs and parties. He coaxes them away from the bar when they've drunk too much, and calms angry bouncers when his charges misbehave. One of Mo's clients always throws his titanium American Express Black card on nightclub floors when he gets drunk. "He thinks if he hits the floor at a certain angle, it will make sparks," Mo said. Mo ensures he always gets his card back. Another of his clients, a politician Mo wisely did not name, once drunkenly propositioned a group of nineteen-year-old girls at a bar. Mo made sure nothing happened. "He was horny, and I was protecting him," Mo said.

His clients see Mo as a reliable fixer. Sometimes they hire him to drive their intoxicated wives and girlfriends home. "They trust me," Mo said. "Do you know how many wives I've carried to their beds? Beautiful women. Drunk as a skunk." A regular once brought a date back to his office after a wine-soaked dinner for a round of late-night desk sex. The man called Mo at three in the morning in a panic. His girlfriend had grown suspicious, and was on her way to the office. He needed Mo to fetch his hook-up and drive her home, but the woman was too drunk to move, so he carried her to his car and drove her home, stopping three or four times for her to vomit.

I could understand the desire of Halifax's high rollers to have a trustworthy driver and fixer on call, but Mo's clients sounded like horrible people. They behaved like overaged frat boys who, though wealthy and respected by day, required an Iraqi soldier-wrestler to babysit them by night. "They think it is better to hire me, who they trust, who has their credit card and access code and everything," Mo said. "They are going to be safe and no damage is going to be done."

"Right, but do you respect them?" I asked.

"Some I respect. Some I don't respect," Mo said. "Some I consider friends. These big shots are miserable in their personal lives. Not all, but most of them. As much as dickheads as they appear to be, they are human at some level. They are gentle souls. They have a lot of good things they do that gets overshadowed by how they carry themselves."

I wondered just how far Mo's services went. Abetting someone's infidelities and keeping them out of trouble is one thing, but I wanted to know if Mo was doing anything illegal for his clients.

"What do you mean? Like giving blowjobs in the car?"

I laughed. "No. I mean do you get them drugs?"

"No. I don't carry it. I don't buy it. I don't sell it." Only once did one of Mo's clients ask him to pick up a parcel that turned out to be an envelope of narcotics. "But I won't do that again," he said.

"What about sex workers?"

"If they ask me to go to a certain address and pick someone up, I will. But I don't pimp."

"What about rough stuff? Are you their muscle?"

"No, but they use my look," Mo said. His clients have never asked Mo to manhandle anyone, but just having a guy his size in their entourage keeps them safe.

Mo bears genuine affection for some of the men and women he serves. He told me he wept when the wife of one of his clients passed away. "She was a beautiful lady." Still, Mo knows most of his clients aren't his friends. "To them, I am either exotic or entertainment. Or maybe they really feel for me," he said. "Sometimes I don't know what I am to them. I don't care."

We finished our lattes and left the restaurant to fetch Mo's car. He'd moved it to a nearby parkade and parked it in a disabled space, using the phony disabled permit in his glove box he keeps for such occasions. Mo drove to a convenience store, where he bought a pack of cigarettes for Tasha and delivered them to her at the restaurant. "That pack of cigarettes cost me fifteen dollars," Mo said when he returned to the car, "but when I call Tasha and say one of my clients needs a table for four, it is there." We drove around Halifax for almost an hour. Mo pointed out some of his clients' mansions while Eurythmics' *Greatest Hits* played endlessly on his stereo.

Mo's concierge business operates outside the Halifax Regional Municipality's taxi bylaws. Mo might be a licensed driver, but his BMW isn't licensed as a taxi. Mo claims he more than obeys all the official rules regarding safety inspections and maintenance. He purchases new tires for his car, for example, and his insurance policy exceeds what the taxi commission demands in terms of liability—even though his policy isn't commercial and therefore violates the rules itself. Mo doesn't have a meter in his car, but he never demands a particular fare anyway. "If you give me five dollars, I will take it. If you give me a hundred dollars, I will take that, too," Mo said. "But the next time you call, if you gave me five dollars, I won't respond. If you gave me a hundred dollars, I will be at your door before you hang up the phone." Mo doesn't worry about the rules he breaks. The worst the municipality can do is fine him, and they have, but Mo refuses to pay.

In 2018, Mo formally incorporated his business as Elite Concierge Services. He hopes to expand by hiring a team of drivers and inking exclusive driving contracts with high-end local businesses. His drivers will shuttle customers from their downtown hotels to nearby golf courses, say, or bring them on tours of local wineries. Other companies could use Mo's business to ferry their employees to and from sales calls, allowing them to work in the back seat rather than worry about driving themselves. Mo will outfit his cars with refreshment fridges, cigar boxes, and fur blankets so his clients feel pampered. And he will foster relationships with doormen and hostesses, like Tasha, to ensure his clients never have to wait in line at a club or for a restaurant table.

The connections Mo has nurtured with Halifax's moneyed class clearly mean a lot to him, and he will continue to serve his wealthiest clients himself. Like Alex Seliga in Edmonton, Mo earned himself a pass to cross the border from Halifax's working class to its gilded rich. He dines with them and attends their parties. Sometimes he sleeps in their guest rooms. They pay him for his services, but Mo never takes advantage of their generosity. "I don't mooch," he said. When Mo joins his clients for dinner, he'll order just a burger and a Pepsi. Once, when Mo took a client clothes shopping—he'd arrived in Halifax with no luggage—the man told Mo to pick out something for himself. Mo declined, but when the client noticed Mo eyeing a hat and a pair of sunglasses he bought them for him. "The glasses cost $689. They are still in the box. I am afraid to wear them."

Near the end of our afternoon together, Mo returned to something he'd said when he first picked me up. "When I asked you if you were interested in losers, you laughed and asked me what was a loser," Mo said. "I will tell you. A loser is a driver who has been driving for thirteen or fourteen years and is going nowhere. And they are still driving for somebody else. And they are still complaining."

Some drivers simply don't know any better, Mo said. "Those who came from some mountain in Africa or Eastern Europe or Asia or Mongolia and they think they are living the dream." Other drivers envy Mo's success. And why wouldn't they? Mo drives a better car than any of them. He boasts a regular client list of well-heeled Haligonians. And he has escaped the personal politics of dispatchers and the chattering of other cabbies. "Cab drivers will gossip about you even if you walk with a halo on your head," Mo said. "Some of them respect me. And some fear me."

Mo has given them reason to fear him, especially when his "tic" switches on. Once, in a rage, Mo chased a driver for seven kilometres from downtown Halifax to Fairview for giving him "attitude." After the cabbie dropped off his passenger, Mo blocked his taxi. The driver ran away on foot before Mo could catch him. "He left the car and started crying like a bitch," Mo said. "If I had my hand on him in that moment, I would have gone to the extreme."

Police arrested Mo in August 2017 after a similar incident. A cabbie named Joseph Robichaud testified in court that Mo poached one of his fares, a young woman, in front of a downtown restaurant one Saturday night. Robichaud had protested, shouted at Mo, and called him a rapist. Mo became enraged and rushed to Robichaud's car. Finding the driver's side door locked, Mo punched Robichaud in the face several times through the open window and smashed his glasses. "Lucky I had the door closed," Robichaud told a Halifax court. "I was afraid of what would've happened to me. He is a big boy. I'm an old man. I could've been hospitalized."

The court found Mo guilty of assault and mischief and ordered him to pay for the broken glasses, report to a probation officer, attend anger-management counselling, and stay away from Robichaud. At sentencing, Mo suggested that the scratches on Robichaud's face might have been self-inflicted, and accused Robichaud of "stalking" his house. Still, Mo should consider himself lucky. Had a conviction from his 2005 assault charge appeared on his record, he might've gone to jail.

After Mo dropped me at my B&B, I wondered why I liked him so much. Mo was a lifelong bully, a blowhard, and a self-described "peacock." He always felt he deserved more than he was offered, and believed the rules were for suckers. And yet he'd charmed me. Wondering if I'd been conned, I reached out to Jennie King, a friend of the friend who first told me about Mo.

Jennie met Mo when he drove her home from an opening night party at Halifax's Neptune Theatre. Jennie lived in Cow Bay, a rural community about forty minutes outside of Halifax, so she and Mo had plenty of time to chat during the drive. When Mo mentioned he was an artist, Jennie invited him to a charity function at The Neptune the following week. Artists would be painting portraits of local celebrities on ceiling tiles that would then be auctioned off for a mental-health foundation. Jennie quickly forgot she'd invited her cab driver to the event, but Mo didn't. He showed up ready to paint. Instead of painting a portrait of a celebrity, though, Mo painted Jennie. He signed the back "To my good friend Jennie, who inspired me to paint again." Mo became Jennie's regular cabbie after that. "He would drive me home after every opening night," Jennie said. "We would stop and get donairs. Or we'd secretly chain-smoke on the long drive to the country, telling stories." They met for coffee once, when Jennie wanted to commission Mo to do a painting for her husband. "I poked him a few times about it, but he really didn't show any interest," Jennie said. "He just wanted us to be car buddies and tell each other our sad stories."

Jennie found Mo's sad stories intriguing, especially the ones about his life in the Iraqi military. She'd worked with the Royal Nova Scotia International Tattoo, a famed military musical performance group, and knew a lot of soldiers. "But I never met anyone from the other side," she said. Mo had told her he didn't like talking about the wars he'd fought. This reticence surprised me, as he was hardly shy, but he still agreed to answer Jennie's questions. "I grilled him," she said. When she asked Mo if he'd killed anyone, he told her that killing was his job as a soldier. He told her, too, that he suffered long bouts of depression, and would spend weeks in his basement waiting until the darkness ebbed.

Perhaps this is what I found most endearing about Mo. Not his honesty, though I'd never met anyone as unfiltered or as open about their own failings. And not his deliciously subversive role as infiltrator of the kind of polished spaces where coarse men like him rarely find purchase. Maybe I was simply drawn to Mo's vulnerability. I wouldn't meet a driver as strong, or as brash, or as physically threatening. But nor would I meet one as fragile. Everything Mo had endured—war, violence, fear, frustration— both hardened and softened him. An intact strongman could earn my respect, no doubt, but Mo's cracks earned my affection.

Eleven

THE IMMIGRANT
WHO MADE IT

IN HIS 1970 MEDITATION ON TAXI DRIVING, "FARES I HAVE Known," cabbie-journalist Peter Churchill wrote:

> Some of the people you find behind the wheel, the ones with beards and fierce eyes, are men who write poems and plays or paint pictures, men waiting for the world to acknowledge them as poets, playwrights and artists—and pay them for it. Usually it doesn't, of course.

The description made me think of Mo. The world never acknowledged him as the artist he longed to be in his first years in Halifax. But Churchill could've also been writing about William Hawkins, a poet and songwriter who acted as high priest of Ottawa's bohemian underground in the 1960s. In the first half of his life, Hawkins did a stint in prison, studied with Allen Ginsberg, penned songs with Bruce Cockburn, and caroused with Richie

Havens, Jimi Hendrix, Darius Brubeck, and Joni Mitchell. He notoriously spent the better part of a $6,000 Canada Council for the Arts grant on Mexican marijuana, which he smuggled across the Rio Grande and then into Canada. He published five collections of poetry in the '60s and early '70s, and his poems appeared in anthologies alongside those of Margaret Atwood, Michael Ondaatje, Fred Wah, and bpNichol.

The second half of Hawkins' life hardly resembled the first. In 1973, he woke up in a Toronto rehab centre with a body full of alcohol, heroin, and pills. He emerged clean and sober twenty-eight days later and returned home to Ottawa. The following year, Hawkins started driving cab, and abruptly switched from cavorting with his crew of counter-culture rulebreakers to serving the capital's lawmakers. His repeat clientele included members of Parliament, political staffers, and the journalists tasked with covering the nation's business. "The cab was a perfect way to hide out," Hawkins once said. "It was an outlaw existence. Nobody knew where you were. It kept the temptations away." Hawkins had been a prison inmate, a poet, a musician, a junkie, a philanderer and a drug smuggler. Yet it was only after he started driving taxi for buttoned-up Ottawans that he came to consider himself an outlaw.

Leaving behind his bohemian life for the stable interior of a taxi was another sort of border crossing, and Hawkins a sort of refugee. Like Michael Kamara and Kareem Yalahow, Hawkins had escaped chaos and sought sanctuary beneath a roof light. The only difference is the monsters they fled. Michael and Kareem fled the rifle and the bomb. Hawkins the bottle and the needle.

He drove taxi in Ottawa for almost forty years before his death in 2016, enjoying something of a renaissance in his final decade. A book of his selected poems was published in 2005, and was followed three years later by the release of the double album *Dancing Alone: Songs of Bill Hawkins*. Two collections of his older poems appeared in 2010. His complete works were published in a single volume in 2014, a year after VERSeOttawa named Hawkins their first Hall of Honour inductee.

Despite the hometown love, Hawkins never quite hit outside of Ottawa. But if he, like Mo, represents one of Churchill's unacknowledged taxi-driving artists, cabbie-turned-novelist Rawi Hage stands as the exception. The world has certainly recognized Rawi's artistry, and he now resides atop Canada's literary pantheon. Which is a good thing, because Rawi was a terrible taxi driver.

"I had no sense of direction," Rawi told me when we met in a Montreal coffee shop that wasn't a Tim Hortons. Rawi drove a Montreal cab in the early 2000s—around the same time, and on the same streets, as his fellow Beiruti Hassan Kattoua. This was just before GPS-enabled smart phones, when cabbies were still expected to know where they were going. Rawi rarely did. Instead of confessing his ineptitude to his fares, though, Rawi would ask them which route they preferred and prayed they gave detailed directions. The strategy often failed. "At some point you have to acknowledge that you have no clue," Rawi said. He had poor night vision, too, but could not afford eyeglasses. "I couldn't read the street signs and I couldn't see the house numbers." He had to pay for the damage caused by two fender-benders due to his lousy eyesight. Some clients showed compassion for Rawi's deficiencies. Most did not.

Rawi wouldn't charge the riders he frustrated. Nor would he take money from clients he sensed were struggling financially. He waived the fare for mothers with babies in poor neighbourhoods, for example. "And I would never take money from Indigenous people," Rawi said. He shrugged when I asked why. "It was for all the good reasons. It was my private thing." These clients were always grateful for the free rides, but Rawi's benevolence further cut into his earnings. "Between this and my dysfunctionality as a driver, I didn't make any money."

Rawi was a better soccer player than a taxi driver. Growing up in Beirut, he was the fastest winger on his soccer team. Lebanon's national Junior B team drafted him when he was eleven years old, but Rawi never ended up playing for his country. "The war broke out, and everything went to hell." The conflict drew in soldiers from Syria, Egypt, Saudi Arabia, and Israel. "The whole region made Beirut a soccer stadium for all their conflicts," Rawi said. Like Hassan, most of his childhood he spent amid smoke, gunfire, and blood. He recalls cowering as bombs fell on the Christian enclave in East Beirut where his family lived.

The neighbourhood is gone now, levelled after 2,750 tonnes of ammonium nitrate exploded in Beirut's port in August 2020. After the blast, Rawi wrote a sad and scathing column for the *Globe and Mail*. "I am writing this with the knowledge that my childhood home is destroyed," it began. He recalled his youth living through war, and witnessing the massacres, death, and bombings the nation suffered through. In the end, Rawi writes:

> My brother sent me a video of our devastated home. He was silent; there was nothing to say. It seems that when the tragedy is omnipresent and touches everyone, even to breathe, or to complain, is a shameful indulgence. The only noise I heard, as I was attentively listening 9,600 kilometres away, was the inevitable, menacing crackling sound of broken glass, forced upon a shattered nation and its burned homes.

During the civil war, without soccer to occupy him and power cuts keeping the family television off, Rawi started taking photos. He and his cousin shared a camera and became obsessed with photographing falling bombs. "We wanted to see one in the air. To see how it is before it falls," Rawi said. "Because once it falls, it explodes. And you don't see it." Rawi and his cousin never managed to capture a bomb in mid-plummet. "But we almost managed to kill ourselves."

I asked what brought him to Canada. "It's all on Googles, man," he said, annoyed at the question. Rawi clearly didn't want to chat. We'd met briefly years earlier in the hospitality suite at a literary festival, and I suspect he only agreed to talk to me out of professional courtesy. I'd only spend an hour with Rawi, less than with any of the other cabbies, and he bolted out of the café as soon as I clicked my recorder off. I found it ironic that the only professional storyteller I'd sat with was the least willing to tell me his own story. Nevertheless, I was grateful for the time he granted me.

The chaos and thuggery of war eventually chased Rawi out of Lebanon in 1984, when he was nineteen years old. He moved to New York on a visitor's visa, working lousy jobs in tough neighbourhoods for eight years. He waited tables, moved boxes in a warehouse, sold knickknacks, and, for a couple of years, drove a taxi. He also worked as a photographer's assistant, his childhood fascination with photography meshing with his new darkroom skills and affection for solitude. Rawi once told an interviewer: "The most magical thing was when I saw the image surface in the fix. My duties were to prepare chemicals and clean the dark room afterward. I loved the idea of being in the dark alone."

Once his visa expired, Rawi continued to live in the US illegally before applying for refugee status in Canada in 1991. His French-language skills landed him in Montreal—in the winter, of course. He studied photography at Dawson College and Concordia University, graduating with a BFA in 1998. He proved a talented art photographer—his photos still hang on the walls of the Canadian Museum of History and the Musée de la civilisation à Québec—but he couldn't find steady photography work.

"The art scene was much more complex than I thought," Rawi said. "These art schools don't tell you that once you graduate, you're gonna be fucked." Rawi's shyness didn't help, either. "I'm an introvert. I was terrible at communicating with people and I wasn't good at the business side." He landed a few gigs shooting weddings, but the gown-and-tux kitsch offended his artist's aesthetic.

Rawi drifted for a while before enrolling in an MFA program. The decision was strategic. He knew with a post-graduate degree he could find work teaching art somewhere. "Like in a high school or wherever," he said. Rawi needed a job that would allow him to attend his classes during the day, so he applied for a taxi license and attended a two-month training program where he learned about traffic laws, city landmarks, professional courtesy, and other such practicalities. Rawi enjoyed the conversations he had with his fellow trainees. Everyone came from somewhere else. The men shared food and cigarettes during class breaks and tried to one-up each other with stories of struggles endured in their respective homelands. "We compared stuff like that and complained about totalitarian regimes. It was fun."

After graduating from "taxi school," Rawi reached out to his friend Mohammed Solari, an Iranian exile who'd attended the same Dawson photography program and who was also driving cab. Solari helped Rawi get a taxi and introduced him to his cabbie colleagues. Solari worked at a taxi company called Atlas, owned by an Iranian exile. Atlas employed several Iranian drivers who, like Solari, fled Iran after the 1979 Islamic Revolution. "They were all ex-communists who started the revolution," Rawi said. "They all knew each other, and some were very mad at Khomeini." When they wanted to insult each other, they'd call each other Arabs—often in front of Rawi. The slurs never bothered him. He enjoyed the camaraderie.

Despite his poor sense of direction and his weak night vision, Rawi soon came to know the sorts of things that cabbies know.

"There are rules that you learn, either by somebody warning you or you learn the hard way." He learned that if a lone woman with a large bag gets into the front seat of a cab at night, for example, she wants to pay her fare with oral sex. "And that's trouble, because it means she doesn't have any money," Rawi said. He learned to identify, and avoid, drunk passengers who might throw up in the back seat, resulting in a seventy-dollar cleaning bill and a persistent stench. Back-seat blowjobs meant another potential clean-up. Rawi learned that fellatio-inclined couples will wait until they reach a highway before starting, knowing the driver cannot pull over and kick them out. All he can do is keep quiet, and pray they don't make a mess.

Paternalistic and condescending remarks from his wealthy passengers always annoyed Rawi. He hated it when they romanticized his profession with classist comments like "You must have lots of stories." But Rawi conceded that drivers all learn to exploit class differences for business. "We are opportunistic, too," Rawi said. Drivers know the strip clubs frequented by middle-class suburbanites and will circle them after last call to pick up lucrative fares to distant neighbourhoods. Drivers also patrol Montreal's poor neighbourhoods at the end of the month, when residents receive their social-assistance cheques. "They want to go downtown. They want to go drinking. They will leave a big tip," Rawi said. "We used to call it 'the revenge of the poor.'"

Montreal's cabbies have a reputation for rudeness. "We're not polite people," Rawi conceded. In 2018, taxi passengers filed 1,187 complaints with Montreal's taxi bureau, most about drivers' lack of courtesy and unsafe driving. Another Montreal cabbie, who refused to be named, told me his boorishness towards passengers is a kind of bully posturing—pre-emptive self-defense against potential danger, especially late at night. Mean people don't appear vulnerable, he reasoned, and neither do crazy people. If he has a carload of stoned passengers at three in the morning, he'll blast through red lights at 100 kilometres per hour just to convince them he's too unhinged to mess with.

Rawi sees the famed insolence of Montreal's taxi drivers as an expression of their conflict-born toughness. "Most of these guys come from the street. From wars," Rawi said. "We come from places where we learned how to fight." Rawi kept a sharpened screwdriver next to him as he drove, but he never had to use it. "And I never wanted to," he said. Cabbies know every fare entails a real possibility of danger, and this sparked a strange neurosis in Rawi. "You're looking out at the world but talking into this small mirror to somebody behind you who could assassinate you, basically. And you can't do anything about it."

Much of Rawi's story reminded me of Mo Jalil's. As boys, Rawi and Mo both obsessed over the bombs that fell on their cities. They each left their war-ravaged homes and studied art in Canada, and both started driving cab after becoming frustrated by the art scene. And yet unlike with the other cabbies I met, the most compelling thing about Rawi wasn't the stories he told about his life before the taxi business. It was the way he wrote himself out of that business.

Just before he started driving cab, Rawi participated in a photography exhibition by Arab-Canadian artists. The exhibition's curator, Dr Aïda Kaouk, sent Rawi across Canada to take portraits of the artists involved in the show. Dr Kaouk asked Rawi to keep a log of his travels, but Rawi, recoiling at the bland bureaucracy of the assignment, submitted fictional short stories instead. Dr Kaouk loved them. When she next saw him, she held Rawi's hand and praised his talent as a writer.

Encouraged by Dr Kaouk, Rawi wrote short stories in the sparse hours between his MFA classes and taxi-driving shifts. One story included a scene from his boyhood, when he was trying to photograph falling bombs: "The images of falling bombs never revealed anything. After we sent them off to get developed, all we had were photographs of blue skies, a few clouds, roads and the tops of buildings." Rawi sent off a few stories for publication in literary journals and eventually received a $10,000 grant from the Quebec Arts Council to produce a collection. The funding was well-timed: Rawi was living in poverty and feeling the crush of his student loans. Though the collection was never completed, Rawi expanded one story into a novel, *De Niro's Game*, that his friend and mentor John Asfour, a Beirut-born poet who was blinded by an exploding grenade during the Lebanon Civil War, urged him to send to publishers. House of Anansi Press rescued the manuscript from its slush pile and published *De Niro's Game* in 2006.

When the novel was first released, Rawi kept a stack of copies in his taxi and tried to sell them to his passengers. If Rawi was a poor driver, he was an even worse salesman. The few clients who showed any interest in the book flung it into the front seat when they found out Rawi wanted twenty dollars for it. He sold only one copy this way. Rawi figures the man who bought the book didn't believe he actually wrote it.

Six months passed before the Canadian literary scene noticed *De Niro's Game*. The book won two Quebec Writer's Federation awards, including the Hugh MacLennan Prize for Fiction, and was shortlisted for both a Governor General's Award and for the Giller Prize. Rawi's publisher bought him a tuxedo to wear at the Giller gala since he couldn't afford one himself. The book's critical and commercial success didn't immediately make Rawi wealthy, however. Publishers issue royalty payments only once or twice a year, so even bestselling authors wait many months for their cheques to come in. "People thought I was a millionaire," Rawi said. "I was in a very precarious position. I didn't have the money, but I couldn't go back to the taxi full time because I was touring with the book. I was still poor until I won the IMPAC."

The IMPAC Dublin Literary Award, which Rawi received in 2018, was worth 100,000 euros. In his acceptance speech, Rawi Hage extended gratitude to his father, "who always surrounded me and my brothers with books and stories of travels and wonder." He also thanked his mother "who hid me under the dining room table under the falling bombs, and whose farewell tears on the day of my leaving my native Lebanon are printed in my memory." He thanked his publisher, his editor, his friends and colleagues. And then he thanked his old cabbie friend Mohammed Solari. "He kept me alert and awake during those long taxi-driving nights," Rawi said.

Winning the IMPAC eased Rawi's financial anxieties enough that he finally quit driving cab. But though the prize also secured Rawi's place in the upper reaches of Canada's literary world, he still retained his taxi license for another two years. He felt an emotional attachment to the taxi business, but the decision to keep renewing his licence was mostly born of pragmatism. "It was a security thing," Rawi said. "I didn't know what was going to happen. Everyone told me you might have one successful book, but that doesn't mean it is going to secure you for life." Book sales and publisher's advances had been shrinking, even for authors with glittering CVs. Few authors would fault Rawi for treating his taxi like a life raft. Rawi never ended up driving cab again, though, and eventually allowed his licence to expire.

Rawi's second novel, *Cockroach*, earned him another Giller nomination. (He could afford his own tuxedo by then.) For his third, *Carnival*, Rawi broke the promise he'd made to himself never to write about driving taxi. He'd long considered the topic a cliché until the series of late-night conversations he had with author Jaspreet Singh, who wrote his own novels in the same Tim Hortons Rawi used for bathroom breaks during his cab-driving shifts. Jaspreet saw the literary potential in Rawi's cab. Eventually Rawi did, too. When *Carnival* was published, he told the *National Post* that driving a taxi provided him with a "wealth of little encounters" that he could develop into stories. "A taxi could become kind of a chamber for intimacies, lies, tension," Rawi said. "There's this confinement of many emotions and lives."

Carnival follows the life of a taxi driver, born into the circus, named Fly. According to Fly, and to Rawi himself, there are two types of taxi drivers: spiders and flies. Spiders wait at taxi stands for their dispatcher to assign them fares, while flies circle the city streets looking for passengers. Flies are in perpetual motion. As a cabbie, Rawi was always a fly. "I used to get very bored at the taxi stand," Rawi said. "I just wanted to drive. I liked picking up from the street because it was, for me, an adventure. There's an element of danger."

Rawi admires the type of writer who shares his cabbie affection for both risk and autonomy. "I can't deal with happy writers or safe writers," Rawi told the *Globe and Mail*. He prefers writers who, like taxi drivers, occupy society's margins and revel in the kind of solitude born of being an outsider. For this reason, he'd much rather spend time with his former cabbie friends than hobnob with Canada's literati. "They are better storytellers," he said. I couldn't agree more.

Whether he likes it or not, Rawi's four acclaimed novels—2018's *Beirut Hellfire Society* scored another Giller nod—have earned him an honoured place among the literati. In 2019, The Writer's Trust awarded Rawi the $25,000 Engel Findley Award, which goes to a mid-career author "in recognition of a remarkable body of work, and in anticipation of future contributions to Canadian literature." His next contribution will be the book of short stories he began back when he first started driving cab in Montreal.

Rawi once remarked to an interviewer that his success as an author had earned him the label "the immigrant who made it." The comment amused Rawi, but the more I thought about it the more it troubled me. The label implies Rawi somehow rose above his assigned station as a newcomer. As a brown man from elsewhere, his is considered an *over*achievement, one that earns him condescending, and ironic, pats on the head from journalists who've failed to reach the same career heights themselves. I was also struck by the comment's odd singularity. Rawi wasn't seen as *an* immigrant who'd made it, but *the* immigrant—as if Canada's literary scene only had space for one such writer at a time.

But I was most bothered by the implication that an immigrant succeeds only once he stops doing the sorts of jobs immigrants do. Immigrants drive cabs. They deliver pizza. They pour coffee at Tim Hortons, or concrete at building sites like my grandfather did when he arrived from Italy in the 1950s. They certainly don't write bestselling novels. But if they do, then they've made it. We define immigrant success as the ascension out of the brown-collar ghetto of the taxi industry and into white-coloured space.

What of the cabbies who never stop driving? I thought about Jass and Amrit, who transformed mileage into a paid-off mortgage. I thought of Kareem and Michael, who fled African wars to Canada, where hours driving cab allowed their families to live safely and thrive. Maybe these cabbies will never need a tuxedo, but they'll still buy a sharp new suit for their son's or daughter's wedding. And pay for the reception, besides. Society at large won't grant these drivers any prizes, ovations, or gala invitations. I'm certain they don't care either way. But haven't they made it, too?

Twelve

WHEREFORE ART THOU, JENS ANDERSEN?

A 1979 EPISODE OF THE SITCOM *TAXI* FOCUSED ON THE flailing acting career of cabbie Bobby Wheeler, played by Jeff Conaway. A disillusioned Bobby quits acting after another wannabe actor, Steve, lands the lead in an off-Broadway revival of *Romeo and Juliet* with his first New York audition. Near the end of the episode, Bobby agrees to help Steve rehearse a scene between Romeo and Paris in the Sunshine Taxi garage. Sour at first, Bobby mumbles his lines through a mouthful of chocolate bar, but he quickly becomes absorbed in the text. Bobby's emotional performance stuns his coworkers. After a mimed sword-fight leaves Bobby's Paris stage-dying on the garage floor and gasping his last words, "If thou be merciful, open the tomb, lay me with Juliet," the assembled cabbies and mechanics applaud. So does the studio audience. In the end, Bobby decides to keep pursuing his acting career.

The episode is a remarkable bit of television. Two men performing Shakespeare in the oily confines of a taxi garage smacks of the absurd, but the scene-within-the-scene isn't played for laughs. The actors, and the actors portraying the actors, seem serious. Director James Burrows elevates the episode above typical sitcom silliness into something sophisticated and artful—Bobby yearns to elevate himself from hack driver to respected New York actor just as Rawi ascended into the upper atmosphere of CanLit.

But Rawi wasn't the first taxi driver I thought of when I watched Bobby and Steve's Shakespearean *pas de deux*. One of the unexpected consequences of my year among the cabbies is that I will forever associate William Shakespeare—and Bob Dylan, as it turns out—with Edmonton cabbie Jens Andersen.

Like nearly all the cabbies I met, Jens was born elsewhere. Jens' parents brought him to Canada from Denmark when he was two years old. "I wasn't an immigrant," he told me. "I was luggage."

Jens wanted to meet in the English and Film Studies Department at the University of Alberta, so we sat on a pair of musty couches in the hallway outside a student resource room and department administration offices. "This is where it all started," Jens told me as soon as we sat down. It all ended here, too. Several times, in fact. Jens' university career was defined by decades of stutters and stops. He enrolled in political science and sociology in 1971, but flunked out of his freshman year. Next, Jens tried a journalism program at Grant MacEwan College. He wouldn't finish this either, dropping out after a year and a half.

Though he failed as a journalism student, Jens still followed the advice of a favourite professor who told him that in order to become a good journalist he should get a real-world job like serving or bartending. Or driving cab. "Being a cabbie is a perfect antidote for all the baloney theories stuffed into students in the classroom," Jens would later write. "I was acutely conscious of my own sheltered booshwah upbringing and was determined to overcome it."

Jens didn't start driving taxi right away, though. First he travelled to Hay River, Northwest Territories, where he toiled as a general-assignment reporter for a regional newspaper. When the paper folded, Jens returned to Edmonton and delivered mail for Canada Post for two years. "I should've stayed in that job," Jens told me. "I would be retiring right now with a great pension." Instead, Jens quit carrying mail in 1978 and enrolled again at the U of A, this time in biology. He started driving cab on the weekends and during his summer vacations. Jens and a friend named Teddy shared a taxi. Just like Peter and his buddy Bob in Mississauga, Jens would drive twelve-hour night shifts before delivering the cab to Teddy, who drove during the day.

Biology didn't suit Jens. He barely attended classes and dropped out of the program in 1984 without earning his degree. But this second stint at the U of A proved productive for Jens in terms of his journalism, criticism, and exposure to the culture of the time. He started writing for *The Gateway*, U of A's student paper. He penned book reviews before landing the role of arts editor. "I was drifting towards the arts though I was not an artsy person," Jens said. Eventually, he became *The Gateway*'s managing editor.

During his time at the *The Gateway*, Jens wrote hundreds of reviews and editorials, many in a column called "The Chopping Block." I found an online archive of *Gateway* stories and spent the better part of a week submerged in Jens Andersen's university oeuvre. Jens was a deliciously pompous writer. He relished giving bad reviews and countering the prevailing wisdom of the day and never missed an opportunity to wax intellectual. He charmed me. I envied him. I wish I had the brio to write like a young Jens Andersen.

Jens begins a review of the Gregory Bateson book *Mind and Nature*, for example, by referring to glowing reviews by the *New York Times*, *Los Angeles Times*, and the *Washington Post* before writing "In all this there is a lesson, for *Mind and Nature* is trash, a rambling garble of slapdash theories." He declares the book "sloppy flapdoodle." Sometimes, Jens' writing revealed a sort of counter-culture genius. In 1981, he took five photos of artworks from the Edmonton Art Gallery's magazine—among them images of a wooden bicycle chained to a parking meter, wine glasses, and a doughnut on a plate—and reprinted them in *The Gateway* along with a photo of a fluorescent light fixture that had been partially melted during a fire in the Students' Union Building. He invited readers to "Spot the Fraud" and guess which of the six photos wasn't actually a work of art. Jens was characteristically harsh in the editorial that followed. Only the wooden bicycle showed any sign of effort, he argued, but even it was a mere curiosity. "The ultimate question the sculpture asks," Jens writes, "is why any human with a limited time on this sorry world would waste their precious time in such a manner."

I was fond of Jens' four-column editorial defending his use of the Latin "sic," but my favourite of his *Gateway* pieces came from an unlikely assignment to a Hollywood movie press junket in 1982. The thought of a cab-driving Edmontonian undergrad travelling to Beverly Hills, checking into the famed Beverly Wilshire Hotel, then attending the premieres of *Quest for Fire*, *Porky's*, and *Making Love* made me giddy. Jens devotes as much of his Hollywood dispatch describing the junket itself as he does to the movies he was tasked with reviewing. He devotes two full paragraphs to enumerating the amenities of his posh hotel room, remarking on the three telephones, the two soap boxes, and "enough towels to make a window escape from the fifth floor." The luxury got to Jens' head. "I am almost beginning to believe I am a person of consequence," he wrote.

On his second day in Hollywood, Jens gathered with his fellow delegates for hors d'oeuvres but no alcohol. "The legal age in California is 21," Jens writes, "and since our contingent has some underage people in it we must all suffer Coke and 7-Up." Then he went off to the movies. Jens showed some minor affection for the "low grade buffoonery" of teen sex comedy *Porky's*, and appreciated the craft in *Making Love*, but heaped his trademark scorn on the caveman epic *Quest for Fire*. His list of the film's flaws included its portrayal of vegetarian mammoths as oddly ferocious and the curious detail that "actress Rae Dawn Chong almost wears no clothes when everyone in her tribe— even children—does so." At a Q&A following the screening, Jens asked director Jean-Jacques Annaud about his depiction of prehistoric sexuality, which Jens considered "a central point in a film where primitive man evolves in the space of a week from crude dog-style humping to schmaltzy Hollywood-style romantic foreplay." Jens doesn't reveal Arnaud's response to his critique, only that the director "held his ground."

During a post-breakfast press conference on the junket's last day, Twentieth Century-Fox programmers plugged some of their current television offerings. After a screening of a trailer for the series *The Fall Guy*, actress Heather Thomas fielded questions from the assembled delegates. According to Jens, Thomas did her best to portray herself as a serious artist in a serious role—not just "the cheesecake in the show," as he put it, whose wardrobe is limited to shorts and bikini tops. I suspect a paint-by-numbers cop drama like *The Fall Guy* would've bored Jens. I suspect, too, that his ears perked up when Thomas mentioned Nietzsche during the presser. Jens wouldn't have missed an opportunity to show off his erudition, at least not on the page. "I feel like asking Thomas what she thinks of Nietzsche's famous dictum, 'The weak and botched shall perish: first principle of our charity,' and how this saying might apply to the producers of the show," Jens wrote, "but once again my natural tact and diplomacy get the better of me and I remain silent."

Jens was being ironic, of course. His lack of tact and diplomacy constantly infuriated *Gateway* readers, who expressed their distaste in letters to the editor. "The reader is not interested in your sophomoric, masturbatory blather," claimed one. After Jens ended a commentary on a Mozart documentary with an eight-line quote, in untranslated German, from a letter Mozart sent his cousin, a perplexed reader requested Jens "drop down to the level of us mortals when he's trying to review something. This could have been a recipe for strudel, for all I know." One reader called for Jens to be strapped to an electric chair. Another invited him to hurl himself off Edmonton's High Level Bridge. I laughed out loud at a response to one of Jens' music reviews: "Frankly, I really couldn't give a shit how many old records you know by heart, Mr Andersen.... You reviewed 3 albums in 4 paragraphs, spending more time talking about your 'creeping arteriosclerosis' (to which I wish all success)." These crafted responses made me nostalgic for the days before social media and hair-triggered Twitter wars.

After dropping out of the U of A for the second time, Jens continued to drive cab. But he wasn't finished with higher education. In 1992, at the urging of his cabbie-partner Teddy, Jens enrolled for a third time at the U of A to pursue an education degree with a focus on English. Jens was in his early forties by then, and married with three children. He was nearly always the oldest person in each of his classes, but his work ethic hardly matched the stereotype of the overachieving mature student. "I burned out in the teaching practicums," Jens said. "I felt myself going under for the third time. I had to break it to my wife that I was going to bail again." Instead of dropping out, however, Jens transferred from education to the English department in the Faculty of Arts. "I am not a quitter," he told me, apparently without irony.

With English, Jens finally found a program that suited him. He attended classes and completed his assignments and read the books on his course lists. He even managed to crank out a few chapters of a Canadian taxi novel in two of his creative-writing classes. "It was kind of a vague project, sort of autobiographical and very much in abeyance at the moment," he told me. Jens showed a knack for writing literary essays. His paper on John Coulter's historical drama *Riel* won the McClelland and Stewart Essay Prize in Canadian Studies. The award inspired Jens to consider writing his own play about Louis Riel, so he registered for a course in historical drama.

Then Jens discovered Shakespeare, and everything changed. Jens had read a couple of Shakespearean tragedies in high school like everyone else, but the U of A drama course sparked an obsession with Shakespeare's historical plays. "Shakespeare is a very sneaky writer," Jens told me. "He puts things under the surface." Shakespeare's dialogue also reminded Jens of his own life as a cabbie. "Taxi driving keeps you grounded," he said. "It is very reality based. I found that in Shakespeare, too." Jens appreciated Shakespeare's ability to capture the lives and language of the Elizabethan working class: the porters, tavern-keepers, and highwaymen. "All the slang and low talk," Jens said. "Shakespeare seems like a down-to-earth guy."

Shakespeare's best work, according to Jens, is the underappreciated *Troilus and Cressida*. As soon as Jens mentioned the play, he launched into an hour-long explanation of the religious metaphors Shakespeare hid within the text. I've never read *Troilus and Cressida*, nor have I ever seen the play performed, so I spent the hour pretending I understood what Jens was talking about and marvelling at his near-breathless enthusiasm. Jens' zeal peaked as he told me how he'd solved one of the play's most enduring mysteries. He believes he's the first reader in the more than four-hundred-year life of the play to identify a nameless warrior in Act

V who appears wearing "goodly armour" and having a "putrefied core." "I found out who that figure in armour is," Jens told me.

Then, for the first time since his impromptu dissertation began, Jens paused. "I don't know if I should tell you," he said. Jens had solved a centuries-old mystery, after all. Why should he divulge his secret to me? In the end, Jens did tell me who the warrior is, but I won't pass it along. Fact is, I don't really care. Few do. Still, I had to admire Jens' fixation with a question almost nobody was asking about one of the Bard's least-read plays. Jens had stumbled upon a literary Holy Grail no one was looking for.

Jens hopes to publish a new edition of *Troilus and Cressida* that includes his own annotations and four introductory essays. He pitched the idea to the University of Alberta Press in 1998 while he was still a student. The editors passed. "They were very polite," Jens said. "They thought I was crazy." After finally graduating with his English degree in 2000, he pitched the book to Penguin Canada. They turned him down, too. Jens decided to self-publish the book instead, and placed an ad in *The Shakespeare Newsletter* in the hope of soliciting interest and funding. "It garnered absolutely zero response," Jens said. "Including from the *Newsletter*, who probably regarded me as some sort of freak suffering from frostbite of the brain."

Twenty years have passed, but Jens' dream of publishing the book endures. "I've been kicking the can down the road," Jens said. "I still want to do it. But Bob Dylan got in the way."

Jens had long been a casual fan of Dylan's music, but when he re-listened to 1975's *The Basement Tapes* in 2012, his world changed. It was a line from "Crash on the Levee" that first triggered Jens' attention. The song mentions a place called "William's Point," and Jens wondered if Dylan was referring to William Shakespeare. Jens listened closely to the rest of the song. Dylan also sings about a king and a queen, characters that seemed out of place in an American folk tune. And the line "If you go down in the flood / It's gonna be your own fault" reminded Jens of Ophelia's suicide by drowning. Jens started to wonder if "Crash on the Levee" might be written from Hamlet's point of view.

Jens' own intellectual levee burst. He started scouring through *The Basement Tapes* for other nods to Shakespeare. In "Odds and Ends" he found a line that echoed Ulysses' speech in *Troilus and Cressida*. "Tears of Rage" mentions a father and daughter that reminded Jens of *King Lear*. Now thoroughly fixated, Jens started to plug Dylan's lyrics into the Concordance of Shakespeare's Complete Works, an online database that allows researchers to chart the appearance of individual words in the Shakespeare canon. "I found that every song on *The Basement Tapes*, except maybe one, can be traced to a specific Shakespeare play," Jens said. He found this amateur literary sleuthing exhilarating. "It's just like detective books. When I was a kid, I read *Hardy Boys*. This is just like being a Hardy Boy." For Jens, his discovery of Falstaffian echoes in Dylan's "Million Dollar Bash" was akin to Frank and Joe Hardy uncovering the secret of Skull Mountain, say, or solving the mystery of the flickering torch.

I wondered, though, if Jens was sometimes stretching things a bit. Was the "big dumb blonde" in "Million Dollar Bash" *really* Venus from *Venus and Adonis*? Was Dylan's "The Mighty Quinn" *really* a pun of Richard III's promise to make Elizabeth a "high and mighty queen"? Even Jens admitted to a bit of confirmation bias. Still, he directed me to Bob Dylan's acceptance speech for the 2015 MusicCares Person of the Year Award. "These songs of mine," Dylan said, "I think of as mystery plays, the kind that Shakespeare saw when he was growing up. I think you could trace what I do back that far."

For Jens, this not only proved the connection between Dylan's lyrics and Shakespeare, but bound Dylan to Jens himself.

"This is me!" Jens said. "I am tracking back to those medieval plays, too." He joked that Dylan could've received the Nobel Prize for Literature just for figuring out *Troilus and Cressida* before he did. Eight years on and Jens continues to find clues and allusions and literary threads to pull. "An appalling amount of stuff remains to be sorted out," he told me. These are the things he thinks about between fares. "Dylan's songs are always weird, near-impenetrable and astonishing. Don't ever evolve into that mind-blown creature the Dylanologist, I warn thee!" I asked Jens how his family views his obsession. "It's just Dad being Dad," he said.

Jens yearns for a more receptive audience. In 2014, he wrote a six-thousand-word essay about Shakespearean allusions in *The Basement Tapes* under the smart title "The Shakespeare in Dylan's Basement," and posted an excerpt on his blog. "I held the rest back because no one cares," he said. Still, he sent the entire essay out to editors at twenty-three different newspapers. Only Lucinda Chodan, editor-in-chief of the *Montreal Gazette,* responded. Chodan knew Jens from the U of A. She was his news editor at *The Gateway* in 1979 and, according to Jens, used to drive him "to the brink of apoplexy with her insistence on proper spelling and grammar." Despite their history, and Jens' much-improved spelling and grammar, Chodan declined to publish his opus. Jens seemed neither surprised nor disappointed. If, when, and however his *Troilus and Cressida* edition gets published, he will include the Dylan essay as part of the introduction, "plus all the other stuff that leaked out the sides."

After our talk, Jens drove me from the university back to my hotel. He quit driving taxi in 2015 and started driving for Uber. I asked him why. "Curiosity was one of the reasons," he said. Later, thinking back on my time with the Taxi Sheriff in Montreal, I regretted not pressing Jens more about this. At the time, though, my brain was swirling with Shakespeare and Dylan, Hamlet and Ophelia, and the endless Richards and Henrys. To follow up such highfalutin ideas with the banal workings of the taxi industry felt akin to watching *Porky's* after a performance of *King Lear*. I felt satisfied just having spent a few hours with such an affable kook.

Only once my head stopped spinning did I realize that, for Jens, curiosity wasn't just "one of the reasons" he started driving for Uber. Curiosity was everything. Jens first started pushing cab to see the "real world" outside of "booshwah" academia, and he'd devoted much of his life to chasing theories about art and music and literature down deep intellectual rabbit holes. And his inquisitiveness is pure, lacking malice or any motive beyond knowledge. Jens' obsession with Shakespeare and Dylan will never bring him wealth or notoriety. He knows this, but he doesn't care. He remains indifferent to everyone's indifference, mine included.

Jens wants to know things. He wants to figure things out. More than anyone I've ever met, Jens is driven by curiosity. As a writer and traveller, I can't imagine a virtue greater than this.

Thirteen

DRIVING TAMMY MARIE

TAMMY MARIE STARTED HAVING SEX FOR MONEY WHEN she was twelve. Her boyfriend, a thirty-three-year-old cocaine dealer, acted as her first pimp. "He was the person that taught me nothing comes for free," she told me. One night, her boyfriend told Tammy she owed him for the clothes and alcohol he'd bought her. He demanded she have sex with six of his friends to pay off the debt. "I was having sex anyway," Tammy said. "Why not get paid for it?" Tammy chugged three beers for courage, then her boyfriend drove her to the house where his friends were waiting. She was finished in an hour. Each paid her forty dollars. "That was my initial worth, at twelve years old," Tammy said. "Forty dollars."

Tammy's career in the sex trade would last twelve years, during which time she had "interactions" with all manner of men. "Men with photos of their wives and kids on their key chains," Tammy said. "The corporate guys going to a business meeting who just need a blowjob before work. College kids. All walks of life." Tammy always felt the work empowered her; it took nearly twenty years until she came to terms with her exploitation as a youth at the hands of bad men. She'd been trafficked through private homes and the dark rooms at the back of gang-owned Vietnamese restaurants. "My vulnerabilities were taken advantage of," she said. "There were very few people within that bubble that didn't want something from me."

All except for taxi drivers. "I really believe there are angels on earth," Tammy told me. "For me, they have mostly come in the shape of a taxi driver."

The taxi industry has long overlapped with the sex trade. "The connection between the taxi-driver and the prostitute was notorious," cab-driving scholar Edmund Vaz wrote in 1955. According to Vaz, pre-Second World War cabbies in Montreal worked in conjunction with the city's brothels and earned a commission for each client they delivered to their doors. Sex work went underground after the war, and drivers would partner with one or more "call girls." "Because of the quasi 'underground' form that prostitution has taken in this city, it is functionally important that the prostitute work with the taxi-driver," Vaz wrote. "In this way the prostitute avails herself of one of the optimum advertising media which is tantamount to increased income." In Vaz's day, sex workers "advertised their commodity" by handing business cards to drivers at taxi stands, and cabbies in turn would pass along these phone numbers to sex-seeking passengers—known, in the parlance of the time, as "liners" or "flyers."

Driving such clients was a lucrative aspect of the taxi business in urban centres throughout the seventies and eighties. According to Peter McSherry in his book *Mean Streets: Confessions of a Nighttime Taxi Driver*, Toronto cabbies would average between six and seven sex worker fares per night during this period. McSherry recalls a house in Toronto's Annex where, during the mid-seventies, "taxis delivering and picking up 'tricks' were literally bumping into each other in the night." The business boomed further in 1978, after Canada's Supreme Court ruled that solicitation had to be "pressing or persistent" in order to be considered an offense. According to McSherry, this stricter definition of solicitation led to a wave of new sex workers on Toronto streets. "In the core area, all of the side streets were grossly infested with 'corner girls'—for whom there were not nearly enough corners," McSherry unkindly wrote.

These "halcyon days" lasted until the mid-1980s, when street-level prostitution slowly began to diminish in Toronto and elsewhere. Instead of soliciting clients outdoors, more and more sex workers advertised their services in the back pages of newspapers. Then the trade shifted online. These days, the primary point of contact between sex worker and client in most Canadian cities is the internet. In Calgary, for example, less than 20 percent of sexual services are sold on the street. Cabbies still ferry clients to the remaining strolls upon request, of course, though Jens Anderson told me such passengers are "generally of the one-shot, dude-passenger-is-drunk-and-wants-to-get-laid sort." Jens found such fares distasteful, but "johns seldom tell you at the outset of a trip what their intentions are, and in the middle of a trip it isn't easy to refuse cruising the stroll." For better or worse, such fares still belong to the taxi drivers. Since ride-share apps like Uber record each client's name and track his travel route, today's flyers prefer the old-school anonymity offered by traditional taxicabs.

Some taxi drivers solicit clients for sex workers, but such arrangements are relatively rare according to the drivers I spoke to. Hassan Kattoua has colleagues who earn good money acting as both pimp and driver. "But those are very, very few in Montreal," Hassan said. "Most cabbies are respectful and family-oriented.

And if the morals, the customs and religious principles did not prevent them from doing so, the fear of losing their precious permit did." Jens Anderson never pimped for sex workers either, though he isn't sure why. "The pairing seems natural enough, with economic benefits on both sides," he said. "Maybe I just wasn't desperate or opportunistic enough, or the business seemed nasty, or I was just paranoid or cowardly about it."

More commonly, sex workers enter long-term partnerships with cabbies to ferry them to and from their appointments. Having a trustworthy driver-at-the-ready is a professional boon, especially for those who book out-call services. I was curious if the business arrangements between sex workers and their regular cabbies ever evolved into personal relationships. Both groups, after all, navigate the borderland between the lawful and the illicit, and often occupy the same late-night environs. I wanted to know if their life stories ever overlapped. Jens told me he entered into an agreement with an Edmonton "call girl" in 2005 who booked him and his taxi partner Teddy as her regular drivers. The arrangement lasted around three years, but Jens never learned much about her. "We were both a bit cool and guarded, I suppose," Jens said. Though the woman always tipped generously, Jens wasn't fond of such private booking arrangements, called "personals" in taxi lingo. "They tend to be logistical headaches," Jens said.

Jens opted not to partner with another sex worker he met years later, "a chirpy, cheerful young prostitute," who got into his cab. "After a few straightforward indicators of her profession, she came straight to the point: 'Yeah I'm just in from Vancouver and I don't have a taxi driver yet.'" Jens figured the woman wanted him to offer his services. "But I just maintained an awkward pause, perhaps the awkwardest in all my decades of driving."

In some Canadian cities, local law enforcement tries to make use of these professional agreements between cabbies and sex workers for their investigations. The Calgary Police Service's Counter Exploitation Unit encourages active sex workers to join a safety registry that includes information about any of the worker's associates, including regular cabbies. If a worker goes missing, or worse, the registry would enable police to find the worker's last driver to determine, say, the last address she was brought to. Not all sex workers want to join the registry, of course, or cooperate with law enforcement at all.

I couldn't find any drivers whose lives meaningfully intersected with the sex workers they served—or at least I couldn't find any willing to divulge such stories—so I sought out sex workers instead. I felt grateful when a friend introduced me to Tammy. We met at a Starbucks attached to an Indigo bookstore on a Monday afternoon, a rather bland locale considering the conversation we were about to have.

By the time Tammy started selling sex on the street in the mid-90s, much of the business had already moved indoors. The remaining street-level workers—along with their clients, nighttime cabbies, and dope pushers—formed a nocturnal ecosystem Tammy said she never quite fit into. "A lot of people told me I never belonged there, like I stuck out like a sore thumb," Tammy said. "I was always a little bit kinder and nicer and warmer and more open." Unlike many other women working Calgary's downtown stroll, Tammy chatted with the drivers she flagged down. And while her fellow "working girls" had a reputation for ditching out on their cab fares, Tammy always offered to pay in advance. "I'm not going to take advantage of someone in the middle of the night as they're doing their job trying to take care of their family," Tammy said. "And they're not going to take advantage of me while I'm dope-sick, or searching for a trick, or going from place A to place B."

Taxis were Tammy's sanctuaries, her life rafts, and her getaway cars. She knew which drivers would allow her to do drugs in the backseat, "and if I ever was in trouble, I could always flag down a cabbie and they would stop," Tammy said. "I would be able to get in, and if I was scared or was in a harmful situation, they would get me out of there." Once, she got into a fight with a man who then dragged her out of his car and smashed her head against the curb. A taxi driver witnessed the assault and asked Tammy where he could take her. Tammy told him she didn't have any money. The cabbie didn't want any. He just wanted to drive her wherever she needed to go.

Sam was Tammy's most memorable driver. They met when Tammy was sixteen years old after she flagged down his taxi and asked to sit in the front seat. (Riding in the back makes Tammy car sick.) Sam was an experienced late-night driver and could tell Tammy was a sex worker. "The cabbies always know," she said. Sam found Tammy easygoing and fun, more so than the other sex workers he'd driven. After their first ride together, Sam told Tammy to give his cab number to his company's dispatch the next time she needed a taxi. He soon became Tammy's regular driver, and their relationship lasted four years. Sam, who came from Lebanon, had a wife from an arranged marriage and children. This is all Tammy would ever learn about his personal life. She never knew his last name.

Sam saw Tammy about once every two months, when she would call for a ride to a date's house, or to the downtown stroll. "I could also call him at four in the morning if I was stuck in the middle of nowhere. He would come and pick me up," Tammy said. And he would rescue her when a date went sour. "I would say 'Sam, I am in a bad spot. I need to get out of here.' And he would come." For a "working girl" like Tammy, a trustworthy and reliable driver is gold. Often, Sam wouldn't charge Tammy for the rides. Other times, when Tammy was particularly low on money, she'd reach out to Sam to see if he wanted services. "If I needed a quick forty bucks, I could call Sam," Tammy said.

Sometimes he'd be in the mood. Sometimes not. Their relationship lacked all pretense and complication. Each understood their role in the other's life. "I really enjoyed knowing where I stood and what was expected of me," Tammy said. "I knew who I was in his world, and I knew that he valued me enough as a human being that he wasn't going to harm me."

"How old was Sam?" I asked Tammy.

"Probably in his forties," she said.

"And you were in your teens?"

"Yes, I was in my teens," then she paused. She could tell what I was thinking. "For myself, I don't look at that as an exploitative situation," she said.

Her comment jarred me. Sam, after all, was paying for sex with a minor. I had difficulty seeing him as anything other than a predator. Then again, I've never been in Tammy's world. "As far as I go in the lifestyle, and my understanding of what it means to be taken advantage of, I have a different point of reference," Tammy said. The respectful exchange of money and services between Sam and Tammy hardly ranks as exploitation in comparison to the violence and abuse sex workers often endure.

The law disagrees, of course. At the very least, Sam was guilty of obtaining sexual services for consideration from a person under eighteen years, but he also could have been charged with sexual assault. Still, Tammy considers Sam her protector and believes he genuinely cared about her. He tried, for instance, to coax Tammy off drugs and sex work and often reminded her that her mother worried about her. Tammy was unaccustomed to such concern. "It is startling that somebody notices, really," she said. Being a sex worker often means being invisible to society, which is something I'd also heard cabbies say about themselves. "I stood there on a street corner and took up some physical space, but as far as society goes, I didn't exist. I wasn't a human being." People refused to give Tammy the time, or to look her in the eye.

Sam and other cabbies—especially the Muslim drivers—treated Tammy like she had value. "They reminded me I am somebody's daughter. There are people in the world that know nothing about me, who don't have any ulterior motive, and just want me to know that I am worth life." She was also quick to point out that she always felt safer with a cabbie than a cop. "I was never sexually assaulted by cab drivers," she said. "But I was sexually assaulted by police officers. And I was a minor at the time."

Though she stops short of calling Sam a father figure, Tammy acknowledges that he was the only male influence in her life after her grandfather died when she was eight years old. Sam occupied a space in Tammy's psyche that was otherwise empty. "He became a champion and a protector and a male role model that loved and cared about me, and genuinely wanted good things to happen for me."

Their relationship changed in the mid-1990s, when Tammy went from smoking cocaine to shooting it into her veins. "Once I became an IV drug user, I became a different person," Tammy said. "Any goodness in me was taken by the dope." Intravenous drug users occupy the lowest stratum of street life, Tammy told me. "You're almost fine if you are smoking crack, but the minute you stick a needle in your arm you are a classless, dirty junkie." Tammy's long-repressed self-hatred finally manifested in her drug use. "It became apparent to everybody that I just didn't care about myself," Tammy said. "I was sick and I was done and I was hopeless."

Sam cared too much about Tammy to abet her annihilation. "If this is what you are going to choose, don't call me anymore," he told her one night. "I can't watch it. I won't watch it." But when Sam urged Tammy to find help, Tammy urged Sam to go fuck himself. Then she bounded out of his taxi and into the street.

The darkness brought on by the drugs chipped away at Tammy for four months. She started to fray, performing services for clients she'd vowed never to do. She grew increasingly violent and once tried to stab her drug dealer. She remembers telling a taxi driver she was diabetic and shooting up three times during a twenty-minute cab ride. Tammy doesn't know if the driver believed she had diabetes, or if he'd cared either way, but when he dropped her off he said "Well, you sure are sick. I hope you get better."

Sam was on Tammy's mind when she finally checked herself into the Fresh Start Recovery Centre. She thought of Sam again during one of her workshops. "A lady was talking about how we walk through life with a basket on our back and people plant seeds in this basket," Tammy said. "We never know when they're going to take root, but they eventually do. So Sam was one of the people who planted a seed in my basket." Sam came to mind yet again, three weeks into treatment, when the centre granted Tammy her first weekend pass. Fresh Start was located in Calgary's distant south, and Tammy had no way to get home. Normally, she'd hitch a ride, but her addiction counsellors warned her against partaking in risky past behaviours.

So Tammy called Sam.

"I'm in treatment," she told him.

"I don't believe you," he said.

"Well how about this? I'm at Fresh Start. I get a weekend pass. Can you come pick me up on Friday at 4:30?"

After a pause, Sam said "Fine. I'll be there."

Tammy knew Sam thought she was lying. Standing outside the centre when he arrived wouldn't be enough to convince him that she was actually receiving treatment. So Tammy told him to come inside the centre and have the front desk call her. The next Friday, Sam arrived at the centre on time and had Tammy paged, just as she'd asked. When he saw her come into the reception area, he started to cry. He lifted Tammy off her feet in a bear hug, but he was speechless. Finally, on the ride to Tammy's house,

Sam turned to her and said, "I've never seen you look like this. There's joy in your eyes."

Sam picked Tammy up from Fresh Start every Friday after that, and returned her every Monday. He gave her money for cigarettes, too. When Tammy reached her sixty-days-sober milestone, Sam thought they should celebrate. "I want to take you shopping," he said. "You've worked hard. You deserve something. What do you want?"

"I want shoes," Tammy said.

On their way back to the centre, Sam brought Tammy to the downtown Bay. "I chose a pair of god-awful moon-boot-looking sandals. They had six-inch wedge heels and Velcro straps. I just loved them." Tammy kept the boots for years, long after she stopped wearing them. But she could not keep clean. During her fifth month at Fresh Start she relapsed, and the centre asked her to leave. Tammy hitched a ride home. She felt too ashamed to call Sam. "There was no way that I was going to contact him," Tammy said. She never spoke to Sam again.

Tammy eventually got sober, and left the sex trade after almost twelve years. She was twenty-three years old. "I came out of the lifestyle with nothing," Tammy said. "I had an eight-year-old son and I had nothing else. I had to figure things out." Tammy went back to school. She earned a high-school diploma and a certificate in drafting. She bought a house, got married, and found work as a piping drafter, but the transition from sex work and active addiction to a square job proved challenging. "Once you see around the dark corners, you can't unsee what you've seen." She could relate to Calgary's panhandlers and homeless people far more than the privileged do-gooders she shared her drafting studio with. Her challenges worsened in 2014, when severe post-partum depression after the birth her second child, a baby girl, was compounded by traumatic flashbacks from her sex-worker past. "I just didn't fit into this life that I had built for myself," Tammy said. In October 2015, after eleven years of sobriety, she relapsed on crack cocaine.

Then she called a cab. Tammy needed a ride to an outpatient rehab centre in Ponoka, two hundred kilometres north of Calgary. The driver allowed her to drink and use drugs during the whole two-hour journey, for which she paid $480. When Tammy asked the driver about the camera mounted inside the taxi, an innovation since her sex-work days, the driver told her not to worry. He flipped the sun-visor down to block the camera and let Tammy use without being filmed.

The rehab didn't take. As a last resort, Tammy used all her savings to pay for treatment at the Thorpe Recovery Centre in Lloydminster. She drank vodka and smoked crack during the eight-hour bus ride to Lloydminster. Tammy flagged a taxi in front of the Greyhound station when she arrived. Her cabbie could tell Tammy was high, just like Sam always could.

"You new in town?" he asked her.

"Yes, I'm new," Tammy said. "I'm here for treatment."

"Thorpe?"

"Yeah."

"Figures. It is only for work or treatment that people ever come here."

"I have thirty-six hours before I check in," Tammy said. "I need a hotel."

"I know the perfect place," he said. "You can still smoke in the rooms."

The driver brought Tammy to the hotel and gave her his cell phone number in case she wanted anything else. Tammy called him later that night. She needed cigarettes, but was too high and too afraid to leave her room. She'd also run out of vodka, but the cabbie refused to bring her any. "I'm not going to help you kill yourself," he told her. "You're on this kick. That's fine. That's cool. I'll drive you wherever you want to go. But I'm not bringing you alcohol." He knocked on her door a half hour later with a pack of cigarettes, two lighters, and a bottle of orange juice. "In case you're thirsty," he said. "I want you to get some vitamin C."

Before the cabbie left, Tammy asked him for one more thing. "I have to get to Thorpe tomorrow," she said. "And I need to be there by four o'clock. Can you please come to my room and get me at three-thirty? I'm not going to be able to call you. I'm probably not even going to want to go. But please, will you come and get me?"

"Of course I will," he said. Then he left Tammy alone.

Tammy still needed vodka. She girded herself, left the hotel, and waved down a taxi. She jumped in the front seat, as was her habit, and asked for a ride to the nearest liquor store. This driver could tell Tammy was stoned, too, and could smell the last of the vodka on her breath. He turned to her and said "You are such a beautiful soul. You deserve to be so joyful. Why are you putting this poison into your body? Why do you do this to yourself?"

"Because I'm sick and it doesn't fucking matter anyways."

"Your life matters," he said. "Your life matters."

The driver brought Tammy to a liquor store then back to the hotel. After she paid him, he said "Wherever you go in life, I wish you the best and I wish you joy."

As promised, Tammy's previous cabbie knocked on her door at exactly three-thirty the following afternoon. Tammy was still stoned. And scared. And she hadn't finished her crack. She wasn't ready for Thorpe. While the cabbie stood and waited, Tammy called a friend in Calgary. "I don't know if I can do this. I don't know if I can go. I still have dope left."

"Flush it, Tammy," the friend said.

The driver watched as Tammy emptied the last of her crack into the hotel toilet. "You're amazing," he said, and he began to cry. "Let's go. Let's get into the cab." On the way to Thorpe, the cabbie confessed he was a severe alcoholic. He found Tammy's courage inspiring. The man carried Tammy's bags into the centre for her and wished her luck. Tammy believes she wouldn't have made it to treatment without his help. Like Sam, and the driver from the night before, Tammy would never see this cabbie again. He never told her his name.

Tammy got clean again, and stayed that way, but she's been undergoing trauma treatment for the last three years and has not returned to her drafting job. "It's been a hard struggle," Tammy said, "I got out of sex work, and now the healing matters. Along with that, taking little pieces of gold and the people I met along the way that had an impact on my life." Her Lloydminster cabbie was one of these people.

But no driver means as much to Tammy as Sam. She only saw him once again, years after their last trip to Fresh Start. "He was picking up a fare and I was walking by. I had to do a double-take. We just made eye contact as his fare was getting in. Then he drove off." I told Tammy that I found this sad, but Tammy shrugged off my desire for a Hollywood ending. "In my life, I found that people didn't stay," she said. "Or they stayed and then they would leave." Tammy still thinks of Sam often, though. She still hears his voice telling her that she's worth something. That she deserves happiness.

"He just wanted me to be okay," Tammy said. "And I am now."

Fourteen

THE LONG JOURNEY OF NATHAN PHELPS

GOD HATES FAGS. ACCORDING TO THE WESTBORO BAPTIST Church in Topeka, Kansas, God also hates America, Canada, and Islam. God hates transgenderism, "the most recent blitzkrieg of raw Satan-inspired rebellion." He hates Alicia Keys and Justin Timberlake ("The fags love him, and he them. His filth justifies their filth," says the WBC). But God hates fags most of all.

God also hates Nathan Phelps. At least that's what Nate thought on his eighteenth birthday in 1976, back when he still believed God existed. At midnight, the precise moment he legally became an adult and couldn't be dragged back, Nate stepped out the door of his family's Topeka compound and fled the Westboro Baptist Church. He loaded a few belongings into the old Rambler he'd bought secretly for $350 and drove away. "I left there believing, with the same certainty that the sun is going to rise in the east, that around the year 2000 Christ would come and I was going to hell," Nate said. "I knew I would suffer for an eternity."

Nate had suffered a lot already. He spent the first eighteen years of his life cowering under the tyranny of his father, Fred Phelps, the extremist Calvinist preacher who founded Westboro Baptist Church in 1955. The WBC's congregation consisted, then as now, almost entirely of the Phelps' extended family. Fred fathered thirteen children, so the pews were kept full. Each day, the family gathered in the chapel to hear the pastor give sermons filled with Old Testament fire. Fred Phelps' God was no loving shepherd. He was a vengeful and demanding lord.

So, too, was Phelps himself. The former Golden Gloves boxer ruled over his family with cruelty and never spared the rod. Phelps wrenched his wife's arm out of its socket for one transgression, and sheared her hair off for another. Nate remembers being bent over a church pew while his father punched and spat on him. He regularly beat Nate and his siblings with a pickaxe handle, and had leather straps custom-made for whippings.

I'd not speak to a taxi driver with a more complicated relationship to his family than Nate Phelps, and none who was as philosophical about his border crossings. I first met Nate in Calgary, shortly after his father's death in 2014. Knowing what I did about the elder Phelps, I wasn't sure if I should offer Nate my condolences. How do you grieve for a man like Fred Phelps? Nate told me he could only feel the most superficial sadness for his death. "Instead, I mourn the man he could have been," Nate said. Someone with Fred Phelps' obvious intelligence, sharp focus, and relentless drive might have achieved great things had he not devoted those talents to hate.

By all accounts, Fred Phelps was a brilliant lawyer, even though he popped enough amphetamines and barbiturates during law school to end up in the back of an ambulance. When US President Lyndon Johnson signed the Civil Rights Act into law in 1964, Fred saw an opportunity. He took on as many racial discrimination cases as he could, often ones that no other attorney would touch. Black clients would call Phelps first whenever they faced discrimination. The local branch of the NAACP even gave Phelps an award for his work, evidently unaware of his fondness for racial slurs in private conversation.

Phelps was no humanitarian. He was an entrepreneur, papering the courts with civil rights lawsuits. At one point, 80 percent of all the cases in the Shawnee County courts were his. Phelps didn't earn much money from individual cases, since settlements were usually small; instead, he won millions of dollars in verdicts cumulatively, over a very short amount of time. His enthusiasm inspired the Kansas court system to enact new regulations to rein in and discipline scattershot attorneys like Phelps. The State of Kansas disbarred Phelps in 1979 for misconduct in connection to a case against a court reporter who failed to deliver a court transcript to him on time. Ten years later, after nine judges accused him of misconduct, he agreed to stop practicing law in federal courts.

Nate recalled that his father did nothing in half measures. After seeing an ad for the Jack LaLanne exercise system on a Wheaties box, the elder Phelps put the whole family on a running program. Nate remembers their first run: "The old man goes out and gets all his running gear. He packs us all in the car and we go to the local high school. He gets halfway around the track and almost passes out." Despite its unpromising beginning, Phelps continued to impose his exercise regime for nearly a decade. The entire family, even Nate's youngest siblings, ran five to ten miles a day and competed in road races. "He had ten-year-old kids out running marathons," Nate said.

The Phelps family went on fanatical diets, too. Dinners often consisted of steamed cabbage, rose-hip and bonemeal tablets, and little piles of brewer's yeast. Phelps himself embarked on long, dangerous fasts. Nate remembers his father losing over one hundred pounds over the course of a fifty-day purge. "During that time, he told me he was literally communing with God. Getting messages," Nate said. "Even as a kid, I found it a little creepy the way he was talking." Phelps believed these extreme exercise and diet regimens would lead to literal immortality. He'd studied the stories of Elijah and Enoch—the only two figures in the Bible who didn't die. Fred believed he would be the third.

When Phelps died in 2014, "his death turned one of the church's primary beliefs on its ear," Nate said. Not only had the WBC's primary mythology been shattered, the church had also lost Fred's vicious energy and intelligence. Several of Nate's siblings inherited their father's vitriol. Few possessed his vision.

Nate inherited neither. He knew from an early age he could not be the son his father wanted him to be. "If you weren't aggressive like he was in challenging the 'evils' out there, then you would get beat for that," Nate said. "But I just couldn't do it. It wasn't in me to be that way." Nate grew up feeling humiliated by his own softness, by the absence of his father's pugilistic fury, and knew the beatings weren't going to stop. Nate also knew his lack of conviction meant he was not among God's chosen. Nate was going to hell anyway. He might as well get the hell out.

Nate spent his first night of freedom sleeping in a gas station restroom. Then he moved in with his older brother Mark, who had fled the church a few years earlier. Nate and Mark worked together in print shops in St. Louis and Kansas City before having a falling out. "I cut my ties with Mark in a destructive way," was all Nate said. Feeling isolated and alone in Kansas City, Nate made contact with his sisters Shirley and Maggie back in Topeka. They told him that their father had mellowed and wasn't violent anymore. They convinced Nate to return.

The reunion was short-lived. "Within a month I realized it was a mistake," Nate said. Fred Phelps expected his prodigal son to work for free in his brother's law office in return for room and board with the family. He also expected Nate to enroll in law school, an education the family would pay for. Law was the family business. Even though he'd been disbarred, eleven of Fred's thirteen children became attorneys. Nate wasn't interested. When he found work outside the family, they told him to leave. For the Phelps clan, Nate's independence was intolerable. This time Nate would not come back, and he would never see his father again.

Nate moved into an apartment above a Volkswagen repair shop with a couple of friends. "Our couch was a stack of Styrofoam covered by a blanket," Nate remembers. He worked at Wendy's, living off Frostys and whatever discards he could take from the kitchen. Nate and his roommates partied constantly. He spent his Wendy's money on beer and drugs. Weed helped Nate sleep, and he only dropped acid a few times, but he "really, really liked speed." Soon, though, Nate had had enough. He recalls sitting in his 1971 Javelin one night as a party raged in the upstairs apartment. "I was playing 'A Man I'll Never Be' by Boston over and over in the car, crying," he said. "That seems like the point where I realized I had to change directions."

He found another job as a live-in repairman in an apartment complex and started to pull away from the drugs and alcohol. Eventually Nate reconciled with Mark and moved to California to work with him in a print shop Mark had opened a month earlier. He started dating a single mother named Tammi, whom he married in 1986. Things were going well. But although he had every reason, finally, to be happy, Nate struggled to shake the feeling that he was condemned by God. He'd been raised to believe that questioning one's faith is a sinful act. "Every time you start engaging your analytical mind, there is a voice in your head that says the devil is working in you," he said. Nate grew suspicious of his own doubts. He feared something dark and insidious motivated his skepticism. "One of the ways you knew you weren't right with the Lord was if you started asking questions."

Nate sought professional help. He spent over a year with a counsellor who had a theology degree to deal "with the religious side of things." Then he began another round of counselling with a different therapist who diagnosed Nate with post-traumatic stress disorder. At the therapist's insistence, Nate spent two weeks in a California psych ward that purported to help his focus. "I came away from that basically thinking it was a scam," Nate said, though he accepts without question his PTSD diagnosis. To this day, Nate doesn't deal well with strong expressions of anger. He shakes in the presence of other people's rage, even if he is not the target. When he *is* the focus of someone's anger, Nate either shuts down or, on rare occasions, goes "ballistic." "Afterwards, I have a very strong guilty reaction because I hate being like my dad."

Nate's faith truly began to crack in the 1990s, after he became a father. Fred Phelps had taught Nate that children are a gift from God—a blessing that he, a man destined for hell, surely didn't deserve. He suspected God planned to kill his child as punishment. It didn't happen. In fact, he and Tammi had two more children. The year 2000 came and went without the promised apocalypse. Being stood up by the Messiah further weakened Nate's faith. A year later, the attacks of September 11 led to another shift in Nate's philosophy as he watched the towers smoulder and fall on television with Tammi's mother. In her anxiety over the tragedy, she blurted out, "We are not right with God. We've got to get right with God." Nate responded, "Are you out of your fucking mind? You just saw four men fly planes into buildings because they felt they *were* right with God."

After 9/11, Nate began to reject the idea of religion altogether, not just his father's hateful brand of Christianity. He blamed religion, all religion, for the hijackers' actions and for the actions of others who inflict pain in the name of God. Most of the world's population believes in some kind of spirituality, Nate said, and the vast majority do no harm. But a tiny minority—like the al-Qaeda terrorists, or his own father—commit heinous acts that they justify with religion. "Faith has that power because 99 percent of people say that faith is a legitimate arbiter of truth."

According to Nate, even my Catholic grandmother, whose Sunday morning mythology I don't share but hardly begrudge, abets those who use faith to do evil. Her rituals grant tacit approval to extremists. "Your grandmother, even though she's never done any harm as a Catholic, puts forward the notion that we can know something without discovering the truth of it. That we can just know it," he said. The men who flew the airliners into the World Trade Center believed, without evidence, that they would be rewarded for their actions by God. "The broad use of faith is benign. But the broad acceptance of faith as a way to discover truth is dangerous."

"Do you think my grandmother is foolish?" I asked him.

"That's a hard one." Nate paused before answering, and in his pause I sensed a caution born of kindness. Unlike celebrity atheists like Richard Dawkins and Bill Maher, who go after believers as if they were piñatas, Nate did not want to insult my grandmother. Eventually, though, he said, "Yes. She is foolish. But I don't necessarily blame her for her foolishness because it is a collective foolishness. We are blinded by that."

Just as the September 11 attacks changed Nate's view of religion, the resulting wars in Afghanistan and Iraq inspired the Westboro Baptist Church to bring its hateful ministry to the masses. The WBC first attracted attention in Kansas in the early 1990s, when the family started protesting alleged homosexual activity in Topeka's Gage Park. But the church earned global fame, and nearly unanimous scorn, when it started picketing the military funerals of American servicemen and women killed overseas. Dead soldiers, the WBC claimed, were God's punishment for

America's accommodation of sin, especially homosexuality. WBC members, adults and children alike, gathered near churches and cemeteries where they held signs proclaiming "Thank God for Dead Soldiers" and "God Blew up the Troops."

The ensuing media attention emboldened the WBC, prompting it to expand its scope. The church started to protest at the funerals of AIDS victims and any celebrity sympathetic to LGBTQ rights. They picketed courthouses, cultural events, rock concerts, and any individual or institution they considered a "fag enabler." This confused me. I didn't understand how the WBC expected to save any souls with such hateful signs and offensive slogans. Who would ever be converted by such vitriol? Nate told me I was missing the point. He quoted Corinthians from memory: "It pleased God by the foolishness of preaching to save them that believe." According to the WBC's reading of Scripture, all God wants from his elect is to preach his word. "My old man always said, 'Never mind if you save a soul. That's God's job. And if God has already decided who is going to heaven and hell, it doesn't matter. It's none of our business.'"

In addition to its in-person demonstrations, the WBC maintains an active online presence. The church's website, the subtly named godhatesfags.com, includes its extensive protest calendar, sermons, photos, videos, page-long screeds against celebrities, and spoofs of popular songs. I found the online content difficult to take seriously. The song parodies sound like what might happen if Weird Al Yankovic and the meanest girl from Sunday school got their hands on a karaoke machine. Tracks include "Mammas Don't Let Your Babies Grow up to Be Trannies" and a send-up of Prince's "Purple Rain" called "Eternal Pain, Sulfur Rain." The WBC's news releases also trade in absurdities. Shortly before a 2019 NFL playoff game between hometown Kansas City Chiefs and the New England Patriots, the WBC issued a warning to football fans:

You devote your mindshare, money, time, energy, and every other resource God has given you to carry on about every nuance of this silly sport. Right now you are in a particular frenzy about the Kansas City Chiefs, because they managed to win a game. As though all of that unholy idolatrous carrying on isn't bad enough to offend the Lord your God, you raised the ante. How, you ask? By inviting a proud filthy Kansas lesbian—Melissa Etheridge—to come and sing your blasphemous national anthem. It's hard to imagine a more offensive scene. Thousands of drunken louts screaming about a piece of leather, while a proud sodomite belts out your irreverent hymn beneath your bloody flag. You slap your hands over your hearts, shed a tear, and pretend you're righteous. You enrage God with this vomitus mess, so we must warn you that your destruction draws nigh, at the hands of a holy God whose promises are sure.

I found it hard not to laugh out loud at such bloviating nonsense. Surfing through the WBC site certainly entertains, as least for a little while. But the sincerity of WBC's hatred eventually becomes hard to bear. Like Nate, you don't want to spend too much time with the Phelps family.

Nate and Tammi separated in 2005. A few months later, Nate met a Canadian woman named Angela online and moved to Cranbrook, British Columbia. "When I came up here I was a naive son of a gun," he said. He'd thought his California license plate would grant him some cool cachet with British Columbians. But Cranbrook was the in heart of softwood-lumber country, and the industry was in the midst of a bitter trade dispute with the US at the time. "I couldn't get rid of that plate fast enough," he said.

Before Nate received the papers that allowed him to work legally in Canada, he drove part-time for Angela's family's cab company, Star Taxi. Star had a lucrative contract with Canadian Pacific Rail, shuttling crews between railyards or onward to the mines in Sparwood and Golden. "It was a lot of work," Nate said. "I made money hand over fist." As a back-up plan, he also trained to be a card dealer at St. Eugene, a golf resort and casino built out of a converted First Nations residential school. Once he received his immigration papers, though, Nate opted for full-time hours at Star.

In 2008, Nate picked up a fare at the Save-On-Foods gas station. The young man, Trevor Melanson, was studying journalism at the University of British Columbia and had come to Cranbrook to visit his girlfriend. On their way to the airport, Nate and Melanson chatted about journalistic ethics and fair reporting. Nate expressed respect for the BBC, which he considered one of the best news organizations in terms of accuracy. Melanson agreed, recalling a BBC documentary he'd seen about an extremist religious group down in Kansas.

Nate stared at Melanson in his rear-view mirror for a while. "They're my family," Nate said, sliding his driver's license from his wallet and passing it back to Melanson as proof. "He freaked out," Nate said. Nate agreed to give Melanson a phone interview sometime in the weeks that followed. Melanson's ensuing profile of Nate, "Running From Hell," first appeared in UBC's student newspaper. The following year, it was published online in *The. Tyee*, where it received twenty thousand views in short order.

Then Nate started getting calls. A representative from a nonprofit organization called American Atheists invited Nate to speak at its 2009 conference, held defiantly during Easter week each year in Atlanta. Nate hesitated. He'd given the occasional interview about the WBC to media outlets in Kansas, but telling his story at a national conference would escalate things. "It is one thing to poke the bear every now and again. It is another to become their adversary," Nate said. The decision took months to make and caused Nate tremendous anxiety. In the end, he decided he needed to support the people his family continued to harm. He drove his van from Cranbrook to Atlanta. The trip took forty hours.

Before checking into his hotel, Nate drove to a hardware store to buy a pickaxe handle similar to the one his father beat him with to use as a prop during his presentation. "It was intimidating to see one of those things again," he said. A copy of the conference program was waiting in his room. "It was the first time I'd seen what was going on," he said. "And Richard Dawkins was speaking right before me. What the fuck?" Nate was already nervous enough without the added pressure of following one of the world's most renowned atheists. He was well-prepared, though, and his talk earned him a standing ovation.

The Atlanta gig spawned more invitations. Nate told his story at universities and lecture halls across North America, becoming a sought-after presenter on humanism, skepticism, and LGBTQ rights. He believes speaking out can help make amends for some of the emotional trauma his family has caused over the years, especially to the LGBTQ community. The engagements also allow Nate to dispel misconceptions about the WBC, like that it's a cult. The church's views may be extreme, but Fred Phelps was no David Koresh. Nate wants people to understand that his father's sermons, even his most vile diatribes, stayed true to Biblical teaching. "He didn't pull anything out of thin air," Nate said.

Christians who maintain that "God Is Love" simply don't know their Scripture, according to Nate. "There are passages in the Bible that specifically say that God hates. If you don't like that, fine. If you want to ignore it in the creation of your idea of God, fine. But we didn't make this shit up. It's there in the Bible." And while contemporary believers might consider Fred Phelps' version of Christianity a distortion, the core of his dogma was once considered mainstream. "It was what everybody believed,"

Nate said. "If my father was born two hundred and fifty years ago, people would have been quoting his sermons."

While Nate's activism is a reaction to his father's hateful faith, he remains adamant that his atheism is not. He bristles at the suggestion that he wouldn't have abandoned God had he grown up with "regular" Christianity rather than the WBC's harsh Calvinism. "Probably my closest friend in the world said to me more than once 'If you had just been exposed to God in the way that God really is, you would not have any issue with Christianity.'" The idea offends Nate. He stopped believing in God after years of analytical thought, therapy, and often painful internal debate. It wasn't knee-jerk defiance. Taking Nate's faithlessness as a blunt reaction to his tyrannical upbringing dismisses his long journey.

In 2010, Calgary's chapter of Centre for Inquiry Canada—an educational charity devoted to rational, secular, and humanistic thinking—invited Nate to speak. Mike Gray, who was CFI's executive director at the time, recalls Nate's presentation about surviving and escaping his family's church. "Nate stands up in front of the crowd and comes across as unbelievably genuine. Unbelievably kind and caring. And he is just relaying his life story. After the speech, we all just stood there. People didn't know what to do." Later, when Gray mentioned that he was stepping down as CFI's Director, Nate volunteered to take the job. He and Angela moved to Calgary shortly afterwards, though they would split up two years later.

Gray admired the passion and humility Nate brought to the job, especially his devotion to LGBTQ issues. At the time, Gray owned a gay bar in Calgary called Club Sapiens, and when he was short-staffed, Nate would volunteer to come help out as a doorman. Though Nate has a bouncer's build—he's six-four and weighs around two hundred and fifty pounds—he lacks a doorman's typically fierce demeanor. "Nate is almost like a cross between the Pillsbury Doughboy and Santa Claus," Gray said.

"He has this chuckle. All my other bouncers were sitting there with a grimace on their faces. Nate just sits there with his laugh, having a great time. Everything was amusing to him. Everything made him smile. It was great to have him around."

I wanted to connect with the Phelps family in Topeka to ask about Nate. This entailed exchanging direct messages with a wbc Twitter account set up for media requests. After a couple of attempts I managed to reach Fred Junior, Nate's older brother, who agreed to consider a "maximum of five questions" via email. In the end, Fred Junior didn't say much. When I asked him what Nate was like as a child, he said only that Nate was "constantly in trouble." He didn't have any specific recollection of his family's reaction to Nate leaving in 1976, but said that he "can't imagine many were surprised." His family thinks "very little" about Nate's speaking publicly about his life at wbc and considers his gay rights activism "foolish." When I asked him if he ever misses Nate, if he wonders how Nate is doing, and whether or not any fraternal bonds remain, he wrote "no; no; no."

Fred Junior ended his email with two Bible quotes. The meaning of the first, from the Book of John, was clear enough: "They went out from us, but they were not of us; for if they had been of us, they would no doubt have continued with us: but they went out, that they might be made manifest that they were not all of us." The second, from Proverbs, confused me: "Go from the presence of a foolish man, when thou perceivest not in him the lips of knowledge." Since it was Nate who left the church, I didn't understand who Fred Junior was calling the "foolish man." Certainly not his late father and namesake. Then I realized Fred Junior was probably referring to me. I suspect the Proverbs line is his standard sign-off to daft and hell-bound journalists like myself.

I also reached out to Megan Phelps-Roper, Nate's niece, whose 2012 departure from the WBC attracted much media attention. Like Nate, she also gives talks about leaving the WBC, and she published a memoir, *Unfollow*, in 2019. Nate left the WBC before Megan was born, and the two Westboro exiles had never met in person. Still, I was curious what Megan had been told about Nate when she was growing up and suspected she'd be more forthcoming than Fred Junior.

Megan wrote to tell me that Nate and others who left the church were rarely discussed by the family. "They were just understood to be reprobates, worthless, dismissed and rejected out of hand." Shirley Phelps-Roper, Megan's mother and Nate's sister, described Nate as "a thief and criminally rebellious," who should be disposed of and ignored. The family regarded everyone who left the WBC the same way, including Megan's big brother, who left when he was eighteen. They'd grown up together, but Megan quickly dismissed him, too. "The church's culture of maligning and cutting off ex-members is deeply engrained," Megan wrote. "Familial ties are presumed to be worthless when someone decides to leave." The family didn't pay any attention to Nate's LGBTQ and atheist activism, either. "Westboro tends to see *anything* that's said or done publicly by ex-members as a cynical ploy for attention, praise, or financial gain rather than as a sincere expression of our change of heart and mind." At the time, Megan had no reason to believe otherwise of Nate.

Only after Megan decided to leave the WBC herself did she start to question what she'd been told about those who left before her—including her uncle Nate. When she first listened to Nate's public lectures and interviews, she was moved by his ability to articulate his experiences in the church. But she was also dismayed by the way Nate often spoke of all religious believers with "an edge of condescension, disdain, and dismissal that reminded me too much of how my family at Westboro preached at outsiders." Just as the WBC's hollering at non-believers didn't inspire them to repent, neither would Nate's contempt for religion coax believers to abandon their faith.

Megan first spoke to Nate on the telephone about a year and a half after she left the WBC. "I'd had so many impossibly wonderful post-Westboro experiences," she wrote. Megan developed close friendships with many people who'd long been targets of WBC fire: members of the LGBTQ community, Jews, and "mainstream" Christians. "I had given these people the benefit of the doubt, opening up to them and trusting them and hoping for the best, and they had far surpassed my best hopes." Megan also reconnected with other family members who'd left the church before her. "I was very hopeful about the prospect of connecting with Nate, this relative I never knew, and continuing to expand my new family."

But Nate let her down. At the time of their conversation, Fred Phelps lay dying in a Topeka hospice. After securing a promise from Nate that he would keep their conversation private, Megan proceeded to "pour out her heart to him." She talked about her dying "Gramps" and changes at the WBC that had contributed to her decision to leave the church. "Not 36 hours later, everything I told Nate was in the newspapers the world over," Megan wrote. "I was *extremely* upset." Megan learned Nate had threatened to go public with the information she'd shared with him unless his siblings allowed ex-WBC members to visit Fred before he died. He gave the family only twenty-four hours to comply.

They didn't, so Nate went public. On his Facebook page, he wrote:

I've learned that my father, Fred Phelps, Sr., pastor of the "God Hates Fags" Westboro Baptist Church, was ex-communicated from the "church" back in August of 2013. He is now on the edge of death at Midland Hospice house in Topeka, Kansas.

I'm not sure how I feel about this. Terribly ironic that his devotion to his god ends this way. Destroyed by the monster he made.

I feel sad for all the hurt he's caused so many. I feel sad for those who will lose the grandfather and father they loved. And I'm bitterly angry that my family is blocking the family members who left from seeing him, and saying their good-byes.

Media outlets around the world ran the story. Nate also gave an interview to the UK's *Daily Mail* in which he revealed that the church's board of male elders had sidelined Shirley Phelps-Roper, long-time church spokesperson, during some sort of power struggle. Nate said these same elders excommunicated Fred Phelps and kicked him out of the church building after he called for church members to be kinder to one another.

Megan was saddened Nate had shared information she'd told him in confidence without offering her a warning or apology. Megan also noted that Nate had released far more details than necessary—"including, perhaps most egregiously, the name of the hospice, which then became the subject of bomb and biochemical threats." Despite feeling betrayed, Megan didn't want the incident to lead to a permanent schism between her and her uncle. Swiftly discarding someone who offends you was the modus operandi of the church she'd left. She wanted to be better than that. "I learned the lesson that I could no longer trust Nate with sensitive information," Megan wrote, "but I also understood that relationships are a spectrum, rather than an on-off switch, and that I could keep having a relationship with Nate that just wasn't particularly close."

In a recent email exchange, that they both shared with me, Nate told Megan he didn't recall violating her trust, and that the urgency of his ultimatum was a response to both to the family ignoring his messages and his father's impending death. However,

Nate did acknowledge that his actions had hurt Megan. He apologized and wished her the best. At the end of her response, Megan wrote: "I do believe in your good wishes for me, uncle. I hope you know I have them for you, too."

Nate held the director's position at CFI in Calgary for four years, then found work driving for a school-bus company. It was there he met Cindi, who managed one of the bus yards. Nate and Cindi married in 2014 and moved back to Cranbrook the year after Nate got laid off from his bus-driving job. His devoutly Mormon managers blamed Calgary's struggling economy, but Nate wonders if they soured on him after learning of his atheism from a magazine profile I wrote about him earlier that year. I was mortified when Nate told me this, but Nate just shrugged. He was happy to return to Cranbrook, where he still owned a home. "And I am happy to be back behind the wheel of a taxi," he said.

I wanted to meet Nate again, so I took a road trip from Calgary, over the Crowsnest Pass, to Cranbrook. The Rocky Mountain town is "blue collar and redneck," Nate said with affection. During late-night shifts, Cranbrook's cabbies often occupy a downtown parking lot that lies conveniently between the King Edward Hotel bar and the strip club at the Sam Steele Inn. One night, in an incident that Nate claims "personifies Cranbrook," a man charged into the parking lot from the "The Sammy" and started hollering at Nate while he was sitting in his taxi. "He was out of his mind high," Nate said. Nate chased him off, but the man returned to the parking lot later and punched his fist through Nate's passenger-side window, shattering the glass.

Nate is hardly confrontational, and not at all inclined towards violence, but he wasn't going to let this stand. He jumped out of the cab and pummelled the man until he ran away again. Nate brought his cab to the taxi office and vacuumed up the broken glass from the seats and floor before returning to the parking lot. The late-night boozers and bar staff gave him a hero's welcome.

Occasionally Nate's fares will spout horrible things about women or minorities to him from the back of his cab, especially when they're drunk. Nate usually doesn't comment. He's only challenged a customer's racism or misogyny about a half-dozen times. "But I am real gentle about it," he said. "I won't, as a rule, get in anyone's face." He has less patience for the aggressively religious. He remembers driving two men home from an evening prayer meeting. One of the men decided to sit in the front seat next to Nate and started proselytizing to the man in the back. Nate was only half-listening. Such conversations make him cranky. Eventually, the front-seat preacher got on such a holy roll he turned to Nate and asked him if he was a praying man. Nate turned and said, "No. I am a thinking man." The preacher didn't say another word the entire trip.

Nate's position on religion would trouble many believers. Some would no doubt find his rejection of faith as offensive as the WBC's perversion of it. Nate shows them little sympathy. "If we're going to be successful as a species long term, faith is going to have to go away," he said. And yet, I don't quite buy Nate's claim to be a "firebrand atheist." I found him too gentle. I don't doubt his atheism, but despite his clear and genuine antagonism towards religion, Nate occasionally reveals a pliability. He appreciates the aesthetic beauty of religious ritual, for example, and never doubts the sincerity of the devout. "After all, I believe my father was honest," he said. He still catches himself humming old hymns, and Bible verses reflexively pop into his head. Faith is a tattoo.

And Nate surprised me when he admitted he would like to find God. "I've always searched for God," he said. "My position isn't a reaction to my father's theology like many assert. It is a thoughtful conclusion based on evidence, or the lack of evidence.

But throughout that search, I have always gravitated toward claims of proof. Emotionally, I would love to discover God. I let go of my fear of the God of my father long ago, but that doesn't mean I'm not intrigued by the idea. I just require evidence."

Lately, Nate's been thinking more about how abandoning religion means untethering oneself from the implications of what lies beyond death. Nate's father raised him to fear a vengeful God. Losing religion meant losing this fear and gaining comfort in its place; Nate no longer worries about his immortal soul. But this relief also comes edged with consequences. "It suddenly becomes that much more important for my life right now to have some relevance," Nate said. "Because this is it." If nothing comes afterwards, everything matters more.

The implications of his belief, or lack of belief, sharpened in 2019, when Nate's brother Mark died. Mark had long suffered from severe asthma that landed him in the hospital many times, but he'd always managed to recover. But the year before Mark's death, doctors discovered mould had destroyed part of his lungs. His physician insisted Mark wear a vibrating vest to help clear his lungs and prescribed him a combination of powerful drugs. But his health continued to fail. He suffered six strokes within a month's time that paralyzed half his body. Nate and Cindi visited Mark in Arizona a few months before he died. His brother's condition shocked Nate; he knew he wouldn't see him alive again.

Mark's death lead to some poignant conversations between Nate and Mark's widow, Luava. Though Mark left the WBC long ago, he remained a devout Christian. "He had just let go of my father's god and embraced a more loving, compassionate god," Nate said. Nate didn't begrudge his brother his faith, especially during his final ten years when it granted him solace during his suffering. Luava doesn't share Mark's devotion, nor Nate's atheism, but she and Nate both agree that Mark is at peace, whatever that means.

Nate stayed in Arizona for a week after the funeral to help Luava deal with the practical aftermath of Mark's death. He caught himself imagining Mark would approve of this kindness. Such thoughts are hardly uncommon or unnatural for the newly bereaved. Aiding his sister-in-law was simply the right thing to do, and Nate felt good doing it. But the image of his brother smiling down on his efforts from a post-death existence startled Nate. "Do I somehow still, to some degree, hold on to this idea that someone is watching?" Nate asked. He knows, intellectually, that Mark is not looking down on him from anywhere. "But my instinct is to continue to include this idea that there is an awareness beyond death."

The soul may not remain after death, if it exists at all, but memory endures. "What is most important," Nate said, "is what you do today, and how you impact others in your life, so that when you go, there are memories that continue to have an impact on other people."

Epilogue

PHIL BAILEY AND I HAD FOLLOWED HIGHWAY 4 OUT OF Yellowknife, then turned south again towards Dettah, the southern terminus of the ice road that crosses Yellowknife Bay in wintertime. About two kilometres before Dettah, Phil pulled his Chevy off the highway and into the bush. Morning rain had muddied the already rough dirt trail, and Phil worried the truck might not make it all the way to his house. He usually kept a quad parked at the trailhead for this reason, but he'd lent it to a neighbour the previous day. Phil's perpetual smirk didn't budge. He lifted his ballcap, rubbed his nearly bald head, and geared the truck down. We managed to jerk and bounce our way to the end of the road.

This half-hectare of land is part of the Denendeh—the territory of the Dene Nation. Phil's family have had a lease on the property for generations. A rough one-bedroom shack had stood on the property since the 1940s, but was abandoned twenty years before Phil's mother took over and gave the property to Phil. The Dene granted Phil permission tear down the old shack. Five layers of old carpet covered the floors, and the walls were insulated with sawdust and newspapers. Phil built a new house on the spot, or rather he supervised the construction. "I learned that if I want something done right, I hire someone else to do it." Phil lives alone in the house. A diesel generator keeps his lights on, and propane powers his fridge and toilet. "I built an outhouse, but I never used it once," he told me. "I literally burn my shit."

We walked past Phil's house, crossed a patch of wild grass and lichen-splotched stones, and stood on the shore of Great Slave Lake. Beyond the spot where someone had recently stolen Phil's boat, we could see Yellowknife's modest skyline. Phil said he likes to watch the city slowly light up at night, especially during the winter. The rest of the year he sits alone on the water's edge to listen to the waves lap against the smooth rocks. "I'll listen to the birds, too," Phil said. "To the ducks. Lots of swans. The odd beaver comes by. I am surrounded by animals here." One winter's day, along the trail leading to his house, Phil spotted lynx tracks following fox tracks following rabbit tracks. A three-pronged chase frozen silent and still in the snow.

"We used to come out here with all our family and do our cultural stuff," Phil said. His relatives hunted and camped in the woods and fished in the cold lake waters. "We'd throw out a net. Get some whitefish. Dry 'em up. Cook 'em up." Phil showed me the wooden shelf nailed into a tree trunk where his family used to skin fish, and the fire barrel where Phil, according to tradition, torched his grandfather's possessions when he died. Phil had kept only his grandfather's leather shaving pouch.

Phil's grandfather could predict the harshness of the coming winter by the size of autumn's acorns. Once, after Phil "got bit by a bee," his grandfather chewed wild-rose leaves into a poultice to heal the sting. Phil's grandmother knew things, too. She was a shaman, Phil said, who once cured her son's blindness. The Virgin Mary had come to her in a dream and led her down a forest path into a gorge. The Virgin pointed to a patch of moss and whispered that Phil's grandmother should boil the moss until it softened, then smear it on her blind child's eyes. Four days later, he could see again. "They would teach us things," Phil said of his grandparents. "They'd pass on their traditional knowledge to me and my brother."

Aside from the Ikwe drivers I met in Winnipeg, Phil was the only cabbie who hadn't come from away. He was the only driver whose roots ran deep in the place he lived in. Everyone else, even old timers like Andy Reti and Peter Pellier, had made long journeys across oceans and borders before making short journeys between Canada's airports and hotels, downtown bars and middle-class suburbs. A federal government analysis of 2006 Census data showed that over half of all Canadian taxi drivers were born abroad. The numbers in large urban centres were much higher. At least 60 percent of drivers in Montreal, Edmonton, Calgary, Ottawa-Gatineau, and Winnipeg were immigrants, while more than 80 percent of cabbies in Toronto and Vancouver came from elsewhere. A similar study hasn't been done since, but the percentage of immigrants driving taxis in Canadian cities must be even higher now.

Still, all the cabbies I met had laid claim to the cities where they now lived and drove. I thought of something Helen Potrebenko's cabbie protagonist, Shannon, says near the end of her novel *Taxi!*: "the city belongs to those who know it." Shannon's claim felt true to me. But the cabbies' title to these places has little to do with their knowledge of local street names and traffic lights and four-way stops. Regardless of when or from where they've arrived, the drivers' intimacy with these cities gives them a sense of ownership that even some lifelong citizens will never have. The most compelling view of a society is from its margins. Taxi drivers inhabit this borderland. They have ready access to a place's spirit, to its hidden psychogeography, that most of us do not. The cities are theirs.

Phil, though, makes a double claim on Yellowknife. Not only does he have a cabbie's-eye-view of the city, the geography he traverses in his taxi—and in his truck, and on his motorcycle, and in his boat before someone stole it—has always been his and his family's home. I couldn't decide whether it was fitting or incongruous that the last Canadian driver I spoke to was one of the only ones who'd always been here.

Phil's story begins in Fort Resolution, a hamlet on Great Slave's southern shore, where he spent the first years of his life with his grandparents while his mother lived and worked in Yellowknife. His mother sent for Phil and his brother, Joe, when Phil was three years old. "We came here as young Native boys," Phil said. Both spoke only Chipewyan when they arrived, but their mother would only speak to them in English. "As a result, I lost my native tongue," Phil said. The boys faced racism in school, dealing with taunts of "dirty Indian" and being told, with cruel irony, to go back where they came from.

Phil quit school when he was sixteen and scored an apprentice-mechanic job with the territorial government. He played minor hockey, too. "I was a goal-scorer," Phil said. "I couldn't skate worth fuck, but I could score the fucking goals." His scoring prowess earned him a spot on the Northwest Territories' all-star team and an invitation to an under-seventeen tournament at Rocky Mountain House. A good showing could've landed Phil a try-out for the national team, but when he asked for time off from his apprentice job to attend the tournament his boss talked him out of it. "What do you want to do?" his boss asked. "You want to be a mechanic? Or do you want to play hockey? And which is more realistic?" Phil handed in his Cooperalls and never played serious hockey again.

He didn't last very long as a mechanic, either. The government's fleet of vehicles was too small to keep Phil busy, so it contracted him out to gold-mining companies, where Phil gained experience as a heavy-equipment mechanic. But lying under enormous trucks in minus-forty-degree weather and slicing his knuckles open on oily engine parts was hardly inspiring, so Phil eventually pitched his wrench across the garage and decided to go back to school to study computer programming. He started driving taxi, too.

Phil has driven cab part-time in Yellowknife for more than thirty years. He holds the title of Yellowknife's longest serving, and only Indigenous, taxi driver. But these days Phil only drives on the weekends. During the week, he works full-time hours as a system administrator with Child Protection Services. The job grants Phil access to confidential files about cases throughout the Northwest Territories, and he spends much of his day reading heartbreaking and often disturbing reports of child abuse, neglect, and abandonment. These are some of Yellowknife's darkest secrets, and few people know more about the city's abusive fathers and neglectful mothers than Phil. Some even end up in Phil's taxi. "I want to kick the living goddam crap out of them," Phil said. "But I can't do fuck all. I got nothing. I can just look at the guy and say nothing. Swallow my tongue."

In a way, Phil was my mirror opposite. I'd travelled across the country to learn about the hidden lives of Canada's taxi drivers while Phil stays home to learn about the hidden lives of his taxi passengers. We both spent our days absorbed in other people's stories. Phil wouldn't reveal anyone's secrets, of course. And I didn't ask. The knowledge was forbidden to me by law, just as Phil's family's Dene knowledge was forbidden to me by tradition.

Phil was more forthcoming with his own skeletons. Before getting back into his Chevy and returning to Yellowknife, Phil leaned on the side of the truck's bed and revealed some truly dark episodes in his life. I felt grateful for Phil's candidness and honoured by his trust, but his story felt like a confession I shouldn't retell. Afterwards, Phil drove me back into Yellowknife. As he shook my hand to say goodbye, he said "I bet you haven't met a fucking taxi driver like me, eh?"

Perhaps not, but I'm not sure Phil was as unique among the cabbies as he thought he was, the taxi having long been a sanctuary for damaged souls. Back in 1970, Peter Churchill wrote of the industry as "the last real haven for men who need a breathing space between their bouts with life. It is not really a job; it is a refuge." Churchill believed all taxi drivers were tragic figures of some kind. Society's outsiders. Unacknowledged artists. Overeducated immigrants. "Then there are the quiet ones." Wrote Churchill:

> These are the men who have failed somehow, or just lost something; a love perhaps, a business, a profession, even their faith— that basic understanding of what everything is all about in the first place. They need time to digest the cataclysm....

Phil fit this description, as had all the taxi drivers I met. Not because they were quiet—most, thankfully, were not—but because their storylines all intersected with failure and defeat in some way. They'd all lost something before they found themselves behind the wheel.

Mo Jalil failed as an artist, and lost part of his mind in a war zone. Michael Kamara lost part of his body. Nate Phelps lost his faith and most of his family, for better or worse. Somalia's *burbur* robbed Kareem Yalahow of his first family, and the Holocaust claimed Andy Reti's father. Alex Seliga's grand tennis scheme with Iva failed, as did Hassan Kattoua's cowboy campaign against Uber. Sergey lost the nation he loved to the Cold War and became stranded in a country he loves less. Rawi Hage lost Beirut to civil war and his neighbourhood to an explosion. Jackie Hartog lost years of her life to the bottle, and the women of Ikwe later lost Jackie herself. Jens Andersen spent years falling into and out of his studies. Amrit Hothi failed to become a soldier and ended up a cop. Jass Hothi lost a husband before she found Amrit.

Despite having lost a few bouts with life, the cabbies I met with had all shown tremendous resilience and resolve. They crafted a life for themselves, and for their families, through personal sacrifice and long, late hours spent at their steering wheels. Few would find this surprising. Most of us recognize how hard taxi drivers work. We can imagine the drunks and bigots they calmly endure, and imagine the dreams they left behind in faraway homelands. We can admire their work ethic and blue-collared grind. Rarely, though, do we envy them. No one in the back of a taxi longs to switch places with the guy up front.

But to suggest that these drivers ended up behind the wheel simply as a result of personal cataclysms would be to underestimate them. The driver's seat is no loser's perch. What characterized the cabbies I met, more than anything else, was their intellect. All were plotters and schemers. They overcame the challenges they faced by working every angle and bending whatever rules they didn't otherwise break. Masters of their own life stories, their genius didn't always reveal itself in short cab rides from here to there.

Phil studied his way out from under frozen trucks. Jens "solved" Shakespeare and Bob Dylan. Mo manipulated Iraq's military justice system to evade prosecution, and he and Alex both manoeuvred their way into their city's monied classes without ever becoming wealthy themselves. Each of Hassan's anti-Uber hacks confirmed his creative powers just as Rawi's literary accolades confirmed his. Michael could think a long-game like few of his fellow amputees in Aberdeen, while Jass and Amrit deftly navigated the hierarchy of low-paid jobs to build a Canadian life for their extended family. The women of Ikwe designed their own ride-share service to sidestep the cabbies who'd done harm to so many women. I'd set out to find storytellers. Instead I found problem-solvers. I envied their practical intelligence.

I recall what Quentin Ranson told me about Michael Kamara: that had he been born in Canada instead of war-torn Sierra Leone, that he may have become a CEO. The same could be said for many of my cabbies. Considering their obvious cleverness, I could easily imagine Mo, Hassan, Jass, and Alex excelling in business or politics were it not for the geographical accident of their birth. But such hypotheticals diminish what these drivers have, in fact, already achieved. I see little value, and no honour, in imagining who these people might've become when the reality of who they are is so compelling.

On my flight south to Calgary, and on my cab ride home from the airport, I realized I'd stopped seeing taxi drivers as my nemeses. Having spent so much time listening to their stories, I'd grown rather affectionate towards them. I started tipping them more, and exhausted my friends and family with tales of Uber's evils. But I didn't see the drivers as my colleagues, either. I shared little in common with these men and women other than a country. They all endured much more than I had. Slipping into their back seats still feels like crossing a frontier. The taxi is still a border.

There are other such borders, of course, other stories I will undoubtedly miss. When I wrote to Helen Potrebenko about my interest in taxi drivers, she wondered why I wasn't writing about other workers. "When was the last time you read a story about a metal fabricator?" she asked. "A payroll clerk? A cashier in a pasta shop?" Fair questions. They, too, undoubtedly have secret lives, untold in our brief interactions with them. Histories that transcend the bare facts of their origins and occupations. No doubt the workers toiling at every Tim Hortons I visited possess biographies as interesting as the drivers I met. I once might've found Jass behind those counters, after all.

We need to put our phones down more often. We need to listen to the otherwise unheard, and see the otherwise invisible. Only when we open ourselves up to them can we acknowledge the stories that surround us.

I won't pester taxi drivers for their stories anymore, though. Those that want to talk, will. I won't be able to stop them. It'll be enough for me to know I ride in the presence of a life that cannot be contained by the taxi's metal, vinyl, and glass. And it'll be enough for them just to drive.

Pandemic Postscript

MY TIME AMONG THE TAXI DRIVERS ENDED BEFORE THE beginning of 2020. Then COVID-19 arrived. As businesses shut down across the country, provincial governments included taxis on their list of essential services, pushing cabbies to the frontlines of a global health crisis alongside grocery-store clerks, pharmacists, and utility workers. Suddenly, taxi drivers were back on my brain.

Despite being deemed necessary and therefore permitted to work, Canada's taxi drivers found little work to do. The pandemic crushed the business, especially during the early days of the lockdown in late March. Sunshine Cabs, which operates in North and West Vancouver, halted dispatch operations due to the sudden lack of ride requests. Kuber Taxi in nearby Surrey also suspended taxi services. Two-thirds of Vancouver's Yellow Cabs sat, unmoving, as passenger calls fell by nearly 80 percent. In Toronto, the operations manager of Beck Taxi estimated business had declined by 75 to 80 percent. Estimates from the Taxi Association of Toronto were even more dire. They reported business was down nearly 100 percent and the average taxi driver was losing $150 a day. With no clients to drive, many cabbies parked their cars and stayed home.

I started to wonder about the taxi drivers I'd gotten to know. So just as the first wave of the pandemic in Canada started to crest, I pestered some of them again to see how they were managing.

Nate Phelps in Cranbrook told me he'd lost about three-quarters of his income to the pandemic. He first started to worry in the middle of March, when British Columbia's casinos closed. "That's a chunk of our business," he said. "Then we started getting news that the airlines were going to start shutting down. And then they announced that they're going to shut down all the bars and the restaurants. It was probably over a two- or three-week period that this all was developing out. And then suddenly there's no business."

One day in mid-April, Nate showed up to work and found his boss had hung a plastic shower curtain between the front and back seats in all Star's taxis using the same tension bars and curtain rings you'd find in a typical bathroom. Now Nate jokingly offers his clients shampoo when they enter the cab. He and his fellow cabbies also keep a sanitizer-soaked rag in the taxi. Nate constantly wipes his hands, the card-reader machine, any cash fares he receives, and door handles inside and outside the taxi. "You'd think that would be pretty frustrating to try to maintain that, but we're not doing that much business at this time. It's not like it's a big challenge." The drivers wipe down the shower curtains, too, but the sanitizer rendered the clear plastic opaque after a few weeks and Nate's boss had to replace them.

Aside from its shower curtain hack, Star Taxi's safety precautions align with measures taken elsewhere. Cabbies across Canada started adhering to new safety and health regulations imposed by local authorities. Drivers are mandated to wear masks and gloves in some jurisdictions, and to sterilize surfaces between fares. They keep hand sanitizer within reach. Many cities prohibit passengers from sitting in the front seat and restrict the number of passengers to three or less. The City of Edmonton went further than most, restricting all trips to a single passenger unless riders reside in the same household. Some taxi drivers rigged temporary plastic dividers between their front and back seats, or paid upwards of $300 to install plexiglass, in an effort to erect a border wall between themselves and their clients.

Cranbrook saw very few COVID cases in the early days of the pandemic. Nate felt the provincial health authority had things well in hand, and Cranbrook's citizens followed the distancing rules at first. By May, though, young people in Cranbrook had grown bored. "People are just freaking tired," Nate said. "Tired of being cooped up, so they're doing whatever rationalizing they need to do to feel alright with getting together with their buddies and having a party." Nate eavesdrops on passengers swapping conspiracy theories about how the pandemic is a hoax or how more people die of the flu every year, all to justify picking up a flat of beer and carousing with their friends.

Nate receives regular calls to pick up passengers from these illicit gatherings. One Saturday night, his dispatch sent Nate to a party where twenty or thirty people were jammed into a house. Four drunk kids stumbled out of the house and tried to get in Nate's cab. He would only take three. "I'm not letting your buddy sit in the front seat," Nate told them. He wanted all his fares, especially kids who were clearly breaking safety protocols, on the other side of the curtain. While the fourth friend stayed behind and waited for another cab, Nate overheard one of the three remaining passengers in his back seat talk about how someone at the party had "escaped" from Calgary, where the province had closed the bars due to the high rate of infections.

Driving Cranbrook's drunk and irresponsible citizens around worries Nate. At sixty-two, he knows a coronavirus infection could lay him out. "I take this shit seriously," he said. "I assume that if I get it, it's going to be a challenge to survive it." To quell his anxiety, Nate started taking the Ativan his doctor prescribed a year earlier. "And I got another prescription about a month ago," Nate said. The pills are already half gone. "You come home and you're just so stressed that you weren't necessarily as on top of things as you should've been," Nate said. "Like, I touched the customer's door handle before I wiped it. And then your mind just takes off."

But Nate's mainly copes by spreading information, not swallowing meds. He posts updated COVID stats from reference website Worldometer on his Facebook page every single day, including worldwide numbers for both cases and deaths as well as data specific to Canada and the United States. The posts invariably attract comments and accusations from science deniers and conspiracy theorists. Nate rarely takes their bait. He prefers to quietly share the information rather than engage with the trolls and shouters.

The data is more for his own benefit, anyway. "If there's a danger or risk, I go looking for information," Nate said. "I am frantic for information." Nate is aware that his need for practical knowledge is rooted in a childhood spent under his father's cruel reign at Westboro Baptist Church. "I can look back at when I was a kid, and at the dangerous environment I grew up in," Nate said. "Anytime I entered that situation, I was using all of my senses and all of my sources of information—scanning the environment— to see if there's any danger."

Nate's ongoing search for facts about the pandemic is, in many ways, a logical expression of his nature. "Being conscious of every little tick. Every little sound that might mean danger approaches."

Taxi-borne COVID-infections and deaths were inevitable—in Canada and abroad. A study conducted in England and Wales by the UK's Office for National Statistics showed that, between March and May 2020, COVID-19-related death for cabbies and chauffeurs was 65 per 100,000, one of the highest rates for men in general. In Tehran, thirteen taxi drivers had died from coronavirus by the middle of April, and at least three hundred were infected. Thailand's first two COVID-19 cases, and Taiwan's first confirmed COVID-19 death, were taxi drivers. Health officials in Hong Kong started offering cabbies free COVID-19 tests in July 2020 as part of an effort to temper a third wave of infections. After beloved Dublin cabbie "Mick the Moan" Glynn died from the virus, his family released a statement encouraging Dubliners to take the pandemic seriously. "So if my dad's death can hammer home the message about how important it is to stay inside and self isolate," Glynn's son told *Dublin Live*, "then we're happy that his death hasn't been in vain." In Toronto, ten airport taxi drivers died from coronavirus infections during the first few months of the pandemic. Many drivers felt they could've better avoided the virus had the City provided guidance, cleaning equipment, and personal protective equipment earlier on. Some washed their cars with watered-down bleach because they, like everyone else, couldn't reliably source proper sanitizer. Then, in mid-April, City Hall further infuriated drivers by advising potentially corona-infected Torontonians to take taxis to testing sites. Beck Taxi's Kristine Hubbard received a call from a City Hall official who told her that "if people want to get a test and they couldn't drive themselves, they were not to take transit. They were to ask family and friends, which obviously would be a difficult question to ask, and otherwise take a taxi or ride hail." Hubbard argued that COVID-19-positive passengers, or those with COVID-19 symptoms, should be isolated to a dedicated fleet of vehicles whose drivers were both informed and willing to do the work.

At least two Montreal cabbies who worked regularly at Trudeau airport died of COVID-19 during the pandemic's first wave. Dani Atallah, taxi driver and vice president of Regroupement des propriétaires de Taxi de Montréal, told the *Montreal Gazette* in May that while he didn't know the exact number of drivers who'd been infected by COVID-19, he knew, anecdotally, that it wasn't small. "I have friends who have become infected and then infected their families," Atallah said.

The Taxi Sherriff might have been one of them. Hassan Kattoua was working at Montreal's airport when the pandemic started. He'd given up trying to license his own car and was renting a taxi from someone with an airport permit. Hassan admitted he and his airport colleagues didn't take the pandemic seriously at first.

Then, in April, Hassan started coughing. "Maybe some people coughed inside the taxi, or sneezed, or whatever," Hassan said. "And I felt sick." Hassan phoned Quebec's Info-Santé telephone hotline and described his symptoms to a nurse. She told him not to come in for a COVID test, but to self-isolate. Hassan's elderly mother fell ill, too, and Hassan stayed at home to care for her. They both recovered. Hassan never took a COVID test so doesn't know if he, or his mother, were ever infected.

Hassan never went back to pushing cab. Before the pandemic, driving a taxi to and from the airport was a lucrative gig. But the lockdown cancelled flights and killed the airport taxi business. "So now, basically, permit holders are begging drivers to rent cars and go to the airport," Hassan told me. "Most of the drivers in the city left the cars they were renting because it's not worth it. Why would you pay the rent when there are no flights?" Another taxi driver told the *Montreal Gazette* that business was so slow at the airport that cabbies could sit for twelve hours and make only twenty dollars. Hassan decided to stay home and collect federal relief money. The monthly payments didn't quite cover his and his mother's bills, but he was still grateful for the help.

When I spoke to Hassan in the spring of 2020, he predicted the pandemic could end up helping his longstanding fight against Uber. The notion surprised me, but his logic seemed sound. Hassan believed that, once businesses reopened, Montrealers would remain hesitant to take the crowded metro, or city buses. Due to their low-occupancy, taxis and other cars-for-hire would be in higher demand as the safest public transportation option. There was a precedent for this. During the 2003 SARS epidemic, cabbies in Toronto felt the same way. One taxi driver, bemoaning the loss of tourist business, told the *Globe and Mail* "Maybe business will pick up if people are afraid to use the GO train."

Hassan knew the public would feel even safer in taxis if owners installed plexiglass barriers between the front and back seats, so he went to Montreal's Taxi Bureau with an idea. "This thing can be used to our advantage," he said. If the Bureau could convince the provincial transportation ministry, Transports Québec, to subsidize the installation of permanent barriers in all ride-for-hire vehicles, passengers would be shielded from potential infection. "The taxi drivers would be protected at the same time from aggression," Hassan said. "So it's not only for the corona."

The measure might also give taxi owners an advantage over Uber drivers. Because a recent ruling by Transports Québec placed taxis on the same regulatory footing as app-based companies like Uber, the government would have to outfit Uber cars with the same permanent barriers as taxis. Part-time Uber drivers—those who drive to "meet girls and make fun," according to Hassan—wouldn't want plexiglass installed in their personal vehicles. "For example, say a guy that is a real estate agent wants to meet a nice girl. He downloads the app and starts driving Uber. He doesn't care about the money," Hassan said. "The girl is gonna see he has a fancy car. He is dressed in a suit and a tie and this and that. Then he busts out his business card, and blah blah, blah. This guy is not going to put a separation barrier in his car." Requiring all vehicles-for-hire to install plexiglass shields would chase casual Uber drivers off the streets, leaving more business for traditional drivers. The Taxi Bureau did not pursue Hassan's idea. Once again, the Taxi Sherriff's efforts had failed.

Hassan can take some comfort in the fact that Uber has hardly thrived during the pandemic. The financial experts who predicted Uber would finally make money by the end of 2020 never anticipated COVID. The company's second quarter reporting, released in August, showed a 27 percent decline in revenues. Ride bookings were down by almost three-quarters. But while the pandemic hammered the ride-hailing business, bookings with Uber's food-delivery service increased by 113 percent. "The COVID crisis has moved delivery from a luxury to a utility," CEO Dara Khosrowshahi said. As a result, the company's net loss in the second quarter of 2020, while still a troubling $1.8 billion, was still better than the same period in 2019. Uber believes it will be profitable by the end of 2021.

Uber also won't have Hassan pestering it anymore. In August 2020, Hassan texted to tell me he'd finally quit driving cab to open a store in Montreal selling open-box electronics. "No more taxi for me," Hassan wrote. "They have won. And I lost the war because I fought it by myself."

"I am sorry to hear that the Sheriff has turned in his badge," I replied.

"It is still in my drawer," he said. "And my heart."

In Halifax, Michael Kamara's earnings collapsed at the onset of the pandemic as businesses and schools shut down. In March, one of Michael's cabbie colleagues told the CBC that business had dropped by 95 percent. The taxi trade had started to pick up slightly when I spoke to Michael in May 2020. Just as Hassan predicted about Montreal, Haligonians worried about risking infections in crowded city buses, and opted instead for the relative safety of solitary cab rides. Still, Michael figures he has to work between twelve and fourteen hours to earn what he used to make in eight.

"Driving taxi during this time is risky," Michael said. "Only God will save you as a driver." As elsewhere, Halifax taxi companies imposed new safety measures and regulations in response to the pandemic. They installed plastic dividers between cabs' front and back seats, and limited the number of riders in a taxi to three, with everyone in the back. Michael sanitizes his cab constantly, including the card reader, which, along with any cash, gets passed through a hole in the divider. Michael doesn't help passengers with their heavy bags anymore, either. He stays in the cab and clicks the button to open the trunk so his fares can load them themselves.

Michael told me the new measures grant him some sense of safety, but he still feels anxious driving cab. Plexiglass and hand-sanitizer offer no guarantees. "You always have the feeling that something will happen to you," Michael said. "But you have the faith that you are here to make a living. To take care of your family. And whatever condition be with you, you will be able to be cured. It's not like Ebola."

Michael's mother-in-law died in Sierra Leone in the fall of 2014, "during the time of the Ebola." He'd visited the country the previous January, to tend to her after she suffered a stroke, and returned to Canada just before WHO declared an Ebola outbreak in neighbouring Guinea. Just like the rebels who brought death across Sierra Leone's borders in 1998, Ebola quickly invaded Freetown. Ebola infected nearly thirty thousand people in ten countries and had killed more than eleven thousand West Africans by the time the epidemic ended in the spring of 2016. Victims died rapid, gruesome deaths characterized by hemorrhagic fever, black stools, and vomiting.

Ebola didn't kill Michael's mother-in-law. She died at her home with what Michael termed "the stroke disease." But because she passed away in the midst of a deadly epidemic, she was considered an Ebola victim. "When somebody was dying during that time, you die an Ebola patient," Michael said. "Even if you die at home, your family will not get to bury you. The government will bury you. They put you in the same burying ground as Ebola patients." The families of coronavirus victims in Canada and elsewhere were denied their regular rituals of burial and mourning, and so too were the families of those who died during the Ebola epidemic—whether they died of the virus or not.

"Disease is like a war," Michael said. "Everything become mess. Economy become mess. Money-finding become mess. Everything become mess. Everybody is thinking different." The same change of thinking is occurring now in Canada, Michael said, in the midst of the coronavirus pandemic. "Everybody's mind is different. You trust nobody. Even your family. You will not visit your family. It's like we're fighting the war. We're fighting the silent war without weapon."

On March 25, 2020, in response to the pandemic, Indian prime minister Narendra Modi declared a "hard lockdown." "To save India and every Indian, there will be a total ban on venturing out of your homes," Modri decreed, in effect sentencing 1.3 billion Indians to house arrest. Foreign nationals weren't exempted, and close to forty thousand Canadians found themselves stranded in India. "I was one of them," Amrit Hothi told me, "but I had a selfish interest of staying on longer. Because of my father."

Amrit had travelled to India the previous December to care for his ailing father. The eighty-five-year-old former soldier suffered from diabetes, and a severe case of gangrene prompted surgeons to amputate his leg. The hospital released Amrit's father in March, but Amrit stayed in India to care for him during his recovery. "Dad wasn't in good shape," Amrit said. He couldn't walk or bathe himself, and Amrit constantly had to monitor the complicated array of medications his father had been prescribed. "One thing leads to another," he said. "If you give medications for something, something else comes up. It was a jigsaw puzzle for me."

As Amrit cared for his father at home, COVID-19 cases skyrocketed in India. The country had reported only 519 cases and ten deaths when Modi first declared the lockdown. By the time the government eased restrictions six weeks later, nearly five thousand Indians had died from COVID-19 and the number of cases exceeded 173,000. The country was recording around three thousand new cases every day and the number was rising.

The numbers spooked Amrit. "There was COVID everywhere," he said. Many Indians resisted masking and social distancing rules. "They don't really care," Amrit said. "I hope there is a vaccine soon, otherwise in India I don't know what is going to happen." Amrit didn't trust the country's political leaders or medical establishment to keep his vulnerable father safe. Rumours circulated about medical labs working in concert with private hospitals. When wealthy patients came in for a COVID test, the labs would fake positive results and send patients to hospitals for expensive treatments. Amrit didn't trust anyone.

Back in Calgary, the taxi business was collapsing. In March, the president of Checker Transportation Group said nearly five hundred of the company's 830 drivers had stopped driving altogether, including Jass, who suffers from diabetes and hypertension, and would therefore be at higher risk for serious medical problems had she contracted COVID-19. "I told her not to risk," Amrit said. "I was stuck in India looking after my dad. I didn't need more stress." Like Hassan, both Jass and Amrit collected federal government relief funding to pay their bills while their taxi stayed parked. "The government was nice giving us five hundred dollars a week. I am thankful," Amrit said. "Canada is heaven compared to India. It is heaven. One should respect that."

Amrit returned to Calgary in the middle of July to renew his nearly expired taxi permit. He planned on heading back to India and to his father once his papers had been filed, but he was too late. Amrit's father died just two weeks after Amrit landed in Calgary. Amrit had been at his father's side for nearly seven months, throughout his hospitalization and recovery, but he wasn't there when he finally passed away. I offered Amrit my condolences. "What can you do?" was all he said.

I last spoke to Amrit in October 2020, on his first day driving cab in more than ten months. It was Jass' first day back, too, of course. "I was kind of nervous," Amrit admitted. "After three trips I feel okay." Amrit wears a mask while he drives, and sanitizes his steering wheel, card reader, and back windows between every fare. He considers Calgary's mild autumn weather a blessing because he can keep the windows down, but he worries about what will happen when winter comes.

Amanpreet, Jass and Amrit's daughter, and her husband finally moved out of the family home earlier that month. The couple bought their own place in Airdrie, a few kilometres north of Calgary. "The house feels empty, but it is good for them. They will learn a lot. Now they will realize how life is. I'm proud."

"This is such a good country," Amrit said. "Such a beautiful country."

In Winnipeg, Christine Brouzes wasn't sure Ikwe would be deemed an essential service. "Our mission is to provide transportation option to taxis. So as long as taxis are on the road, we should be on the road," Christine argued. City authorities, overwhelmed by other pandemic priorities in the first few weeks of the pandemic, were too busy to give Christine a definite answer. So Ikwe instituted new cleaning policies for their vehicles and insisted that their volunteer drivers wear masks and keep serving their members as usual.

But few Ikwe volunteers wanted to drive during the pandemic. Ikwe had more than fifty regular drivers at the beginning of March. By May, only five were left. The volunteers told Christine and the other administrators they feared contracting the virus, or bringing it home and infecting their families. Christine wonders if they'll ever come back. She also worries some will "lose their spark" for the organization. Others will remain fearful, or have spouses who will discourage them from driving because of the ongoing risks of COVID-19 infection. Some drivers will no doubt seek more lucrative, less risky ways to spend their evening hours. Christine wonders if Ikwe will lose volunteers to Skip the Dishes or other such delivery apps, where drivers can earn an income without gambling on their health by having strangers in the car.

As Winnipeg's businesses shut down, the demand for rides tumbled. Christine told me that even Chery, an "Ikwe addict" who used to drive ten hours nearly every day, hadn't given a single ride in weeks. "We just feel kind of defeated and heartbroken by an invisible thing," Christine said. With so few members having anywhere to go, Ikwe decided to offer rides only during the day and early evenings. That way members could still be shuttled to doctor's appointments and for grocery runs.

The decision to stop late night service was difficult. "In our low-income areas, everybody was still partying and getting together," Christine said. Winnipeg's bars were closed, but people disregarded social distancing rules by partying in private homes, as Nate had witnessed in Cranbrook. "We didn't want to be contributing to that potential spread," Christine said. Ikwe also didn't want to put their drivers at risk of infection by giving rides to passengers they knew were acting irresponsibly. The new policy weighed heavily on Christine and the other volunteers. "If a woman feels unsafe taking a taxi or walking a long distance, we want to be there for her. What if she walks home and gets picked up and harmed on the way by a stranger?" Christine said. Refusing to give rides at night conflicted with Ikwe's central mandate of keeping women safe.

Many didn't respond well to the new rules. Some members were "downright rude" and abusive when told they couldn't book rides at night. Christine seems forgiving of this behaviour. She believes the pandemic's pressures have lowered the inhibitions of the women Ikwe serves. "It's just as if everybody is fed up and on edge and will quickly show how they feel," she said. Passengers let fly emotions and tempers they once suppressed. But while some are quick to anger, others express disproportionate gratitude. These days, an Ikwe member is as likely to tell a driver to fuck off as she is to tell her "I love you."

When I first visited Winnipeg, I was struck by the community of women Ikwe had created. Drivers like Jackie, who'd found a source of adult friendship through Ikwe that had previously been elusive; or Chery, who credits volunteering for Ikwe for helping her overcome her shyness. Tim Hortons socializing seemed to mean as much to the women of Ikwe as the driving itself. The pandemic crushed this. The drivers exchange little parking lot gossip anymore. At the beginning of the lockdown, they'd stood between their cars and chatted with each other over the roofs, but the compromise satisfied no one and didn't endure.

"If COVID and the social distancing lasted a week or two, I don't think that this would have changed who we are," Christine said. "But it's gone on long enough now that the social connection is gone. It is stifled." Nor can technology replace the sort of spiritual nourishment Ikwe's volunteers got from their community. "There's no virtual way to do that. There's no connecting online. There's no Zoom meeting to do that."

I texted Mo Jalil in Halifax and asked how his new concierge business was doing during the pandemic. It wasn't. "Unfortunately, the corona put everything on hold and I had to sell my car," he said. "I am thinking of a change, but have NO CLUE what to do." When I called Mo a few days later, he told me that once the pandemic hit Halifax, the high-end clients he depended on didn't need him anymore. "Most of them stayed in their cottages or estates," he told me. "They could just stay away from everybody. They had live-in help who could drive them around."

Mo hadn't lost his honesty. He told me that his ego has prevented him from returning to driving a regular cab, and that he was too proud to even speak to the taxi drivers he used to work with. "I didn't want them to know what kind of situation I'm in," he said. "It is some kind of personality flaw I have." Some of his friends suggested he get into delivery or trucking. Others said he should try getting a job as a freelance artist. He briefly considered applying at Halifax's two animation houses, "but maybe they prefer little Chinese girls, or young artists. Someone they can slap around."

"I'm sorry you had to sell your BMW," I told him. "I know you loved that car."

"It was my pride and joy," Mo said. "But it was useless, and it started to cost more to keep. I'm thinking, if I'm going to change careers and do courier or personal shopper or Uber, I'm not going to drive around with a BMW 7 Series. I'll get a hybrid or something with a big trunk." In the meantime, Mo is helping connect an engineer friend with some of his wealthy former clients. The engineer has designed a "hospital-quality" portable ventilator that can provide oxygen to thirty patients at a time. "What he is looking for is *Dragon's Den*-kind of investors," Mo said. The scheme sounded dodgy to me. Who invents cutting-edge medical equipment in their spare time? I was relieved that Mo didn't appear overly committed to the project. "I'm trying to help him out. A couple of guys were going to call me back. Nobody did."

"What are you doing right now?" I asked him.

"I don't want to sound negative, but I'm totally lost," Mo said. "Part of it is pride. Part of it is wishful thinking. Part of it is hoping for the worst, and there will be an opportunity because I'm a risk-taker. I don't know. To be honest. I am totally in the dark. I don't have a clear direction."

Mo found a direction the following September. He started producing halal and kosher Middle Eastern food products for restaurants and grocery stores. He makes three varieties of *basturma*, an air-dried cured beef common in the region—an Iraqi version, a Turkish-Armenian version, and a Syrian-Lebanese version. "Iraqi is the best," he said. Such halal products already exist in Halifax "but they mostly suck ass," Mo said. He also smokes fish and will start making sausages. "I am totally blind to the industry," he wrote to tell me. "All I have is good recipes and faith. I am just going with my guts and balls and happy-go-lucky."

At the end of our conversation, Mo told me he had an even better idea. "But I need a smart person like you," he texted. "It needs big balls too. I am driving on the highway right now, but I really want to talk to you, cuz YOU might be the key for my new idea." I told Mo I was intrigued. And I was. All the cabbies I'd met were such wonderful schemers, and while I couldn't imagine going into business with Mo—or anyone—being potentially included in one of his plots felt delicious. I was honoured.

I told him to call me whenever he wanted. He sent me a winking emoji as a response, but I still haven't heard from him.

Acknowledgments

FIRST OF ALL, I'D LIKE TO THANK THE DRIVERS, THEIR families, friends, and colleagues that took the time to talk to me and who appear in these pages: Peter Pellier, Michael Kamara, Quentin Ranson, Sergey Chudinov, Andy Reti, Hassan Kattoua, Kareem Yalahow, Mary Apsimik, Jass and Amrit Hothi, Alex Seliga, Iva Jackson, Nathan Phelps, Megan Phelps-Roper, Mike Gray, John Duffy, Christine Brouzes, Chery Lee, Debbs "The One Who Yells," Jackie Hartog, Jessica Hartog, Tammy Marie, Mohammed "Mo" Abdul Jalil, Renée Forrestall, Jennie King, Rawi Hage, Jens Anderson, Lucinda Chodan, and Phil Bailey.

I am also grateful for those who took the time to speak to me but who do not, for whatever reason, appear in the book, especially Violet Baptiste, Michelle Lee, Brenda Rocchio, Tesfai Dmitzu, Aheibam Kiran Kumar Singh, Mohammed Reza, Bashir Hussein, Gerry Manley, Bruce Cockburn, Sneezy Waters, rob mclennan, Roy MacSkimming, Mark Blevis, Cameron Anstee, Ken Rockburn, Chris Wells, Zach Wells, and Cassandra Hawkins.

April Crowchild, Emelie Peacock, Shaun Hunter, Meghan Grant, Sharanpal Ruprai, Ruth Shead, Elisabeth Vallet, Amber Dawn, Omar Mouallem, Trevor Melanson, and Corinne Smith all provided support, advice, or encouragement of one kind or another. Thank you.

I am profoundly grateful for the writers and scholars whose own work informed this book, especially Lorne Foster, Peter McSherry, Karolyn Smardz Frost, Peter Churchill, Sean Mills, Abdulhamid Hathiyani, Monisha Das Gupta, Sarah Sharma, Linda Polman, Ibolya Grossman, Donald Davis, Kate E Murray, Kimberly Berry, Helen Potrebenko, Mike Heffernan, and Edmund W Vaz.

Thanks to the Calgary Public Library and the Yellowknife Public Library for providing me a place to work on this book. I am especially grateful for funding from the Alberta Foundation for the Arts, the Canada Council for the Arts, and Access Copyright.

I was thrilled to work with Dan Wells, Emily Donaldson, Vanessa Stauffer, Michaela Stephen and the rest of the Biblioasis crew, and with Jackie Kaiser and her team at Westwood Creative Artists.

Notes

Introduction

[7] "It is almost a rite-of-passage in contemporary urban Canada...": Lorne
Foster, "The 21st Century Taxi Driver: An Examination of the Hidden
Injuries of Race in Urban Canada," in *Racism, Culture and the Law:
Critical Readings*, ed. Reza Barmaki (Toronto: APF Press) 133–164.

One

[14] "By 1981, Canada's immigrant population...": Census Canada data, 1971
and 1981.

[14] "There are some people who would complain if it rained...": *Globe and
Mail*, July 7, 1975, 5.

[16] "They considered their purported lack...": Abdulhamid Hathiyani,
"Professional Immigrants on a Road to Driving Taxis in Toronto," in
Our Diverse Cities 4 (2007): 128–133.

[17] "New York cabbies covered up...": Monisha Das Gupta, "A View of
Post–9/11 Justice from Below," *Peace Review* 16:2 (2004): 141–148.

Two

[21] Sebastian Junger, "The Terror of Sierra Leone," *Vanity Fair,* August 2000.

[23] Linda Polman, *War Games: The Story of Aid and War in Modern Times* (Kindle Edition: Penguin Books, 2011): 62–63.

Three

[49] "Toronto City Hall had limited the number of new drivers..." Donald F Davis, "The Canadian Taxi Wars, 1925–1950," in *Urban History Review/Revue d'histoire urbaine 27* (1) (1998): 7–22.

Five

[80] Information about female cabbies is from Kimberly Berry, "The Independent Servant: A Socio-Cultural Examination of the Post-War Toronto Taxi Driver," PhD Thesis (University of Ottawa, 2006).

[80] "The Council also worried..." information from Kimberly Berry "She's No Lady: The Experience and Expression of Gender Among Women Taxi Drivers," Master's Thesis (Saint Mary's University, 1997).

Six

[102] "In the two years after his murder..." from Berry, "The Independent Servant."